POLITICS AND LAND USE PLANNING

The London Experience

POLITICS AND
LAND USE PLANNING
The London Experience

STEPHEN L. ELKIN

CAMBRIDGE UNIVERSITY PRESS

Published by the Syndics of the Cambridge University Press
Bentley House, 200 Euston Road, London NW1 2DB
American Branch: 32 East 57th Street, New York, N.Y. 10022

© Cambridge University Press 1974

Composed in Great Britain by William Clowes & Sons, Limited, London, Beccles and
Colchester

Printed in the United States of America

Library of Congress Catalogue Card Number: 73–80486

ISBN: 0 521 20321 X

First published 1974

For D, M, and M

CONTENTS

		page
	Preface	ix
1	Introduction	1
2	The machinery of local government and town planning	13
3	World's End: housing in West Chelsea	27
4	Offices and congestion in the central area: Centre Point and St Giles Circus	53
5	The political environment of councilors	74
6	Deliberation and the delegation of authority	116
7	The authority and the applicant: problems of choice	141
8	Planning, values and rationality	165
	Index	188

PREFACE

Studies of land use planning in American cities have generally emphasized the difficulties and shortcomings of the enterprise. Indeed some observers have said that planning cannot be successfully carried out in the context of American cities. Yet it has often been claimed that in London planning has been successful. How then is this claim to be understood and evaluated? It was this question that prompted the following study.

The initial question was gradually encompassed by a more general interest in the problems of social choice and rationality. Public planning of any kind is basically an attempt to improve the quality of the choices communities make for themselves, i.e. to improve the level of rationality. Together, the various aspects of the problem of rational choice for communities form one of the threads of the study. The empirical analysis of London planning and the evaluation thereof, as contrasted to the situation in American cities, is meant as a case example to advance the discussion of problems of societal choice.

A second thread is provided by comparisons between politics in large American cities and London. The concern with such a comparative perspective arises out of a general interest in British–American contrasts, but it also has a more theoretical basis. Over the past 15–20 years, American political scientists have given considerable attention to politics in American cities. But increasingly the need for non-American cases has been felt so that questions of the existing and proposed theoretical content of the study of urban politics can be sensibly addressed. This study is meant to aid this inquiry: one useful mode of theorizing is the confrontation of hypotheses with the rich empirical material generated in case examples.

The theme of social choice (and that of the status of the study of urban politics) does not depend for its development on an analysis of the present (1973) practices in London. If a concern is theoretical, then evidence from different time periods is appropriate and even essential. However, if the interest is in description of present day London politics, then a study of the city in the early and mid 1960s might seem to be only of historical value. This issue is particularly pressing if the political arrangements have been substantially altered, as is the case in London. The present study is of politics and planning under the London County Council, the general purpose authority for the city, which was supplanted in 1965 by a metropolitan area government, the Greater London Council. Nevertheless, if the continuities and changes from political patterns under the LCC to those under the GLC can be isolated, then the understanding of contemporary London politics will be enhanced. A discussion of the LCC is then a useful benchmark for the analysis of present patterns.

The principal change in London politics from the early 1960s to the early 1970s is a citizenry growing more knowledgeable of and involved with local government decision-making. This is associated with higher levels of conflict both in and outside of government and with an increase in expertise on the part of locally appointed officials in the analysis of public policy alternatives as decisions have to be justified more often in public forums. The context of these features, which also exacerbates conflicts and puts a greater burden on experts, is a declining resource base for the city. Under the LCC, the economy of London was buoyant and the general resources available to the city at an acceptable level, but the GLC is in a generally weaker position. On the continuity side, the most prominent features are, not unexpectedly, in the area of norms and values. Although there is evidence of a changing political culture, manifested in an increase in citizen organization, emphasis on a community-wide perspective in policy-making (as contrasted to a focus on aggregating the interests of particular neighborhoods) remains in evidence. In the same vein, the legislative role which emphasizes deliberation as against bargaining also has persisted. In short, there seems to be a juxtaposition of a citizenry becoming more concerned with issues and more active in local politics with a set of institutional arrangements and political patterns appropriate to a more hierarchical politics. This tension and its development may well be common to other areas of English politics and to the degree that this is so, political patterns under the LCC are suggestive of English politics more generally in the early 1960s just as the changes from this point are also of more general interest.

The principal sources of data for the study are interviews with London officials and the files of the London County Council. In addition, some leaders of community organizations and central government officials were interviewed and some use made of the files of the Chelsea Borough Council. The interviews were conducted in 1965 and in 1969–70; the overwhelming number of those interviewed in the latter period were also interviewed in the former. Virtually all senior local officials involved with planning in the early 1960s were interviewed, as were a considerable number of councilors similarly involved. In the body of the study, quotes from interviews conducted in 1965 which refer to practices under the LCC are given in the present tense; those from 1969–70 interviews are given in the past tense.

All told some 500 hours of open-ended interviews were conducted. This format was employed because, aside from using those interviewed as informants, the principal concern was to elicit information on role conceptions, views of the public interest and other norms. In general, the aim was to comprehend how participants understood their job and their organization. It was important to be sure that those being interviewed comprehended the distinctions involved, and this could best be accomplished by loosely structured interviews. In the absence of extensively tested instruments, more structured interviews run the risk that distinctions are in the questionnaire and not in the mind of the interviewee. The relatively unfamiliar cultural setting in one sense defines the problem and in another may be said to simply complicate the task of eliciting meaningful responses in interview situations.

The interviews and particularly the files were used to develop six case studies, two of which are presented here. The cases supplement the data from the interviews, particularly with regard to decision-making procedures.

Unless otherwise indicated all quotes in the study are either from interview documents or from local authority files. No names are provided, either for the source of the quotes or at any point in the analysis. This was the understanding under which access was granted.

The study would not have been possible without the generous assistance of the officials of the London County Council and the Chelsea Borough Council. I am also grateful to the considerable number of people who commented on various versions of the analysis. James Q. Wilson and Sam Beer of Harvard University and Oliver Williams of the University of Pennsylvania bore the principal burden of commenting with patience and grace. Others who helped include Edward Banfield, Robert Backoff, David Donnison, J. A. G. Griffiths, Peter Hall, Russell Hardin, Brian McLaughlin, Rhodri Morgan, Richard Rose and Jim Sharpe.

I should also like to thank my wife for her emotional and intellectual support. She bore the greatest burden of all.

The study was supported by grants from the Joint Center for Urban Studies of Harvard and MIT and the Centre for Environmental Studies, London.

October, 1973   SLE

1. INTRODUCTION

Control of the use of land is a major problem in all large cities. In both developed and developing nations, local and central authorities have tried in a variety of ways to shape the physical layout of their cities and metropolitan areas in the realization that how land is used has profound consequences for the well-being of their citizens. From what is already known about such attempts, most of which draws on American practice, it would seem that efforts to control land use, roughly, to plan, are intimately bound up with the way in which politics is carried on within the cities and metropolitan areas and at higher levels of government.[1] The intricate and close relationship between politics and planning at any level should now be a commonplace, but at the least it is clear that many implications of this, generally reluctant, marriage have not been analyzed.

Some studies of politics and planning have concentrated on the recalcitrance of non-planners, and particularly of elected officials, when faced with planning proposals. In others the concern has been to demonstrate how politics, by which is usually meant bargaining and competition between elected representatives, has penetrated into the planning process. The typical argument in both kinds of studies has been the tenacity and imperialism of existing political patterns and the comparative weakness of planning.[2] The starting point in these analyses, sometimes unstated or unexplored, is the incompatibility of the logic of planning with the logic of the political arrangements in which planning seeks to operate, the difference largely being one of public policy as a product of conscious choice of ends and means versus public policy as an aggregation of a variety of interests and viewpoints.[3]

Planning and politics in London present a different picture. Accepting

[1] See, for example, Oliver Williams, *Metropolitan Political Analysis* (New York, 1971); Martin Meyerson and Edward C. Banfield, *Politics, Planning and the Public Interest* (New York, 1955); Alan Altshuler, *The City Planning Process* (Ithaca, 1966); David C. Ranney, *Planning and Politics in the Metropolis* (Columbus, 1969); and Francine Rabinowitz, *City Politics and Planning* (New York, 1969).

[2] For studies dealing with planning in other than a land use context and which are concerned with the impact of politics, see the following. Stephen S. Cohen, *Modern Capitalist Planning: The French Model* (Cambridge, Mass., 1969); Andrew Shonfield, *Modern Capitalism* (London, 1965); Aaron Wildavsky, *The Politics of the Budgetary Process* (Boston, 1964); and Charles L. Schultze, *The Politics and Economics of Public Spending* (Washington D.C., 1968).

[3] See, for example, Altshuler, *City Planning* and Meyerson and Banfield, *Politics*.

I

the logical tension between the two, there are still empirical variations, particularly in the extent of the imperialism and tenacity of politics. Thus, land use planning in London provides an opportunity to explore the potential of planning when political patterns do not present a serious impediment to the definition of community purposes and the selection of means to serve them. Most generally of interest is an explanation of the insulation of the planning authority and an examination of the consequences which flow from this situation. The former indicates one central concern of this study: why is it that decisions which had high impact in terms of residential and commercial patterns, decisions which one might think affected some of the central values of the citizenry, were treated by London citizens and public officials alike as if there was little doubt *who* should make the decisions, *how* they should be made and in a general fashion, *what* the decisions should be. The implications of the latter will be considered below.

POLITICS

The insulation of the planning authority, and the attendant low visibility of planning decisions, is illustrated by two major land use projects. Whereas in large American cities such decisions are among the most controversial, if not *the* most controversial, the examples suggest that this was not the case in London. Even decisions having considerable impact on land use patterns generated limited involvement and controversy by American standards.

In a study of property development in England, concentrating mostly on London, Oliver Marriott describes at length the development of a site which has come to be known as Euston Centre. The development according to Marriott, is worth more than 100 million dollars, covers an area of approximately 13 acres, and contains about 100 shops, 160,000 sq. feet of showrooms, a factory, luxury flats, a garage for 900 cars, and two office towers of 17 and 34 stories, high blocks by London standards. The only newspaper to pick up the story of the development did so when the project *was already under way*, when it noted that the London County Council was building an underpass adjacent to the site 'but there is nothing to show that the area is being transformed into what amounts to a miniature new town'.[1] The fact is that one of the largest developments of any sort in London was discussed and decided upon by the local planning authority without any public discussion.

The second example concerns a proposal for a housing development by a public authority. In 1964, Islington Borough Council[2] sought planning permission from the LCC, the planning authority for the area, to clear an

[1] The *Evening Standard*, quoted in Oliver Marriott, *The Property Boom* (London, 1967), p. 165. The original statement appears in capital letters.
[2] For a discussion of the London boroughs see Chapter 2.

old privately-built housing estate and replace it with public authority flats. After informal consultations with LCC planning officers, who agreed that some action needed to be taken, an application for the building of the flats was submitted. For various reasons not relevant to the present discussion, the Town Planning Committee of the County Council did not act on the application within the period designated by law, and the borough lodged an appeal based on what under the law could be interpreted as a refusal. Until some time after the application for permission was submitted by the Borough Council, there was no publicity for the project. Residents on the site and those living in the surrounding area were unaware of the proposal to redevelop and of the consultations. They only gained knowledge of these matters when the borough discovered it required permission from the owners of a protected London square, which was part of the proposed site, if they wished to build on it. One of the owners passed on the information to a resident of the area. In short it was possible for the planning authority to consider an application for a public housing project and to negotiate with the public authority planning to build it without any of the area residents being aware of it.

Contrary to expectations engendered by a study of American urban politics then, governmental decisions in London were discussed and made largely by public officials. Citizens and their spokesmen played a comparatively limited role and knowledge of local affairs was not widely dispersed. The explanation of this state of affairs principally resolves itself into an analysis of two problems. First, we need to delineate the characteristics of political cleavages in London as compared to those in large American cities, particularly their comparatively limited extent in the former. We then need to trace the roots of the London pattern and indicate some of the consequences for the behavior of public officials. Secondly, the low level of interest group behavior in London as compared to large American cities must be described and the factors associated with this situation and its results isolated.

As already implied, one major consequence of the factors just touched on was the autonomy of public officials, especially elected representatives. This had other roots, particularly the norms and values held by them; similarly, the legislative role of representatives influenced the extent of autonomy. The last two and variables clustered around them were associated with another salient characteristic of the LCC, viz. the dominance of an analytical mode of organizational coordination.[1]

The defining characteristic of this mode is the assumption held by organization members of shared objectives which can be used to guide decision-making. In the case of the LCC the manifestations of analytical coordination were the delegation of effective authority by most elected

---

[1] See the discussion of analytical versus political processes in James March and Herbert Simon, *Organizations* (New York, 1958), p. 130.

officials to a small group of their number and to some of their nominal subordinates, viz. local government officers, and the deliberative process pursued by the latter two.

Clues as to how the discrete problems just discussed can be brought together are provided by a strand in the theory of organizational behavior which is concerned with the impact of an organization's environment on its internal processes and structure. Although this work has focused almost entirely on either business organizations or public bureaucracies, not on representative bodies, and it has been largely concerned with organizations as a whole rather than the members that compose them, some of the concepts developed are useful for present purposes. Particularly, the focus on the level of certainty of the environment and the impact of this property on the concentration of influence within the organization is of importance.[1]

In London, the high level of certainty in the political environment of elected representatives is the explanatory variable around which much of the analysis revolves. Similarly, in the discussion of large American cities presented here, it is the low level of certainty which is crucial. For our purposes, the political environment of elected representatives is that aspect of their total environment which is relevant for purposes of getting and staying elected, i.e. the citizenry of the LCC and particularly their own constituents.[2] The level of environmental certainty can be defined as a product of two principal elements, variability and predictability.[3] Environments may then be variable but certain because of high predictability. Or they may be certain even though little information is held or available because their behavior varies little.[4]

Certainty in the political environment of elected representatives refers to variability and predictability in the content and intensity of demands

[1] See, for example, William Dill, 'Environment as an Influence on Managerial Autonomy', *Administrative Science Quarterly*, 3 (1962), 409–33; John Child, 'Towards a Theory of Organization, Environment and Performance of Work Organizations', London Graduate School of Business, March 1970; Richard Norman, 'Organization, Mediation and Environment', Swedish Institute for Administrative Research, March 1969; Tom Burns and G. M. Stalker, *The Management of Innovation* (London, 1961); Paul Lawrence and Jay Lorsch, *Organization and Environment* (Boston, 1967), and James D. Thompson, *Organizations in Action* (New York, 1967).

[2] For a perceptive discussion of the problems of defining and measuring environmental properties, see William Dill, 'The Impact of Environment on Organization Development', in Sidney Malick and Edward H. Van Ness (eds.), *Concepts and Issues in Administrative Behavior* (Englewood Cliffs, N.J., 1962).

[3] Cf. F. E. Emery and E. L. Trist, 'The Causal Texture of Organizational Environments', in F. E. Emery (ed.), *Systems Thinking* (Harmondsworth, Middlesex, 1969).

It is important to distinguish an uncertain environment from a threatening one. An organization may be in a situation of considerable dependence on environmental elements which do not share its ends, and thus be operating in a threatening environment, but at the same time the behavior of these elements may be, for example, highly predictable.

[4] A number of problems are not addressed here including whether uncertainty is simply a measure of the extent to which organizational members perceive an environment to be uncertain, or whether it is to be defined and measured from the point of view of the observer. Here, elements of both approaches are utilized. See Dill, 'Impact of Environment'.

made by environmental actors as well as changes in the size of coalitions that may form to promote particular courses of action. The high level of certainty in the political environment in London was associated with the prevalence of delegation and deliberation, just as the low level of certainty in large American cities is associated with their absence.[1] However, as suggested, environmental properties are the starting point since the perceptions and norms that representatives and other public officials held are also crucial in explaining the characteristics of the LCC.

In attempting to characterize planning politics in London using the concepts introduced, or others that appear in the body of the study, comparisons to land use politics and general political patterns in American cities are invaluable. Indeed the comparisons helped in developing the appropriate concepts in the first place. In addition, the comparisons help to establish relationships between variables and to make judgements of 'more or less' by providing an explicit reference point. American cities are (and were) referred to both as individual cases[2] and for characteristics and relationships that are typical of the whole range of large, mostly older, mostly eastern and mid-western cities.[3]

The extent to which the characteristics of large American cities focused on in the present study are in fact typical is worth some comment. There has been a good deal of discussion about the distribution of power in American cities and how to study this matter, and some of the issues raised are pertinent here.[4] The arguments between the principal protagonists have pointed to the existence of two levels for the exercise of power, viz. public policy decisions themselves and what gets on the civic agenda in the first place. Taking note of this distinction, the description of decision-making in American cities as being characterized by participation of a variety of actors which is presented in succeeding chapters seems accurate. Whatever one might say about the 'meaningfulness' of participation in

[1] Certainty in the political environment is also associated with the orientation to complex choice problems evidenced by those concerned with LCC planning. See Chaper 7.

[2] The particular cities considered are New York, Syracuse, New Haven, Chicago, Minneapolis and St Paul. This reflects the extensive work done on these cities and the attention given to land use politics in the studies. See Wallace Sayre and Herbert Kaufman, *Governing New York City* (New York, 1960); S. J. Makielski, Jr., *The Politics of Zoning: The New York Experience* (New York, 1966); J. Clarence Davies, *Neighborhood Groups and Urban Renewal* (New York, 1966); Roscoe Martin, Frank Munger *et al.*, *Decisions in Syracuse* (Bloomington, 1961); Edward Banfield, *Political Influence* (New York, 1961); Meyerson and Banfield, *Politics*; and Altshuler, *City Planning*.

[3] Here the most useful discussion is by Banfield and James Q. Wilson, *City Politics* (Cambridge, Mass., 1963).

In the main body of this study, American cities are discussed in the present tense, while for the LCC the past tense is used. This is meant to indicate that the features of the former which are analyzed are still present even though, as a matter of fact, the studies on which the analysis is based were done in the late fifties and early sixties for the most part.

[4] See the bibliography in Charles Bonjean *et al.* (eds.), *Community Power: A Behavioral Approach* (New York, 1971).

many or perhaps most American cities, for both particular decisions and for the setting of the civic agenda, multiple actors are involved.[1] Moreover, less in the past but increasingly in the present, at both levels groups low on both a status and income hierarchy have had considerable say. They have by no means dominated nor perhaps have they been successful in promoting various schemes, but they have succeeded in blocking particular decisions and in putting a variety of problems on the civic agenda. To this extent their participation has become increasingly meaningful. Stated somewhat differently, the question of the extent of pluralism or elitism in American cities is not directly pertinent to this study. At the least, London and American cities *are* different in the directions specified here; there may however be some dispute as to how different they are, and over the normative qualities of the American situation.

It is also worth noting here that the methodology pursued in this study, viz. case studies and general interviewing growing out of them, is not open to some of the criticisms of the 'mobilization of bias' school.[2] One of their central arguments seems to be that looking at concrete decisions obscures the workings of this bias, i.e. the impact of the 'dominant values and the political myths, rituals and institutional practices which tend to favor the vested interests of one or more groups, relative to others'.[3] The appropriate reply is simply that there is no reason why a researcher cannot go from questions about how particular issues are resolved, whether they are 'key' or not, to questions such as why these particular matters were being addressed and not some others. Some researchers may not in fact raise this question, but that is hardly damning unless it is demonstrated that they somehow cannot or are much less likely to do so than researchers that utilize some other approach, and neither of these has been demonstrated. At any rate, a substantial portion of what follows the case examples in this study is in fact directed at such matters as why certain kinds of issues didn't arise and why particular groups were inactive.[4]

A second methodological (and theoretical) question must be briefly raised, namely the issue of comparability or equivalence. This is a major consideration in all comparative work, but perhaps especially so in comparative

[1] How the 'meaningfulness' of participation would be ascertained is not clear. Any suggestion that it is a matter of actors getting what they want in some more or less consistent fashion faces the problem that this probably excludes meaningful participation being very widely dispersed.

[2] E. E. Schattschneider, *The Semi-Sovereign People* (New York, 1960), p. 71.

[3] Peter Bachrach and Morton Baratz, *Power and Poverty* (New York, 1970), p. 11.

[4] The crucial (and perhaps irresolvable) issue in discussions of power structures is probably: who 'should' be interested in any particular decision, the content of any civic agenda, or any institutional arrangement. This applies to all schools equally, most obviously to the mobilization of bias scholars, but also to those who focus on concrete decisions since the latter are interested, no doubt, in who doesn't get involved as well as the former. Some exploration of why groups who might be thought to benefit from one or another resolution of an issue but who don't participate is often of considerable value. See Raymond Wolfinger, 'Nondecisions and the Study of Local Politics', *American Political Science Review*, 65 (1971), 1063–80.

urban or local politics. Here we face not only problems of defining measurement procedures which produce equivalent readings in very different contexts, but also the question of *what* to measure. At this juncture in comparative local level analysis, empirical research, if only of a trial and error kind, is as useful a strategy as pursuing discussions of conceptual schemes and measurement problems.[1]

The comparison with American cities has led to a strong emphasis on what may be called the consensual dimension of London politics. Some participants who have read the analysis presented here have commented on this and have pointed to greater conflict than is indicated in the study. This reflects among other things a difference in perspective between participant and observer. However, none of those interviewed described the over-all situation as conflictual so that the emphasis derived from comparison is not markedly divergent from the views of participants. The interrelationships of the distinctions between participant and observer and conflict and consensus constitute one of the central problems of social science. Both distinctions point to the fact that the social world can only be viewed from a particular stance; it is not somehow *there*. The important thing is to be aware of the necessarily partial perspective.

PLANNING AND RATIONALITY

The second major concern of the study grows out of the impact of the features of land use politics in London that have just been enumerated. If the LCC had few political problems which might impede its attempts to define the appropriate course of land use development[2], how did it fare in attempting to do so?

If we are to consider this matter, it would be useful to be able to place the LCC within the context of planning organizations generally. In short, some definition of planning and planning organizations would be helpful. The principal difficulty to be met is to provide a definition which at the same time focuses on the logic of the planning process, as opposed to other ways of making decisions, and is also useful for studying organizations which contend that they are planning and are generally reckoned to be doing so. The task is more easily stated than accomplished since if we make planning very distinct from other kinds of decision processes, more than likely it will be found that many 'planning' organizations are not that at all, i.e. they don't

---

[1] For one attempt to define appropriate concepts for comparative urban inquiry see Stephen L. Elkin, 'Comparative Urban Inquiry: The Potential of Organization Theory', American Political Science Association, September 1972, Washington, D.C. In general, see Adam Przeworski and Henry Teune, *The Logic of Comparative Social Inquiry* (New York, 1970) and Robert T. Holt and John E. Turner (eds.), *The Methodology of Comparative Research* (New York, 1970).

[2] It also had for the most part sufficient legal authority. See Chapters 2 and 5.

match up to the specifications. On the other hand, to simply take at face value the claim made by any organization that it is engaged in planning is not very useful if we wish to inquire into similarities and differences in such organizations; a definition which has greater empirical import is required for comparisons. The tension then is between a definition which is useful for empirical research and one which helps in defining the logic of social choice processes.

With these dilemmas in mind, planning will be defined in the succeeding discussion as the investment by an organization (or larger social unit) of a 'substantial' amount of its resources in consciously defining the policy ends it wishes to serve and the most effective means of achieving them. In the language of Chapter 7, such organizations devote considerable resources to an economizing approach. Planners then are the bureaucrats who carry the principal burden of defining such ends and means; in this approach they may make more or less use of an economizing approach. Since all organizations may be defined as purposive,[1] presumably all of them therefore devote *some* of their resources to defining ends and means, but clearly other concerns are evidenced as well, particularly organizational maintenance. However, planning organizations devote more resources and can perhaps in this sense be said to be more purposive than other organizations. The definition emphasizes the intellectual dimensions of the process, leaving aside the thorny question of power to implement what has been selected,[2] and does not focus on the extent of an organization's skill in defining ends and means. The last prevents excluding some organizations which, although they expend considerable effort in trying to define their purposes and the most effective means of serving them, do not manage to be very successful.

By concentrating on investment of resources, empirical work is facilitated since we may inquire into the extent to which such behavior is occurring. However, if we set the definition of 'substantial' too high we run into the danger noted: many organizations generally considered to be engaged in planning will be excluded. Since it is hard to see how this threshold could be established except by looking at a variety of organizations, and something like this problem attends other crucial features of planning definitions, any approach is likely to run the same or similar risks. On the other side, the concern in the definition for ends and means points to the logic of the process and suggests that town or city planning is simply part of a more general orientation to problems of collective choice.[3]

[1] Cf. Amitai Etzioni, *Modern Organizations* (Englewood Cliffs, N.J., 1964), p. 3.
[2] Cf. Etzioni, *Organizations*, p. 3.
[3] For other definitions of planning see: Yehezkel Dror, 'The Planning Process: A Facet Design', *International Review of Administrative Sciences*, 29 (1963), 44–58; Robert A. Dahl, 'The Politics of Planning', *International Social Science Journal*, 11 (1959), 341–50; Herbert Simon, Donald W. Smithburg and Victor A. Thompson, *Public Administration* (New York, 1950), Chapter 20; and Banfield 'Ends and Means in Planning', *International Social Science Journal*, 11 (1959), 361–8.

The definition of planning just offered points to the central issues in the succeeding analysis of the LCC's attempt to control development. As planning involves selection of ends and means, in the control of development this required the performance of two related tasks: using the system of giving permissions for development as a means to the authority's ends, and convincing applicants to accept ends additional to what they otherwise would prefer. In the event, the LCC was not a very successful advocate in its negotiations, nor very adept at using development control decisions to serve wider ends. This happened even though it was in a position to dominate the negotiations given its legal powers. The analysis of why this was the case turns on the fact that the authority was a poor economizer. The orientation to the problems of choice presented by development control and the conception of the city held by those who were mainly responsible for operating the planning machinery meant (logically meant) that they could not execute the tasks just noted very effectively.

The negotiations that grew out of the authority's attempts to convince applicants are an example of what would likely characterize any kind of comprehensive land use planning where there is a private sector. They also share features with what will transpire in situations in which land use development is in the hands of public agencies, but agencies which have considerable or complete autonomy from the reviewing authority. In short, the LCC has much in common with any land use control system likely to be developed or already in operation in both western and eastern industrialized nations. The central fact in such development control processes is, or is likely to be, that as long as those who do the actual developing are not part of the same agency which reviews development applications then the latter must not only know what it wants to see done, but must convince applicants to do it. It is argued here that the last depends on the first, at least where the planning authority already is in a position, as the LCC was, to define its ends and select its means.[1]

Two questions of fundamental importance are raised by the LCC's limited success in its negotiations with applicants. First, what were the consequences, particularly in terms of the distribution of benefits and costs and of criteria derived from democratic theory? These results clearly had other roots, which indeed extended beyond any factors peculiar to the planning system, so that an examination of the impact of development control must be placed in the wider context of salient features of general political patterns in London.

---

[1] In a more extended way, the ability to convince applicants is associated with certain environmental characteristics, as these affect the orientation to problems of choice that members of the planning organization, and particularly planners, bring to bear. Environments which confer advantages on planning agencies by promoting autonomy of organizational members may reduce the incentives to develop those intellectual skills required for effective negotiating; conversely such skills may develop most readily when the requisite autonomy is absent. See Chapters 5 and 7.

Second, if the LCC didn't manage very well, can *any* organization do much better? One of the long-standing controversies in the discussion of decision-making for large collectivities is the extent to which such bodies in fact can act in a reasonably rational manner.[1] Although this is a particularly complex and elusive issue, as well as perhaps being the underlying concern of much of social science and public life, there is no easy way to avoid entering such risky waters in a book about planning, and so using the LCC's efforts as a springboard some general considerations will be advanced.

The principal concerns of the study, then, are captured in four questions. *How* did the London authority act, *why*, and with *what* consequences? And, is it *possible* to do any better? Chapter 2 describes the legal powers of the planning authority and provides some necessary background about the structure of government in London and about town planning. Chapters 3 and 4 are case studies which illustrate the limited citizen activity in London, the autonomy of planning officials and the difficulties the LCC had in advocacy. Readers familiar with the basic features of governmental structure and planning in London may find it possible to skip Chapter 2 (and possibly the case studies, although these are utilized in the succeeding analysis). Chapters 5, 6, and 7, discuss how and why the authority acted as it did. The concluding chapter presents an evaluation of the planning authority's efforts and examines its activities in the context of some general propositions about rationality.

A NOTE ON THE CASE STUDIES

The use of case studies has a number of advantages, particularly in helping to capture the workings of a complex organization. Through them a whole series of relationships are suggested and it is possible to decide which are worth pursuing further in more wide-ranging interviewing and which should be best laid aside. In the same vein, cases suggest the direction of relationships and this too can be pursued in such interviews. However, the use of case studies raises the obvious question of how 'representative' or 'important' the cases chosen are. There is no easy answer to the question, but the considerations that guided the selection of the ones to present for this study can be noted.

Most often cases are chosen because of their controversial nature or because of their intrinsic interest. These criteria, which are hardly unambiguous and may not even be valid, were in fact not found to be very

---

[1] See, for example: Charles E. Lindblom, *The Intelligence of Democracy* (New York, 1965); Lindblom and David Braybrooke, *A Strategy of Decision* (New York, 1963); Wildavsky, *Budgetary Process*.

useful for the present study. In the United States at least one can pick controversial cases under the hypothesis – not necessarily a good one – that under stress the system will be exposed in all its glory. In London, the choice of cases on the basis of their controversial quality was defeated by the fact that public controversy over land use was not common. For this study, the judgement of those acquainted with planning decisions was utilized; this meant either local government officials or those professionally concerned with planning in some fashion. This was supplemented by two simple assumptions. First, more than one type of land use problem ought to be examined. Therefore, one of the case studies presented deals with housing and one with commercial development in the downtown area. This was meant to guard against any possible important differences in behavior in different types of land use decisions. The second assumption was that large cases would be more useful than small ones; cases in which the decisions involved large-scale developments and in which the choices were complex would be more revealing than small cases. This assumption was made not only because the larger cases ought to bring out what conflict there was more easily, i.e. the addition of a wing onto a house was not likely to upset many people very much, but also because one of the concerns of the study was to understand the problem of rationality in the context of complex choices. Clearly then, complex cases were a necessity. Finally, if the cases are supplemented by extensive interviewing of a general nature, as was done for this study, the more blatant errors of selection can be avoided.

The analysis of the LCC as presented here, with its evident concern for what might be loosely called the intellectual dimension of planning, must be seen in tandem with the equally important, and perhaps even more discussed, problems of the requisite authority and concentration of influence for this enterprise. While the former certainly presents decidedly complex issues for resolution, some small hope for progress may be held out in that practitioners and scholars are increasingly facing up to what is at issue. However, the latter, perhaps by definition, does not seem so amenable to inquiries which aim at producing recommendations for public authorities which seek to do effective planning. More importantly, it appears likely that the minimum concentration of influence and authority required to operate a planning system will become increasingly difficult to find in both England and the United States as larger and larger numbers of citizens take an increasingly critical stance toward government in general and become more forceful advocates of views which grow out of this orientation. This suggests that we need not only to think about the intellectual problems of planning but about such matters as new political arrangements to cope with such changes and performance standards for public authorities which focus on more than the extent to which the authority achieves ends it sets for itself. What follows then may be construed among other things as an inquiry into what may be lost or gained in the decline of a citizenry willing to allow public officials to make many of the decisions which shape the community's well-being.

2. THE MACHINERY OF LOCAL GOVERNMENT AND TOWN PLANNING

During the period of the LCC's existence there were a variety of functional units known as London. These included the City of London (the financial area at the center of the County), the statistical metropolitan area, the London Transport area, the Post Office area and the Metropolitan Police district. There were also water, electricity and gas authorities that covered the region. Aside from these, there was the general purpose government for the County of London, i.e. the London County Council, and it is this authority that is of principal concern in this study (see map on page 14).

The political history of London for our purposes begins in 1888 with the Local Government Act of that year and the creation of London County and its governmental machinery, the London County Council. Before that, government for London was a remarkable patchwork of overlapping authorities with diverse constituencies and diverse sources of authority. Into this the Metropolitan Board of Works was propelled (in 1855), which subsequently however succumbed to scandal, and in 1888, while the English local government system was being revamped, that of London underwent a similar reorganization, although as an afterthought.[1] Such treatment of London was consistent with the general attitude of the central government toward the city, namely one of antagonism.[2] The 1888 Act created an administrative area of 117 square miles, the decision being based not on the results of any particular analysis, but conveniently using the area previously served by the old Board of Works, which in its turn was based on the old 'Bills of Mortality Area'. As Margaret Cole has commented in a study of London government, 'to delimit a capital city by Act of Parliament on a basis of death registers and main drainage (one of the functions of the Board of Works) is surely one of the oddest methods that can ever have been evolved'.[3] Following the precedent of not giving the local government for

[1] Frank Smallwood, *Greater London: The Politics of Metropolitan Reform* (Indianapolis, 1965), p. 61.

[2] Herbert Morrison has commented that 'for some curious reason Parliament has seemed to have a fear of order, dignity and cohesion in the government of the capital'. Quoted in Smallwood, *Greater London*, p. 57.

[3] Margaret Cole, *Servant of the County* (London, 1956), p. 36.

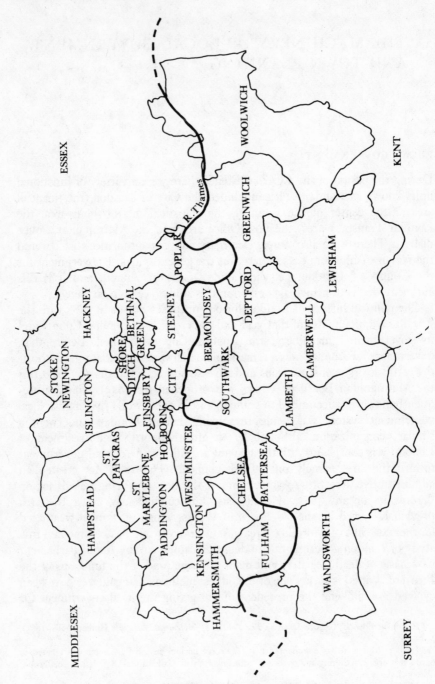

Map 1   The Administrative County of London

London control over its own center,[1] the City of London was not included in this 117 square miles.

In 1894 there was a second local government act which dealt with 'second-tier' authorities, i.e. the lesser units within the major units that had been established in 1888. London was excluded from this act, although the County did receive the full treatment in 1899 under separate legislation. This legislation, however, departed rather markedly from that covering the rest of the country. Here again the animus of Parliament was at work. It was said that London's problems were special, as indeed they were, but a large measure of their 'specialness' was the fact of antagonism. The 1899 Act created twenty-eight second-tier units in the County, called metropolitan boroughs. The aim was, as a student of these matters comments

to undermine the interest and authority which the London County Council had aroused from its inception...The Act had as its main object the establishment of centers of political opposition which would harry and frustrate the radical spirit of the London (County) Council.

And furthermore there was

no attempt to make them [the boroughs] partners in the common task of governing London. [Instead]...each of the 28 metropolitan borough councils was to have its own mayor and alderman, with their robes of office, gilt chain, a mace, and all the other insignia calculated to encourage the feeling of their separate civic consciousness.[2]

Over time, with time favoring the LCC, the breakdown of functions between the County Council and the boroughs came to be as follows:[3] the London County Council assumed responsibility for fire services, main drainage and sewage, 'overspill' housing, in-County housing, main highways and bridges, welfare and personal health services, education, town planning and street improvements and parks; the metropolitan boroughs were charged with street improvements, rating (taxing),[4] public lighting, refuse removal, museum and library services, baths and wash houses, cemeteries, local parks, slum clearance and housing (shared with the LCC), local sewage and drainage, local regulation and inspection functions, the registration of births, marriages and deaths, and town planning (minor).

The 1899 Act also perpetuated the special status of the City Corporation, in that the City was not designated a metropolitan borough and was allowed to enjoy a unique (amongst the sub-units within the County) degree of local autonomy and to retain its particular local election system and government organization. The City government and the County Council did over

[1] Smallwood, *Greater London*, p. 62.

[2] William A. Robson, *The Greater London Boroughs*, Greater London Papers, No. 3 (London, 1961), pp. 6–7.

[3] This is more or less as they were at the time of the demise of the LCC.

[4] See the remarks in Chapter 5 on taxation.

time build up a set of relationships that helped to coordinate their activities. However, the central core of London was legally independent in many key areas.

The result of these various acts was to place the outer portion of greater London under a system of local government that was used all over the rest of England and Wales and which differed from that used in the County of London. Complicating the governmental situation for the London area even further, additional governmental units were constituted after 1900 to deal with special functions. These included a Metropolitan Water Board (1902), the Port of London Authority (1908), the Gas and Electricity Boards (1950), the London and Home Counties Traffic Advisory Committee (1924), and the London Transport Board (1933). As a consequence of the local government acts and of the creation of statutory authorities (special districts), there were between 100 and 200 governmental units serving greater London at the time at which the metropolitan area reorganization took place.[1]

THE ORGANIZATION OF THE LONDON COUNTY COUNCIL

Under the terms of the 1888 Act and its subsequent amendments, the County Council that was to govern London was to be composed of four types of public officials – elected members, aldermen, officers (local government civil servants) and special appointments (outside experts appointed to serve on various committees).[2]

During the late 1950s and early 1960s, the Council consisted of 126 councilors (members) elected every three years in three-member districts and 21 aldermen (1/6th of the total number by statute), who were chosen by a majority vote of elected members for six-year terms and who held the same powers as elected members. This was for a population of over 3,000,000 people. It was customary for the composition of the aldermen to reflect the partisan composition of elected members. The constituencies for Council elections were conterminous with those for national elections.[3]

The Council conducted most of its important business in committees. These committees had delegated power and only certain very important matters were reserved for the full Council.[4] Much of the work of the com-

---

[1] In terms of numbers, London was clearly behind such masters as the New York metropolitan region with roughly 1,400 governments and Chicago with roughly 1,000. The broad estimate for London reflects the variability of definitions as to what constitutes 'greater London'. In general, see Greater London Council, *London Statistics, 1954–64* (London, 1968), pp. 5–8.

[2] In most authorities these appointments are made to the Education Committee.

[3] From 1934 until 1965, the Labour Party controlled the Council. Before that time (1907–34) the Municipal Reform Party (the name the Conservatives used then) held a majority. For the development of local party organizations in London, see Ken Young, 'Political Party Organization', in G. W. Rhodes, *The Government of London: Reform in Action* (London, 1972).

[4] Herbert Morrison, *How London is Governed*, 2nd ed. (London, 1949), p. 4. Those matters reserved to the Council were 'questions of principle' and finance. In general, see Morrison, p. 44ff.

mittees was carried out in sub-committees which could also have authority delegated to them. This was especially true of the Town Planning Committee which dealt with development control permissions,[1] and the Education Committee. The latter committee was required by law to meet in public; in order to avoid the possible effects of public debate on the conduct of business, most of the business was conducted in sub-committees closed to the public and subsequently presented to the full committee. The importance of the committees can be seen in the practice of 'chairman's action', a procedure which allowed a chairman, vice-chairman or other authorized member of a committee, sometimes in consultation with a leader of the opposition party, to decide on committee business between meetings if the matter was deemed urgent or of minor importance. Also, the chairman and vice-chairmen of the various committees, along with the leadership of both parties (generally the same group of people with the addition of the Leader of the Council), were authorized to take action on behalf of the Council when committees were not in session. The committees were organized along functional lines with the addition of two for purposes of co-ordination, the Finance Committee and the General Purposes Committee.

The leadership of the Council was in the hands of the Leader of the Council who was the head of the majority party and in some ways resembled the Prime Minister.[2] Both he and his counterpart from the opposing party, the Leader of the Opposition, had the right to attend any committee meeting. As noted, the various committees were structured in similar fashion with a chairman elected along party lines and also opposition leaders. The jobs of the Leader and of the chairmen of the more important committees were virtually full-time jobs requiring at least four days a week.[3] The average back-bench member probably attended approximately a hundred Council and committee meetings a year. All of the members and aldermen were unpaid.[4]

The total number of LCC officers amounted to somewhat over 12,000, including administrative, clerical, professional and technical personnel. Of

---

[1] The application sub-committee (of the Planning Committee), which handled most development control cases, met every week while the full Council was in session. The sub-committee was broken into panels of three members who rotated at the weekly meetings. The panels were chaired by either the Chairman or Vice-Chairman of the full Committee (both from the majority party) or by those holding the same position on the sub-committee (also majority party members). Controversial and important applications were handled by either the sub-committee or the full Committee. The panels handled mostly routine applications and applications for small-scale development.

[2] William Eric Jackson, *Achievement. A Short History of the London County Council* (London, 1965), p. 52. See also Morrison, *London*, pp. 63–5.

The Council was nominally headed by the Chairman of the Council and the Vice-Chairman, both of whom represented the majority party, and a Deputy Chairman who was a member of the minority party. They all served for a term of one year and their offices were largely ceremonial.

[3] Jackson, *Achievement*, p. 61.

[4] The organization of borough councils roughly paralleled that of the County Council.

these, approximately 500 were employed in the town planning section which formed a part of the Architects' Department. The total staff employed by the Council, including the Fire Brigade, teachers, manual workers, etc., was about 76,000. By comparison, Chicago, a city of roughly comparable size, has of the order of 100,000 employees, including school teachers. The officers were organized in departments divided along functional lines more or less paralleling the organization of the committees. The departments were headed by chief officers who were civil servants, not political appointments. The chief administrative officer of the Council was the Clerk. The conditions of service of officers were established by negotiations between the representatives of the Council and the LCC Staff Association.[1]

TOWN PLANNING

Although American cities employ planners and have something called city planning, the precise nature and goals of the enterprise are not at all clear. Whatever planners do, it certainly is not comprehensive control of land use, and therefore a country which seems to have instituted just that, and has been concerned with town planning in some legislative form since at least 1909 (the first Town Planning Act) is of some interest in this regard.

The concern for town planning grew, at least partly, out of a self-serving and patronizing, yet ultimately public-regarding concern, for working-class living conditions and public health. As William Ashworth notes in a study of the origins of British planning, this concern had two dimensions – aesthetic/architectural, and social.[2] The social dimension stressed poor housing conditions and their effects on the inhabitants of a large portion of cities. Wretched slums were breeding disease and lack of respect for the law, it was argued; economic loss to the employing classes was one result. The earliest response to the slums came in the form of public health and housing legislation and it was out of this type of legislation that town planning grew. The latter too was intended to ameliorate the impact of the slums on the total population. However, the implementation, or the proposed implementation, most often came in the form of attempts to arrange the physical environment. Street widening, moving houses apart, providing parks and in general providing for amenity[3] were some of the more favored devices. This was the architectural dimension. Among promoters of planning a somewhat naive connection was made between improving physical condi-

---

[1] The settlements that were reached by the two participants on wages were in accordance with settlements on pay increases made by a National Joint Council (APTC) which dealt with conditions of service for most of the other local authority officers. The translation of these latter settlements into pay scales for LCC officers was done by the local negotiators.

[2] William Ashworth, *The Genesis of Modern British Town Planning* (London, 1954), Chapter 3.

[3] See Chapter 6 for a definition of this term.

tions and improving social relationships, a naivete which still exists to some extent in the minds of practitioners.

The first piece of legislation to use the term 'town planning' was the Housing, Town Planning, Etc., Act, of 1909. This Act empowered local authorities (local government units such as county councils) to prepare schemes for controlling the development of new housing areas. These powers were an extension of existing ones and built on legislation in the public health and housing fields.[1] The emphasis was on raising the standards of new developments. Interestingly, the 1909 Act did not specify what town planning involved, only what it did *not* involve. It was not to deal with the remodeling of existing towns nor the replanning of badly planned areas. The Act merely listed nineteen matters to be dealt with, but because of the cumbersome administrative structure, the problem of land taxes and the First World War, few schemes were attempted under this legislation.

The first revisions of the original Act came in 1919. It did little to change the basic concept of the previous legislation. However, it did make some significant innovations in the area of working-class housing. The 1919 Act accepted the principle of state subsidies for housing; thus began the growth of the council house system. The standards for these housing developments are directly relevant to an understanding of present-day planning. The houses were to be built at not more than 12 to the acre, which usually meant that they had to be built on open spaces on the periphery of towns. The standards required by the Act reflect an already great emphasis on low density living, even for the lower classes, and also suggest that state provision of good accommodations for the worse-off in the society was seen as reasonable by at least some of the leadership of the country.[2]

The increasing suburbanization of the inter-war years posed new problems with which the 1932 Town and Country Planning Act was designed to deal. Specifically, control was extended over all land, whether developed or not. The Act, however, was rather cumbersome and inflexible. Planning schemes had the force of law and took so long to be approved that development often took place illegally with the attendant difficulties of removing it after the fact. In general, up until the post-war period and the passage of the new planning act, planning was largely ineffective.

In the 1920s and especially in the 1930s, the idea of limiting the growth of London in the context of industrial location patterns added a new dimension to the thinking about town planning. While historically there have always been voices that wished to limit the size of the metropolis,[3] now for

[1] J. B. Cullingworth, *Town and Country Planning in England and Wales* (London, 1964), pp. 16–17. The following draws heavily on Cullingworth's book, especially Chapter 1, pp. 16–25.

[2] Indeed, the Act called for three-bedroom houses with kitchen, bath and garden.

[3] As far back as Elizabeth I, Englishmen have been thinking about limiting the size of London. Witness the proclamation issued by Elizabeth I in 1580 which prohibited the growth of the City of London: 'Where there are such great multitudes of people brought to inhabit in small rooms,

the first time extensive thought was given to the relationship between the depressed character of some of the areas of Britain, the growth of London and the location of industry. The problem of depressed areas was, of course, made more acute by the Depression, and in 1934 the Special Areas Act was passed and an administrative structure set up to promote economic activity in the various sections of the country.[1]

After several years of trying to promote economic growth in the depressed areas, the Commissioner of England and Wales concluded that while some things could be done, 'the further expansion of industry should be controlled to secure a more evenly distributed population'.[2] While this was well in line with ideas afoot about national planning, it would have required major political departures. To deal with the implications of the Commissioner's proposal the government of the day set up the Barlow Commission. This Commission (reporting in 1940) was to inquire into the present and future trends of geographical distribution of the industrial population, and into the costs of industrial concentration and ways to remedy it. The Commission concluded that

...the disadvantages in many, if not in most, of the great industrial concentrations, alike on the strategical, the social and the economic side, do constitute serious handicaps and even in some respects dangers to the nation's life and development, and we are of the opinion that definite action should be taken by Government toward remedying them.[3]

Although there were obvious advantages to concentration, the Commission concluded that these were outweighed by the disadvantages, among which it counted: high site values, traffic congestion, and the effects on work efficiency of long journeys to work. The Commission recommended, among other things, garden cities, satellite towns and trading estates to remedy urban congestion.[4]

On the rather more difficult problem of London the Commission commented that a 'balanced distribution of industry and the industrial population so far as possible throughout the different areas or regions in Great Britain' and an 'appropriate diversification of industries in those areas or regions' would be desirable.[5] In short, the concentration of population

whereof a great part are seen very poor, yea, such as must live of begging or by worse means, and they heaped up together, and in a sort smothered with many families of children and servants in one house or small tenement; it must needs follows, if any plague or popular sickness should by God's permission, enter amongst these multitudes, that the same would not only spread itself and invade the whole city and confines, but that a great mortality would ensure the same, where her majesty's personal presence is many times required.' (Quoted in Cullingworth, p. 204.)

[1] The major depressed areas were the North East Coast, West Cumberland, industrial South Wales and the industrial area around Glasgow.

[2] Quoted in Cullingworth, p. 23.

[3] Quoted in Cullingworth, p. 24.

[4] Cullingworth, pp. 24–5.

[5] Quoted in Cullingworth, p. 25.

around London should be reduced. The Commission also recommended that new administrative machinery be set up at the central government level which could set forth and enforce the policies to achieve the desired ends. The Barlow Commission recommendations were accepted by the government and continued to be one of the bases of post-war policy for London and the country.

The effects of the war at home gave added support to the Barlow Commission recommendations. The building of new factories in the depressed areas to serve war needs showed the feasibility of the proposals and the bombing of the country turned what might have been a visionary scheme into a necessity. Some program was required to repair the war damage. It was now necessary to give consideration to replacement of the bombed factories and of bombed cities in general.

The enthusiasm for social change generated by the war was also important in encouraging support for planning policies and machinery. The Uthwatt Committee on Compensation and Betterment (land values), the Scott Committee on Land Utilization in Rural Areas and the Beveridge Committee on Social Insurance and Allied Services, all sitting during this period, reflected such concerns. The ideas of planning 'schemes' and regulation were to be supplemented and to some extent replaced by a broader vision – one that would take a 'positive' and wide-ranging view of land use.

The London advisory plans

The various ideas about the ends to be served by town planning for London found their first great expression in two advisory plans prepared under the direction of Professor Patrick Abercrombie.[1] One plan was for the area of Greater London, the other for the County of London.[2] These plans, building on the Barlow Commission report, brought together many current ideas concerning amenity, open space, low density living, housing for the working class, industrial relocation, limiting the size of London and social and economic planning, and placed them in an original framework.

These advisory plans did not have statutory status, although in 1945 the County Council adopted some of the major principles of the *County of London Plan* including those for density, open space, residential mixing of social classes and location of industry. They were not very thorough in their analysis, having been prepared under somewhat hurried conditions. The architects of the plan worked with census data from 1931 (the last

---

[1] Patrick Abercrombie, *Greater London Plan, 1944* (London, 1945) and J. H. Forshaw and Abercrombie, *The County of London Plan* (London, 1944). Forshaw was chief architect of the London County Council.

[2] There was also an advisory plan for the City of London prepared under the direction of the City Engineer.

census) and without very good projections of the likely post-war economic, demographic and technological changes. The plans were important because they represented an attempt by one of the foremost planners of the time to explore new concepts and bring together old ideas, and on this basis to project a future picture of London as it could and ought to be.

In 1946, after several reviews of the Abercrombie proposals for London and its environs, the government announced through the Minister of Town and Country Planning its support of the major features of the plans. The Minister noted that the proposals made by Abercrombie (and Forshaw) were in accord with the recommendations of the Barlow Commission already adopted by the central government.

The advisory plans contained a very clear idea, indeed a graphic idea, of the way in which London and its environs should look and included the following main features: (1) a concentric ring pattern of residential densities with the highest at the center and a general tapering off to the periphery; (2) maintenance of a single main center for the area, i.e. there were no proposals for building up competing centers; (3) a pattern of radial and ring highways; (4) rebuilding of large portions of the center to new standards and the relocation of some industry; (5) a greenbelt to be maintained and expanded around the built-up portion of the city; (6) a series of new towns to be created outside of the built-up area to take some of the excess population of the central city; (7) a limit on the size of the population of the metropolitan area.[1]

Abercrombie's plans attempted to integrate a number of historical biases concerning land use, ideas about planning in general and for London in particular, and various proposals for social policy. The plans brought together the major aspects of thinking about planning, namely, planning as a way to improve the conditions of the working class, planning as a way to preserve amenity, and city planning as a tool of social and economic planning. Consistently informing the various ideas and approaches was the widely held and historically legitimated idea of limiting the size of London. In general, by integrating and extending existing ideas about London planning, the advisory plans paved the way for a consensus about the development of the metropolis.[2]

Abercrombie's plans were heavily architectural in their orientation. They conceived of the metropolitan area as having a spatial, physical form which could be pictured on a kind of map. Planning, and thus its major expression, the plan, was an activity which would guide the physical and spatial growth of the city towards desired ends expressed in physical and spatial terms. For London, the problem became one of designing the given space and

[1] Donald Foley, *Controlling London's Growth: Planning the Great Wen 1940–1960* (Berkeley, 1963), p. 58.

[2] Foley, p. 52.

physical structures in a way that would serve the major end of constraining the growth of the city.

The 1947 Act and the 'Development Plan' for London

The next major step in the development of planning ideas and machinery was the 1947 Town and Country Planning Act which served as the basis of the post-war planning system for England and Wales. The 1947 Act resolved a good many of the problems of the earlier planning legislation. Now virtually all development was subject to planning permission and provisions were made for the promotion of development by local planning authorities (county councils and county boroughs). All development rights and development values were nationalized and owners of land thus owned only existing (1947) use rights and values. Compensation was to be paid 'once and for all' for development rights out of a national fund and developers were to pay a 100 per cent charge on the increase in land values resulting from development.[1]

The 1947 Act enjoined the local planning authorities, of which the LCC was one, to construct a development plan for the area of their concern. Pursuant to this, the LCC started preparation of a plan for the County of London which under the terms of the Act was to have statutory status. It was to cover roughly a twenty-year period with a focus on the first five years and revisions every five years afterward. Under the terms of the law the County Council had to conduct a survey of the area before preparing the plan. Among other things the survey was to deal with the physical features of the land, population and economic trends, social structure, land use status and trends, and the projects proposed by other governmental agencies in the area.[2] The survey did not reveal to the LCC any need for substantial changes in Abercrombie's proposals or the principles adopted by the Council in 1945. By and large, it was decided to retain the proposals and modify them according to what the survey revealed, or simply to include others that reflected the already existing situation (which might be difficult to alter).[3] For example, the density survey revealed that Abercrombie's density zones were in line with the broad pattern of existing densities within the County and so with some revisions they were incorporated into

[1] See Cullingworth, *Town and Country Planning*, p. 32 and Chapter 4 below. The treatment of development rights and compensation has gone through many changes since 1947. In the present situation, developers no longer pay any development charge. See Cullingworth, Chapter 6.

[2] For a summary of the survey, see London County Council, *Administrative County of London Development Plan, 1951, Analysis* (London, 1951), pp. 9–14.

[3] At the time the Council was preparing the *Plan* it did not, of course, have the data from the 1951 Census. This could only be used in the *Review* (London County Council, *Administrative County of London Development Plan. First Review 1960*, County Planning Reports, vol. 1 (London, 1960). Therefore, aside from the data from the survey, the 1931 Census was still the only comprehensive data available.

the *Development Plan*.[1] To some degree, the Council had to take Abercrombie's proposals on faith. There were no well-developed alternatives, nor was there sufficient research to justify a completely different approach. The advisory plans represented the received wisdom on planning for London combined with some ideas from one of the leading planners of the day.

The density zones the LCC introduced in the *Development Plan* for the control of development were 200, 136, 100, 70 and under 70 persons per acre, the highest being at the center and the lowest at the periphery.[2] The variations in density levels were designed to reflect, among other things, proximity to large open spaces (the Royal Parks at the center), the price of land, and level of demand. The existing evidence suggests that the adjustments were arbitrary, not being based on any careful attempt to evaluate the various factors. But this is not surprising since the Council was following the proposals of Abercrombie who wished to zone the *whole* County of London at the same level (100 p.p.a.). Abercrombie conceded that this was impractical and so made some adjustments. The density levels were pre-eminently designed to serve a single set of values – those concerned with residential space and amenity. All other factors such as housing demand, transport, type of household, were apparently secondary.[3] At the beginning, the density controls were to be used temporarily to reduce the population of London, the aim being to overspill some of the population, rebuild to the new standards and then attract the people back to a better city. The population target for the County was 3.3 million people.

The *Development Plan* by law included a town map showing land use, a program map showing the proposals planned for the next five years and to some degree for future periods, and a written statement setting out and describing what was to be accomplished. This statement included the designation of comprehensive development areas (see below). In its various parts the *Plan* also included proposals for housing, schools, transportation, open space, standards for development (density, day-lighting etc.), special areas and so on. Most of the proposals for capital development were submitted either by departments of the Council other than Planning – for example the Housing Department – or by other bodies concerned with the London area, such as the London Transport Executive.

The *Development Plan* was submitted to the Minister of Housing and

---

[1] The use zones also generally followed the existing distribution of uses.

[2] These figures should be contrasted with figures from some large American cities. In New York (excluding Manhattan) and Boston, the highest densities run about 450 persons per acre (it is not clear whether these are net residential acres) with sections of Manhattan reaching 1,300 p.p.a. The highest densities in Chicago average around 163 p.p.a., in Philadelphia 150 p.p.a. and in Seattle, 62 p.p.a. Quoted in Nathan Glazer 'Housing Problems and Housing Policies', *Public Interest*, 7 (1967), p. 26.

[3] See Forshaw and Abercrombie, *County of London Plan*, p. 79. See also Chapter 7 below. The same approach was carried over by the LCC into open space. All areas of the County were to have the *same* complement of open space regardless of differences in types of neighborhoods and their inhabitants.

Local Government (which had superseded the Ministry of Town and Country Planning) in 1951. The *Plan* was publicized and a public inquiry also held. The latter resulted in over 7,000 objections being filed. Most were withdrawn or dealt with by negotiations and the remaining ones were settled at an inquiry conducted by Ministry officials. The Minister's approval was given to the *Plan* after some relatively minor modifications in 1955.

In 1960 a review was completed and submitted to the Minister. Again publicity was given and again an inquiry held into objections which resulted in the basic features of the original *Plan* remaining unaltered. The review produced some minor modifications in residential densities and also indicated the planning authority's concern about the increase of office use in the central area.[1] After the Minister had proposed some modifications, a second inquiry was held to deal with the modifications and the revised *Plan* was approved in 1962.

The 1947 Act provided for a variety of planning powers which were to be used to achieve the goals set out in the *Plan*. However, the *Plan* was not intended only as a detailed picture of the future. The emphasis was also on flexibility, the relation between future states and flexibility not being considered.[2] The most important power assigned to the planning authority was development control. Under the 1947 Act everyone who proposed to undertake a 'development', which was interpreted to mean any 'substantial' change in the use of land, had first to apply for permission.[3] Not only private developers but also public authorities were required to seek permissions. In the case of the borough councils, this permission had to be obtained from the LCC. When the LCC itself wished to undertake development, it was required to seek approval from the Minister of Housing (as well as obtaining approval from its own Planning Committee). Central government ministries did not need permission to develop, but were expected to consult with the planning authority. The same applied to the statutory undertakers, i.e. public utilities and special districts.

Under a variety of circumstances, applicants could appeal a decision of the LCC to the Minister who then would generally hold a public inquiry (he could have held a private hearing). This was a common procedure when

[1] See Chapter 4.
[2] See Chapter 7. Also see Desmond Heap, 'English Development Plans for the Control of Land Use', in Charles Haar (ed.), *Law and Land: Anglo-American Planning Practice* (Cambridge, Mass., 1964), pp. 79–80 and Charles Haar, 'Comparisons and Comments', in Haar, *Law and Land*, p. 259.
[3] Lewis B. Keeble, *Principles and Practice of Town and Country Planning*, 2nd ed. (London, 1959), p. 286. Permission is even required for changes in the design and appearance of buildings. Keeble, p. 286.
Permissions are most often given, especially in large developments, to outline applications. These applications state the general features of the development and if permission is granted the specifics are subject to approval.
The LCC generally received over 10,000 applications for permission to develop in any given year. Of these it usually approved between 80 and 90 per cent. See GLC, *London Statistics 1955–64*, p. 157.

permission was refused by the County Council. As well, if the LCC wished to approve an application which constituted a significant departure from the *Development Plan*, permission from the Minister was required, who would hold an inquiry. The Ministry of Housing and Local Government was thus supposed to be an enforcer of equity and a coordinator of planning activities.

Development control was the principal means by which the Council attempted to serve its planning ends. However the 1947 Act and the various acts which preceded and followed it granted a variety of other powers. Among these were: comprehensive development areas, new towns and expanded towns. The first is a process by which public acquisition of land is used to redevelop or develop a large area. This may be done, for example, in areas of war damage, areas of obsolete development or bad layout, or where land is to be developed as a whole for any purpose defined in the development plan. The land may be developed by the planning authority itself or by a private developer or both together, but the authority must draw the plan for the area.[1] As to the new towns, eight were built to serve London in the post-war period under development corporations set up by the central government and helped by the LCC. Expanded towns are those towns with which the LCC entered into agreements to accept some of the Council's overspill population. The LCC helped pay for these expanding towns by rendering financial and other forms of assistance to the receiving authorities.

The ideas informing the planning of London were aimed at serving one basic end, viz., the containment of London and its surrounding region. While the population of the County in fact declined, it would be difficult to attribute this solely to the efforts of the planning authority. Indeed, it may well be that the efforts of the LCC and its successor have played second fiddle to demographic changes that were already in progress. However, while the population of the County and the conurbation has been declining, the population of the areas in the wider London region has been growing. It has not proved possible to contain the London region. Partly as a result of this failure and partly as a result of better data and more sophisticated approaches to metropolitan planning, the Abercrombie orthodoxy and the ideas in the *Development Plan* have been challenged in recent years. There are those who now argue that it is necessary to accept the continued growth of the London region, and future planning for the region may well look more kindly on it.[2]

[1] Cullingworth, *Town and Country Planning*, pp. 247–50.
[2] See Chapter 7 and, for example, Peter G. Hall, *London 2000*, 2nd ed. (London, 1969) and J. H. Westergaard, 'The Structure of Greater London', Centre for Urban Studies (ed.), *London: Aspects of Change* (London, 1964). The 1971 Census figures show substantial declines in the population of the GLC area, thus indicating a continuation of existing trends in the built-up area of the region. Partly in response to this the GLC has become concerned about the continuing economic vitality of London. See Chapter 5.

3. WORLD'S END:
HOUSING IN WEST CHELSEA

INTRODUCTION

Chelsea was one of the small inner boroughs of London. It had somewhat under 50,000 population and was at the west end of the central core of the County on the north side of the Thames River. (See map on p. 34.) The borough was predominantly composed of middle-class and upper-class people with a small enclave of working-class residents in the western portion at World's End. Parts of the eastern end of the borough had been privately renewed, as many of the old working-men's cottages were turned into pleasant little residences for the better-off who wished a fashionable Chelsea address. This process of private renewal had also started in the western section of the borough, although to a lesser extent than in the east.

The struggle for a desirable Chelsea address was limited by the relatively short supply of residential land in the borough. It had a total of 382 residential acres, making it the fifth smallest borough in this regard (excluding the City). Its over-all density was more or less average for the County, being approximately 115 persons per acre. In the *Development Plan*, the borough was zoned at 136 p.p.a.[1] The price of land in the borough was rather high compared with other residential parts of the County, although probably not the highest. Partly as a result of this, Chelsea did not have as much open space as some of the other residential boroughs.[2] However, it was only twelfth out of 29 in terms of open space deficiency according to the LCC.[3] It had in fact a total of over 76 acres of open space of which about half was open to the public and roughly an additional third characterized by limited access. The rest was private open space. There was little,

[1] The average density figure for the borough and the zoned density taken together make it seem that there was, according to the *Plan*, room for expansion. This is misleading. First, the existing average density hid areas where the density was, in fact, considerably higher. According to the terms of the *Plan*, the densities of these areas was to be reduced. Chelsea was in fact designated as a borough to be overspilled. In general, the population of the County at the time of this study was below the proposed one (3,200,484 to 3,300,000). Again this is misleading in a sense similar to that just noted. The plan was not to reduce the size of the population but rather to shift it around in the County so as to improve standards of accommodation and also to overspill some people, improve the area, and then attract them back.

[2] Aside from being a residential borough, Chelsea also contained one of the large shopping areas of London, viz. King's Road and Sloane Square.

[3] *Analysis*, p. 221.

if any, unused acreage in the borough, and, therefore, any addition to the stock of open space would have to have been at the expense of other uses. The result of this, as well as the high cost of land, was that the LCC had proposed the smallest addition to the stock of open space for Chelsea of all the boroughs. (The boroughs themselves could also add to the stock.)

The Conservative Party dominated Chelsea politics starting before World War II; the Labour Party in the late fifties and early sixties (the time of the case study) had few representatives on the Borough Council. The LCC through these years was dominated by the Labour Party. The fact of party differences *per se* did not guarantee differences of opinion between the two authorities, but in the case of Chelsea, the fact that it was a Tory borough took on special significance in the eyes of the LCC. One student of London politics put the matter this way.

Whereas Westminster and Hampstead [Borough Councils] are good Tories, that is, they are Tories but they do provide good services, Chelsea is viewed in Labour circles as being particularly unenlightened – perhaps the nearest one gets in London to the pre-welfare state Toryism of the rural shires.[1]

Added to this, the LCC felt that the Borough Council had not done all it could in the past in the area of planning, particularly in the area of open space. One senior LCC planner commented that

...there is a difference in perspective between the two authorities. The borough is a housing authority and only that; it is only really interested in building houses and not in roads, open space and so on. The LCC as a planning authority has to take a broader view. In fact the Ministry has pointed out to the LCC that Chelsea should have more open space. However, Chelsea hasn't been too keen on providing it. They keep saying that they'll deal with it in the next project.

The borough on its side, felt that given the built-up nature of the area and the cost of land, provision of additional open space was difficult at best. All told, relations between the borough and the LCC were not very harmonious.

HOUSING MARKETS AND HOUSING POLICY IN LONDON

The population of the Administrative County of London in 1961 was just over 3.2 million. This was an increase from a war-time low of 2.3 million but still a decline from the turn of the century population of over 4 million. Except for the upsurge caused by population returning after the war, there had been a steady decline in the County population since at least 1920.[2] These population figures suggest that the total demand for housing in the central city area would not have increased after World War II (leaving

---

[1] Personal communication from L. J. Sharpe.
[2] See *Analysis*, Chapter 2.

aside the question of loss of housing due to bombing). A declining population ought not to generate an increasing total demand. The actual picture was, however, somewhat more complex. While the population of the County declined, the number of households declined substantially less, and the number of separate dwellings actually increased.[1] There was, in fact, a complex population movement in and out of the County. As far as can be determined, what happened was as follows. Families with children moved out, often leaving behind old parents who had lived with them and who often still required individual dwellings. Coming in were young people and young married professionals, often without children.[2] In short, the average size of households in the County was declining so that rather than the demand for housing declining, at least for smaller dwellings, it increased.[3]

Taken altogether, however, these various factors should have produced an overall improvement in housing conditions. In fact, the excess of households over dwellings fell from 300,000 in 1951 to 169,000 in 1961. However, some groups benefited considerably more from this decline than others. To understand why, the following facts must be noted. Empty land in the County was very scarce and new building proceeded very slowly.[4] From 1948 until 1960, the total number of houses built in the County was roughly between 8,000 and 12,000 per year; this included all housing authorities, housing associations and private enterprise. There was practically no building by private enterprise for rent.[5] The housing most likely to remain in the

---

[1] D. V. Donnison, *The Government of Housing* (Harmondsworth, Middlesex, 1967), p. 333. The following account relies heavily on Donnison. For a brief review of post-war housing policy in England and Wales see Donnison, Chapter 5. For a broader review, see J. B. Cullingworth, *Housing and Local Government in England and Wales*, The New Town and County Hall Series, No. 8 (London, 1964), and by the same author, *Housing Needs and Planning Policy* (London, 1960).

[2] Hall, *London 2000*, pp. 95–9.

[3] In 1951, the average household size in the County was 2.82 persons. In 1961, it was 2.66. For England and Wales, the average size in 1951 was 3.19 and 3.11 in 1961. In 1951, the average household size in Chelsea was 2.45; in 1961 it was 2.12 (Hall, *London 2000*, p. 96). Abercrombie in his original population projection for the LCC area and its environs was not aware of the interrelationships between population size, household size and housing demand. He concentrated on the first and the third. In England, it wasn't until around 1960 that the importance of household size for housing demand was appreciated. Donnison, *Government of Housing*, pp. 171–2.

[4] A Chairman of the Housing Committee of the LCC commented on the shortage of land as follows: 'The other reality is that housing always has had overriding priority. I have never known the Council to refuse money for housing. The shortage of land or the building industry shortages have slowed us down, but never money. Even under the last [Conservative] government when there were cutbacks we didn't slow down our housing program. We are entirely limited by the rate at which we can clear land. This, even more than the building industry is our limit, not financial restrictions.'

[5] In general, private industry built comparatively little housing in the County. From 1945 to 1960, private developers constructed about 12 per cent of the total new housing units. The various housing authorities provided about 86 per cent in the same period. The rest were constructed by housing associations. (From data supplied by the LCC.) This partly derives from a socialist suspicion of landlords; the LCC was by and large not interested in promoting private building. Housing was to be a publicly provided service. As Donnison comments, 'In this country, government tends to draw clear distinctions between private and public enterprise and to treat the profit

rental sector was older houses that could be sub-divided, and older flats. Self-contained rented houses which were suitable for families with children were more likely to be lost to slum clearance or to owner occupation. After the war, and until about 1955, local housing authorities made good progress housing families from their waiting lists, i.e., putting families who had requested council housing into such houses. After that, slum clearance gained momentum and the new housing was used more to rehouse those who had been displaced than those on the waiting lists. In 1950, its best year, the LCC rehoused 12,000 people, 84 per cent of whom had been on the waiting list. However, in the sixties the figure was more like 7,500 persons per year rehoused with less than a quarter coming off the waiting list.

Those who gained from this situation were: (1) people whose homes were being demolished by slum clearance; (2) people who did manage to make it off the lists; (3) families whose children had left thus giving them (the parents) additional space; (4) those who had contacts and could get the better, rented housing; (5) those who could afford to buy a house. Those who lost out were the poorer sections of the community and large families, especially if they had to live near the center of town because of their jobs. Two other groups tended to lose, viz. recent movers to London who were without contacts (young, single people, for example), and foreigners, often non-white, with low incomes. Add to the factors noted, the old age of many of London's dwellings,[1] the war losses that had to be made good,[2] and the natural process of displacement, and the result was that the housing situation for at least some sections of the community was very difficult. It is these groups who tended to share dwellings,[3] live in substandard dwellings[4] and languish on the waiting lists.

The housing situation for London can be summed up in the following figures which relate the demand for housing to the supply available. In 1961, the excess of demand over supply was 121,000 units.[5] To this must

motive with a suspicion equally chilling, whether derived from socialist hostility to capitalism or aristocratic contempt for those "in trade".' Donnison, *Government of Housing*, p. 180.

[1] In 1949, the last date for such data for London County, almost 75 per cent of the housing in the County was built before 1916, 25 per cent before 1870.

[2] About 10 per cent of the buildings in the County had been destroyed, 10 per cent were damaged and uninhabitable and 10 per cent were damaged but inhabitable. *Analysis*, p. 28.

[3] Almost 550,000 people shared dwellings in the Greater London Council area in 1961, 125,000 of whom did not have exclusive use of either stove or sink. General Register Office, *Census 1961, England and Wales. Greater London Tables* (London, 1963–4).

[4] About 55 per cent of all dwelling units in the County in 1961 were unsatisfactory. General Register Office, *Census 1961, County Report, London* (London, 1963). A satisfactory dwelling would have the following: piped cold and hot water; water closet; and fixed bath.

[5] As Hall notes (*London 2000*, pp. 104–9), these figures for excess demand are ideal figures. They do not measure actual shortages but rather what people 'might decently expect to live in'. They also include a vacancy rate of 3 per cent.

be added the unsatisfactory housing units, and any natural demographic increase. Hall arrives at a maximum figure of 629,000 total new dwellings required for the years 1961 to 2000. The minimum figure would be 343,000 for the same period. To meet the maximum figure would require somewhat over 15,500 new units per year; to meet the minimum figure would require roughly 8,500 new units per year. The total new construction for the period 1950–61, on a yearly basis, averaged just over 9,000 new units. In the long term, then, if standards are not revised upward and no distinctions are made about the type of housing necessary to meet the various types of demands, housing supply will catch up with housing demand defined at minimum levels of acceptability. However, this would mean some large section of the population languishing in unsatisfactory housing for extended periods. To meet the deficit in a shorter period would require a great mobilization of resources.

Chelsea

In Chelsea, the amount of substandard housing in 1961 was 33 per cent of the total.[1] The number of people on the waiting list for a council house in the borough as of 1964 was just over 1,300. Of these nearly 300 had been on the list for over 10 years and the average length of time a family had to wait to be rehoused in Council property was 11 years. The Borough Council's record in attempting to meet this situation was about 1,000 new units constructed in the period 1945 to 1958.[2] This put the Borough Council 26th out of 28 boroughs in the provision of total number of council housing.[3] On a *per capita* basis the Borough Council did somewhat better, ranking 19th. In the post-war period, the LCC built no council housing in Chelsea. This was the only metropolitan borough of which this was true.

Several factors help to explain what might be construed as a less than satisfactory response by the Borough Council to the housing situation. At least the following factors were relevant: the high cost of land; the size of the borough which made rehousing difficult; the built-up nature of most of the land; the social composition of the borough which meant less demand for subsidized council housing; the intermittent credit squeezes of the post-war period; the changes in housing subsidies (the last two apply to all housing authorities); and the fact of renewal by better-off private owners. Added to this, there was some suggestion of indifference to council housing

[1] *Census 1961, County Report, London.*

[2] In addition, private building added an additional 500 dwellings in the same period. *Review,* p. 87. The total number of dwellings in the borough was just under 20,000. *Census 1961, County Report, London.*

[3] *Review,* p. 87.

for long periods on the part of the Conservative Party in the Borough. A weak Labour Party points in the same direction.

Calls for higher density

As a result of pressure on housing resources in London, various people spoke out in favor of higher densities. The call for increased densities was given formal status in 1962 by the Conservative Minister, Sir Keith Joseph, in several speeches, White Papers and Ministry circulars[1] and in a letter to the LCC. As early as 1959, the organization representing the metropolitan boroughs (who were housing authorities and thus were preoccupied with this problem) made it known to the LCC that it would like a review of the density issue so that the boroughs could, within the directives of the *Development Plan*, provide more housing than was allowed at present. This point was again made by the body, the 'Metropolitan Boroughs Standing Joint Committee' in 1960. In reply to the 1960 representation, the LCC indicated that it would make some limited allowances at the quinquennial review of the *Development Plan* to be presented in 1961 and in fact did so. But, in general, the allowances were small and the LCC was determined to rely on the original densities as the major means to insure 'adequate' living conditions within the perspective of the *Plan*.[2]

The LCC in fact was long suspicious of lowering housing standards, and particularly density standards. The attitude of the authority was well expressed by one senior planner.

The main object of controlling densities in London is to secure good living conditions. An excessive number of persons per acre leads to unsatisfactory conditions. Even by using the utmost skill in design and modern methods of construction, it is very difficult with high densities to provide all that is necessary for family living. Very little green space around buildings can be made available, children cannot be given really adequate space for play, private gardens are non-existent and privacy at a minimum. Densities of 200 persons per acre, if not imaginatively handled, could repeat the social errors of Victorian tenements. Above 200 persons per acre sheer bulk of building can be oppressive.

Only grudgingly and haltingly did the LCC revise its standards upward to deal with increased housing pressures.

There were relatively few challenges to the prescribed densities in the form of applications for figures well above those prescribed. The challenges that did come were mostly by commercial developers trying to maximize

---

[1] See, e.g., the statement by Joseph in Ministry of Housing and Local Government, *Residential Areas, Higher Densities*, Planning Bulletin No. 2 (1962).

[2] In the review of the *Plan*, the Minister had struck out 200 p.p.a. as a ceiling on density. This is indicative of changing attitudes in the Ministry. The LCC was very much against this.

their investment and these were generally dismissed as commercial propositions of the kind the *Development Plan* was designed to prohibit. However,
in 1962, another kind of challenge arose, noticeable for the sophistication of
the design. This was from a borough housing authority whose values were
not commercial (although obviously economic feasibility was a consideration)
and who presented serious arguments why even under the perspective of
the *Development Plan* and if need be, outside of it, there was reason to
allow high density housing in those areas not upgraded at the review. This
attack could not be dismissed so lightly.

THE CREMORNE ESTATE AND THE EXTENDED AREA

After World War II, the Chelsea Borough Council started on a council
housing scheme in the West Chelsea area, which was completed in 1956.
The project was built at the prescribed density of 136 persons per acre and
covered an area of 9.5 acres. As a senior officer of the Borough Council
noted: 'At the time, the boroughs were afraid of the LCC and so we took
the density zones as given.' During the planning of the scheme, a plan was
drawn up by the architects of the development which also included the
adjoining area known as the World's End section of West Chelsea. At the
completion of the Cremorne Estate, as the project was known, plans for the
second phase of the development lapsed, owing to high land costs and rehousing problems.

In 1955, the Town Clerk wrote on behalf of the Borough Council to the
Architect of the LCC (under whose nominal head the administration of
planning was carried out) asking that the programming of the extended
area (World's End) be pushed forward to the next period, i.e., after 1971.[1]
The Clerk noted that moving the programming up would encourage those
interested in renovating their homes to do so, since the fear of demolition
would be put off for almost 20 years. The LCC replied that to put the
area in the subsequent programming category would be impossible as this
was reserved for projects of great significance whose development was
uncertain. The County Council also noted that the appropriate time to
seek reprogramming was at the first review of the *Development Plan* when
it would decide whether the programming ought to be deleted entirely.
There the matter lay until 1960 when in the course of the quinquennial
review of the *Plan*, the LCC suggested that rather than delete the programming, the borough should proceed in the indicated period (6–20 years).
The County Council based its decision in part on the fact that the borough
already owned some of the property in the area.

---

[1] This would be the third programming period, 20 years (from 1951) and beyond. The first
period was 0–5 years; the second was 6–20 years.

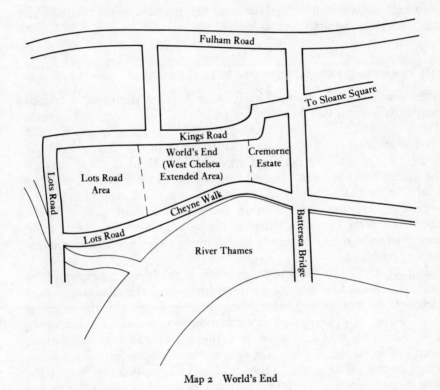

Map 2   World's End

At this juncture, a number of circumstances came together which convinced the Borough Council that it had to act in the World's End area. Aside from the fact that the programming still remained (although this would still allow private development), several other factors emerged. Under a 1955 Act, housing authorities were forced to start giving up houses requisitioned during the war (this was to be completed by 1960).[1] This meant that the borough would have an addition to its housing burden consisting of those who were turned out and had to be rehoused. In addition, in 1960 a new Chairman of the Housing Committee was elected who considered herself to be on the left-wing of the Conservative Party and strongly committed to schemes of social justice, which seems to have been something of a departure from her predecessors. Another reason the Council felt compelled to act is that it was clear to the councilors and officers that World's End was the last major housing site that would be available for some time.[2] Undoubtedly, the most important factor was the gradual change in thinking on the density issue alluded to above. It was clear to the Borough Council that as long as it could only rehouse at 136 p.p.a., which was the zoned density, any scheme would contribute little to coping with its housing difficulties.

Meetings with the County Council

In 1961, the Borough Council started to give serious consideration to a housing scheme for World's End. After some preliminary discussion within the Council, an informal meeting was arranged with a planning officer of the LCC who was in charge of redevelopment in the area. The meeting took place in December with the Borough Council being represented by its relevant officers. The result was an agreement on the area to be included in the development (12.2 acres) as well as some indication by the LCC officer of what the County Council might accept. It was agreed that the area for purposes of calculating density should be considerably larger than the site to be actually built on. The major point here was the inclusion of the original Cremorne Estate. It was agreed that for purposes of density the two areas (Cremorne and World's End) could be considered together with the density being calculated as an average of the existing density on Cremorne plus the expected density in World's End. This was clearly an advantage for the Borough Council as it allowed more people to be housed on the World's End site than if density was calculated solely on the actual area to be redeveloped since the Cremorne Estate had a relatively low density. The LCC planner indicated that the County Council would probably look favorably on a density of 170 p.p.a. average on the two sites. He further said

---

[1] *Requisitioned Houses and Housing (Amendment) Act, 1955.*

[2] To let private parties redevelop might leave the borough with the stigma of a poor housing record, given the impending metropolitan area reorganization.

35

that the LCC would also expect that the scheme include one acre of open space per one thousand persons.[1] It was clear that, at this stage in the discussions, the LCC was inclined to be generous and go well beyond the zoned density and to demand less than the open space presumably required by the *Plan*.[2]

The next contact between the two authorities came little less than a month later and was in the form of a letter from the Chairman of the Borough Planning Committee which said that the borough was interested in an overall density figure of 250 p.p.a. (i.e., an average density including the Cremorne Estate). The Chairman noted that the proposed development was near the Thames River and near a large public park, both of which, in light of LCC statements in the *Review*, might merit a higher density. The Chairman also objected to the requirement of one acre of open space per thousand population as it would, he contended, make the scheme difficult to execute since it would mean fewer people could be housed.[3]

During this period, the LCC planning officers were crystallizing their attitudes toward the project. Originally, as one planner put it, 'we were somewhat at sea as to what density to accept. On the one hand, the borough was pushing for a high density, on the other, we knew that the [Town Planning] Committee was inclined to be rigid on such matters.' However, it was agreed, as another planner commented, that 'a town planning case could be made out for the figure of 170 p.p.a.' Another officer noted that when the then Chairman of the Planning Committee granted a raise in the zoned density, he usually allowed a density equal to the next level, i.e., 170 p.p.a. in this case. In this particular case, the Chairman, in fact, had said that he would accept 170 p.p.a. It is clear from the correspondence and reports that those in the LCC actively concerned with the case favored granting a density of 170 p.p.a.

No more contact between the two authorities occurred until the middle of February (1962) when a meeting took place which this time included members as well as officers. Several methods of developing the area were canvassed, with the borough pushing for densities of 250 persons per acre and the LCC Planning Committee Chairman allowing that 200 p.p.a. might be permitted across both sites if some additional building were done on the Cremorne Estate so that the new site would not be overcrowded. The open space provisions were also discussed. But whereas the LCC felt that it had emphasized that in order for 200 p.p.a. density to be allowed, the open space provisions had to be adhered to, the borough thought that it was getting

---

[1] The ultimate LCC target for open space was 4 acres per thousand, the interim target figure was 2½. In calculating density for an area, public open space was not included in the acreage.

[2] The *Plan* was not very clear as to whether in large developments the open space standard of 2½ acres per thousand had to be met on the site itself. This was to become a point of contention. See below.

[3] There were roughly 1,900 people on the World's End site, at a density of 176 p.p.a.

an unconditional offer of this density. This difference did not come out until some time after the meeting. The principal outcome of the meeting was that it was agreed that the Chelsea Council should write to the LCC asking for a 200 p.p.a. density and the LCC Chairman would endeavour to see that it was approved.

After the Chairman had made his offer of 200 p.p.a., he realized that he might have been too generous. He found little support from members of the Committee who were wary of such high densities, nor from planners who, though inclined to be generous with the borough, were against going so high. They were particularly upset because they felt that there was an understanding with the Chairman about the appropriate density for the project (i.e., 170 p.p.a.).

After meeting with the LCC, the Chairman of the Borough Planning Committee wrote to his counterpart, putting in writing the latter's offer and indicating the borough's acceptance. The Chelsea Chairman said that if 250 p.p.a. was unacceptable to the LCC, the 200 p.p.a. would be accepted by the borough as a rockbottom figure. Even though this might not allow elimination of the waiting list, it would permit substantial inroads. In response to the borough's letter, LCC planners indicated in a report to the Planning Committee their preference for 170 p.p.a. overall.

The main report suggests that by developing the new site at 200 p.p.a., an overall figure of 170 p.p.a. would be reached, providing for a net gain in housing of some 550 persons...This is the highest figure we could recommend and even so, some high buildings would be inevitable, with civic design problems and possible difficulty through aerodynamic effect upon the near-by chimneys of the Lots Road Power Station. It should be possible at this density to meet these points, but we would expect this to be impracticable at any higher figure. In any case, having regard to these difficulties...we would suggest that the committee do not specifically agree to a density above that for which the area is zoned, but ask the Borough Council to submit a sketch.

In March, events became somewhat confused. While the borough debated whether to submit an application at the figure of 200 p.p.a. over the combined Cremorne and World's End areas, the LCC realized that it was somewhat vulnerable owing to the unexpected generosity of the Chairman, which he now regretted. A strategic withdrawal was called for. The first hint of the withdrawal came when the two authorities exchanged transcripts of what had taken place at the February meeting. The LCC record emphasized that even if an offer of 200 p.p.a. was made by the Chairman, difficulty was still expected and also that the offer was qualified by need for open space. The borough's rendition did not mention such a qualification.

The next step in the withdrawal came in a meeting in March between officers of the two authorities. Aside from confirming the elimination of 250 p.p.a. density figure, the point of interest of the meeting was that the

LCC planner was not prepared to offer any specific density figure. The retreat was confirmed in a subsequent letter to the borough which said that without a sketch of the proposed development, the LCC would not consider *any* increase in density. The letter concluded by saying, that 'the Council would be prepared to consider some slight increase in density subject to the submission of a satisfactory scheme'.

During this same period the borough had decided to submit an application for an average of 200 p.p.a. for both areas realizing that 200 p.p.a. was the highest density the LCC would accept in light of the previous meetings. Curiously, the application was not accompanied by a sketch scheme. On 30 May the LCC Town Planning Committee turned down the application. The notice of rejection stated 'that such an overall density is considered excessive'. Furthermore, without a 'sketch scheme' the LCC said, a 'congested layout' would result. Also any sketch would have to deal with the problems associated with the neighboring power station. The letter went on to say that room must be left for a primary school, the area for which was not to be included for density purposes. This was the first time the school was brought up, except for a brief mention in the February meeting and the borough was baffled.[1] In the planners' report to the Committee which preceded the above refusal, they recommended that the County Council turn down 200 p.p.a. but they stated that the Council should recommend a density of 170 p.p.a. However, in its instructions to the planners, the Committee said that the LCC 'would be prepared to consider...a density somewhat in excess of 136 p.p.a.' with a school site and satisfactory design arrangement. This was the phrase that appeared in the letter of refusal to the borough.

An application with a sketch

Chelsea's response to the LCC refusal was to prepare a sketch plan of a development scheme at a density of 200 p.p.a. It was submitted in July. Although the LCC was no longer interested in 200 p.p.a., as indicated by the previous refusal, the borough went ahead. The sketch confirmed the worst fears of LCC planners: it was a crude piece of work[2] which was designed to demonstrate that it was physically possible to get the required number of people on the site and still have room for open space and a school. The sketch conspicuously failed to show that a 200 p.p.a. density development could be designed while achieving architectural merit and promoting amenity. It confirmed the LCC in its position that densities of 200 or above

[1] The 1951 *Plan* showed a proposed primary school, but in the *Review* all such symbols were deleted. The school was also shown in the *London School Plan* of 1944.

[2] The sketch contained two massive, Y-shaped, concrete, 26 story apartment blocks with simple markings for a school and open space.

were unworkable. However, having now met the LCC's requirement for a sketch, if a refusal was forthcoming, the borough could lodge an appeal with the Minister.

The LCC's response to the sketch scheme indicated that it was somewhat bemused by the new application and planners wrote to the borough noting their unhappiness with the new application and asking whether, in fact, a formal review of it was desired. The Chelsea Council in its turn wrote an angry letter saying that it had submitted a sketch scheme in order to confirm a promise made by the LCC Planning Chairman that 200 p.p.a. was acceptable. One further round of letters, which contained essentially the same arguments, was exchanged. This took events up to August 1962.

Not unexpectedly, the application was formally refused in November 1962. The letter said that the density was 'excessive' and that, moreover, 'the height, bulk and massing [of the buildings] would mar the skyline and spoil the traditional views as seen from the river'. Amenities would be 'prejudiced', and architectural problems were not satisfactorily dealt with, continued the Council. Also not dealt with was the effect of high buildings on the nearby power station. The LCC then stated that it would be prepared to accept an average density of 150 p.p.a. for the Cremorne Estate and World's End. Before the Committee had stated that the maximum allowable density would be 150 p.p.a., LCC planners had argued that the Committee should turn down the application but not specify an acceptable density figure and wait upon a more reasonable sketch. It seems clear that while the planners were unhappy with the borough's behavior, they were not prepared to close the door to further negotiations by saying that the LCC would accept so much and no more. Members, however, would not commit the Council to anything but a small increase in the existing density without an intelligent plan for redevelopment. The initial feeling that a 170 p.p.a. average was satisfactory was in part based on good will, which was subsequently dissipated. It is interesting to note that the Borough was, in fact, apparently willing to accept a figure of 170 p.p.a. overall if a higher density was not forthcoming.[1]

After the refusal of the sketch scheme, the borough was faced with the question of whether to ask for an appeal before an inspector of the Minister. The Leader of the Conservative Party on the LCC, who was elected from a Chelsea constituency, counselled an appeal based on his knowledge that the

[1] The Chairman of the Borough Housing Committee, in a letter to a Chelsea M.P. said that the figure of 170 p.p.a. was really suitable; permission at this density would allow rehousing of people on the site and some cut in the waiting list. This view was confirmed by the Town Clerk on the same day in another letter to the M.P. The Clerk noted that 150 p.p.a. was out of the question (this was after the last refusal), that 200 p.p.a. over the whole area would result in about 280 p.p.a. on the actual building site which was probably unacceptable, so that the borough would accept a figure of 170 p.p.a. which would allow some inroads on the housing list. A Chelsea officer when reading a draft of the case study and coming across the assertion that the borough would have accepted a 170 p.p.a. density, wrote in the margin, 'Never'.

Minister (Sir Keith Joseph) was in favor of high density schemes. In a letter to the Borough Council, he said that he 'kn[ew] the Minister has views about increased density in certain places which are likely to coincide with yours'.[1] He noted, however, that as the Minister had to decide the appeal, no approaches could be made to him on the matter. The borough went as far as preparing the grounds of appeal, but when they sought advice from a lawyer who specialized in representations at planning inquiries, they were advised that in order to make a stronger case, they should commission an intelligent scheme by a well-known architect. If this was rejected by the LCC, then, given the Minister's views, they would certainly stand a good chance at the appeal. The advice was taken and one of the finest architects in the country was called in and asked to prepare a high density scheme for the area.

Some objections to the redevelopment and other interim events

When the various applications were submitted, the proposed development received some publicity in the Chelsea newspaper. This was in addition to the required notification of the residents living on the projected development site. Reaction to the project was split. The World's End area was actually two neighborhoods of more or less equal size. One section principally consisted of renovated houses occupied mostly by the better-off. This renovation was an extension of the process that had taken place over much of the eastern section of the borough. The other section was in appearance much as the first section would have been had not attention been lavished upon it. The houses were generally badly in need of repair and some were without basic amenities. The reaction to the proposed development closely followed the differences in the property. Those who had sunk goodly sums of money into their properties were loathe to be cleared off,[2] while those who lived in the deteriorating houses were very pleased. Protestors were more vocal than supporters. The objections were, however, temporarily stilled when the borough decided to prepare a new scheme for the area. The objectors decided to wait until the next round, i.e., until the new scheme was to be considered by the LCC.[3]

Another interim event was the Borough Council elections on 10 May 1962 and, although the redevelopment was discussed, business was as usual, the Tories winning easily.

[1] Borough officials already knew this first hand. One official noted that at a party the 'Minister himself gave considerable encouragement to the submission of a plan for a high density scheme'.

[2] These people invested in houses in the area when they saw that the Borough Council was not moving rapidly toward redevelopment of the area.

[3] It is important to note that if the LCC approved the new scheme, the objectors would have been shut out. A public inquiry was generally possible only if the planning authority rejected an application, since it was only an applicant that could request one.

A new scheme

After the LCC's rejection of the scheme there was a brief hiatus in the contacts between the two authorities as the borough had its new proposals prepared. The next contact between the two authorities took place between LCC officers and the architect employed by the Borough Council. In this meeting LCC planners again noted that any density in excess of 150 p.p.a. over the Cremorne and World's End areas combined would not be acceptable. They also mentioned the problems associated with high buildings and revealed that the nearby power station was to be modernized and thus had to be taken into account in any development. LCC planners also noted that a new major road was coming into the area which made any large scale project uncertain. Finally, they raised the question of utilizing in an expanded project a tract of land (about 28 acres) next door to World's End, which was known as the Lots Road area. It was zoned as industrial but the LCC could rezone it residential, they said. This was an attempt to get the two authorities together in what otherwise might turn out as a deadlock. In the end, the borough decided to disregard the LCC's reluctance to allow a high density and high buildings and to let the architect continue to construct a scheme which had an overall density of 200 p.p.a., contained several high buildings and which would house approximately 2,500 people.

Negotiations on expanding the site carried on for several months, with the Planning Chairman of the LCC (by this time there was a new Chairman) showing some interest, but with the major burden being shouldered by the planners. One of the major stumbling blocks between the authorities was an agreement over who would be responsible for rehousing any people displaced from a wider scheme. Discussions proceeded through December 1963 but by early January 1964 the borough was beginning to feel that the offer to develop Lots Road was a diversion. A senior officer of the borough expressed it this way.

The Lots Road offer was a red herring. It would have meant further delay since plans were nebulous for the area. Also, because it was zoned for light industry this would have meant a process of negotiating this change. Anyway, since the area did have residences this would have meant the overspill problem would have been harder to deal with since more people would now be involved.

To decide on what course of action to take in the face of the apparent collapse of what had looked like a promising suggestion, the Chairman of the Borough Housing Committee, the Clerk and a few other members and officers closely acquainted with the events, held a meeting at the home of the first. It was at this January meeting that the borough firmly decided to pursue a strategy of bringing the matter to the Minister. The consultant architect suggested that they concentrate on the original site (World's End) and do a first-class scheme designed only for it. It was decided that when the scheme was completed great publicity should be given it so as to impress the Minister with its worth. It was also decided that, as the Minister knew of the new plan, it would be wiser not to try and see him but rather, after the LCC's probable refusal, an informal approach might be considered. One of the borough councilors, who was also a member of the LCC noted that it was certain that the scheme would be rejected as he had been unable to find much support for it in either party. It was finally agreed that an appeal should be attempted as soon as possible so that it could be decided by the present Minister who was known to favor high density schemes.

Soon after the meeting, the application for development was submitted. This prompted the LCC planners to try again to reach agreement on development of the whole area (i.e., including Lots Road). They saw that the borough's architect was a man of outstanding ability, as evidenced by his earlier work, and now, by his proposed scheme; to let pass this opportunity for a fine piece of development would be foolish. A meeting was called with the Borough Council officers on 20 February to work on the problem again. Present besides the officers of each authority was the borough's architect. One of the LCC planners started off by saying that the World's End area could be divided up into three areas, the existing Cremorne Estate, the proposed development site (World's End), and the contiguous site (Lots Road). He said that discussions with the Engineers' Department had finally resulted in information about the line of the proposed new road. After allowing space for a proposed secondary school on the Lots Road site, it was felt by the LCC planners that if the remaining land (i.e., remaining in the Lots Road area) could be rezoned residentially, a case could be made out for submission to the County Council Planning Committee for residential development (for the three areas) to a total density of about 170 p.p.a. This would allow development to a figure of 186 p.p.a. on the gross areas (including the school area) of Lots Road and the World's End site, which would allow for rehousing of all existing residents with no overspill problem.

The Borough Council representatives then asked whether the planners had in mind the immediate development of the World's End site at a density of 186 p.p.a. It was replied that this was the case. The borough engineer then went on to say that it was difficult to consider the planners' proposals until more was known and this might take many years. In the meantime, the borough had a scheme which could be proceeded with immediately and which was 'just the type...the Minister said should be regarded favorably for high density schemes'. Furthermore, the LCC planners' proposal would barely allow rehousing of the existing population. An LCC planner replied that the borough's scheme showed great architectural merit (he himself was an architect), 'but reminded the borough engineer that the density figure that it produced, i.e., 250 p.p.a. (on World's End taken alone), the London County Council officers could not argue favorably for at any committee meeting of the County Council'. Moreover, the LCC could not consider rehousing more than the existing population within the proposed development because:

...new housing development must be geared to existing and planned services as a whole, i.e., education, open space, etc., and approval could not be given to plans, however good they might be, for development of individual sites if it was known in advance that these types of services were inadequate.

The borough's architect then asked whether, if the figure of 170 p.p.a. average for the three sites was agreed to, it would be possible to still use his scheme on the one site and then reduce the number of people on the second (Lots Road) so as to average out to 170 p.p.a. The borough engineer supported this approach vigorously. An LCC planner agreed to look into this suggestion and on this note the meeting ended.

The scheme that the borough's architect had prepared contained a dual use of land (i.e., service facilities, especially parking, on the ground, the building placed on a podium over the service area), elimination of through roads into the site and eight tower blocks of varying sizes from 12 to 19 stories (the highest was 185 feet).[1] LCC planning officers reported their reaction to the scheme to the Committee: they repeated that it was a development of 'great merit and considerable architectural promise', but it was unsatisfactory from the point of view of density and high buildings; the latter particularly because of the proximity of the power station. Included in the report was a closer scrutiny of the question of development of the Lots Road area. The principal point of discussion was the borough's proposal of a high density nucleus on World's End and low density development on Lots Road. It was felt that this 'would give rise to a very large and unacceptable overspill of population (in Lots Road) unless the Borough Council undertook to rehouse the existing residents in the Lots Road area in the accommodation to be built (in World's End) as the commencement of a continuing operation of comprehensive redevelopment of both areas'.[2] The

---

[1] The architect explained his scheme this way. 'The point briefly is that when the 136 persons per acre was established, the situation with the automobile was a very different one. It was possible then to build medium high buildings and create a reasonable environment but it was not now possible to do this if proper provision is to be made for car storage. It is at about this density that one is obliged to cover the whole site with cars or find some other means of storing them. My argument was that once one crosses this barrier and cars have to be stored underground (or somewhere) that it is economic sense to increase the density significantly so that the burden of engineering costs for car storage can be shared by a larger number of dwellings. The alternative would be to restrict densities to, say, 90 or 100 persons per acre...All this proves is that development concepts should not be rigid and it is unreasonable to use density as a test of amenity or quality of environment.'

[2] The Chairman of the LCC Planning Committee described the problem of an overspill agreement as follows. 'Given an agreement on overspill, I might have accepted the [borough's architect's] scheme or something like it. In fact, this offer was made to the borough. The agreement

planners also said that their discussion of density for Lots Road and World's End 'did not take into account the substantial area of open space which should be provided in conjunction with the redevelopment' of the whole area. They noted that on the basis of the interim standard of open space adopted in the *Development Plan*,[1] 11.75 acres of public open space out of a total area of 40 acres, would be needed for World's End plus Lots Road, of which 3.3 acres was to be for the former. The borough's proposals for World's End included, according to the planners' calculations, 1.1 acres of public open space. Should the LCC allow a high density nucleus and not require adequate open space, when the time came for the development of Lots Road, should the LCC do it, *it* would be responsible for a large investment in open space and concomitant housing for the overspill population.

The report dealt with another issue which was to take on increasing significance, i.e., the modernization of the nearby power station. The main point of interest was that the scientific advisor to the LCC felt that while the proposed modernization would certainly reduce the amount of possible pollution, it was inadvisable that buildings adjacent to the station be over 120 feet.

Subsequent negotiation on the matter became very involved. Concerned with the power station were the London Transport Executive who owned it, the borough, the LCC and the Alkali Inspectorate of the Ministry of Housing, who are scientific advisors to the Minister on such matters. At issue was whether the proposed modernization could be altered to take account of the redevelopment and whether indeed the emissions would constitute a danger. The issue was effectively resolved by the Inspectorate saying that they felt that any danger was minimal. If the matter came before the Minister their views would likely prove determinate.

A call-in by the Minister

On 12 August, the Minister decided to call-in the application under powers granted him by the Town and Country Planning Act. This procedure ended the possibility of an agreement between the two authorities on Lots Road, or in general. At the time that the Minister called in the application, the LCC wrote to the Minister stating its objections to the proposed development. The letter recounted previous objections, but also included a new basis for refusal. Mention has already been made of the LCC officers'

---

was to be based on the fact that the LCC if it allowed the high density in [World's End], would have to supply most of the open space in Lots Road. To compensate the LCC for this, the borough would have to house some of the displaced people [from Lots Road] in their project.' An LCC planner working on the case, commented however, that an overspill agreement 'was no more than a pious hope'. It was clearly in the LCC's interest to get the borough to accept responsibility for rehousing overspill population from Lots Road. On the borough's part, they hoped somebody else would be responsible for the problem.

[1] As noted, the standard was 2½ acres per thousand people.

attempt to get agreement on the Lots Road area as part of a comprehensive scheme. Even though the borough had not taken up the idea in terms acceptable to the LCC planners, the latter, at the behest of the Planning Committee, continued their investigations. At the time of the call-in, the LCC still felt that the Lots Road area was worthy of consideration and stated in the letter that it would like to see this area and World's End treated together. The Council noted that the present proposals for World's End were thus 'premature'. The LCC also told the Minister of its intention to amend the *Development Plan* in order to rezone the Lots Road area from industrial to residential.

One other point is worthy of consideration here. Mention has already been made of the question of open space and the LCC's confused position on the matter. As the Council was developing its position on World's End, the points stressed were density and the problems of the power station. These were the points made in the letter to the Minister. Open space was not mentioned, although it had been mentioned in some of the reports to the Committee by planners. By the time of the inquiry, the LCC had decided to elevate this to a major concern and to insist on $2\frac{1}{2}$ acres per thousand population. It is not clear why the Council was so insistent in the Chelsea case in light of its flexibility on other applications. What is clear is that it had a great deal of difficulty in deciding how much space would be appropriate.

A revised scheme and other interim events

In light of the discussion over the power station, the borough's architect decided that it was possible to redo his scheme in order to keep it below the level at which the LCC scientific advisor thought undesirable conditions might occur. In this way the borough would be safe on this issue at least. The new scheme was informally submitted to the LCC for its observations in November; of course, the Council now no longer had authority to issue a decision. The LCC scientific advisor was quite pleased with this new proposal and considered it a victory for his point of view. However, the LCC planners felt that the new scheme lacked the merits of the old. More importantly, the density was still too high. The new proposal differed from the old in the height of buildings, although the general arrangement of a dual use of land was continued. The scheme also included more area for open space although the area was not considered sufficient. LCC planners felt, moreover, that from a civic design point of view the old proposal was better. The tower blocks were 'too closely sited in a concentrated form which would be seen in oblique views as a large mass of high buildings obtruding into the skyline'. Again, the argument was made that the new scheme was premature in light of the proposals for rezoning the Lots Road area. All of this information was sent to the Minister in preparation for the forthcoming inquiry. The inquiry date had now been moved up to the new year so that proper consideration could be given to the new proposal.

During the same period, the Chairmen of the two committees involved exchanged some public insults about their respective activities concerning the redevelopment, but these appeared to excite no particular interest outside the public authorities themselves. Meanwhile, the LCC prepared its case for the upcoming inquiry. With this in mind, a report was sent to the Minister outlining the authority's case. The report was primarily the product of the Chairman's view of the matter and was done pursuant to the Committee's authorization that she define the authority's case. The report seemed to rule out using Lots Road as a basis for compromise with the borough and thus upset the planners, but attempts to alter the views of the Chairman were unsuccessful. In looking back on the matter, the Chairman commented that the application 'was like Chelsea's deathbed repentance.[1] They had done almost nothing on housing before and I was not about to help them do a high density project to bail themselves out.'

The redevelopment was also the subject of a debate in the full Council in which the Planning Committee Chairman publicly defended her position by indicating that she would not be a party to the borough's attempt to repent for the size of its housing list. Other Council members argued that Chelsea was near the center of the city and should be allowed higher densities in consequence. The latter line was taken by Conservatives, while Labour Party members tended to support the Chairman.

The inquiry

The inquiry held by the Ministry of Housing and Local Government opened in January 1965 in Chelsea Town Hall. Those present included lawyers for both local authorities, officers of each authority, lawyers for some local objectors to the scheme, and an inspector and a technical officer from the Ministry. The latter was to evaluate the evidence on the air pollution problem. Also present was the architect hired by the borough and the Chairman of the Borough Housing Committee. The LCC Planning Chairman was not present; this was usual as it is felt that the members were not experts and that they and the LCC in general might suffer under cross-examination. By implication, 'political' considerations were not thought to be relevant points of discussion at an inquiry.

Much of the material presented at the inquiry has been covered in the preceding discussion. However, some new information did emerge, mostly concerned with plans for the modernized power station and the LCC's

---

[1] 'Deathbed' refers to the borough's imminent merger with Kensington Borough Council under the London Government Act of 1965.

attitude on Lots Road. On the former, it became clear that the Minister had induced London Transport to make plans for the purchase of a fuel that would give off fewer pollutants and which would be used in the new plant. This would ensure that any embarrassment over the proximity of the plant and the housing would be minimized. The purchase of the new fuel was noted by a London Transport witness at the inquiry.

On the question of how the Lots Road area was to be related to the development at World's End, LCC planners were unable to present any coherent analysis. The problems turned principally on whether most of the open space for the two areas treated together could be provided in the Lots Road section thus allowing a high density development on the World's End site. The major difficulty was that, in fact, the LCC was reluctant to allow such high density development under any circumstances. However, if this high–low approach was not allowed and each section was to provide its own complement of open space (and presumably be built at roughly the same densities) then it is difficult to see in what sense the areas were related. In consequence, it was difficult to see in what sense the World's End scheme could be said to be 'premature', as the LCC contended. The LCC planners at the inquiry compounded the earlier confusion about how much open space was required by now making it unclear where it was to be provided.[1]

Aside from the information on the power station and Lots Road, the most interesting thing about the inquiry was the strategies pursued by the participants. In one sense, an inquiry is not so much an examination of the data (although it certainly is that as well) as a peg on which the Ministry can hang its decision. In this particular case, this relates both to the substantive material presented (e.g., the problem of the power station) and to the way in which the issue was presented. If either of the participants could provide an intelligent way of looking at the problem, even though it went beyond the *Development Plan*, the Minister would find it easier to give a favorable decision. Two of the basic strategies possible at an inquiry are: (1) to try to keep the decision on a technical basis with the *Development Plan* being the focus; (2) to contend that the question is one of policy outside the expertise of officers and of their judgements as set down in the *Plan*. The first is most useful for the LCC and the latter for any appellant, in this case the Borough Council.

The borough, through its lawyers, principally argued that the problems associated with a severe housing shortage in the city should be given greater consideration than the *Development Plan* provided for. The proposed development would enable the borough to make a significant step in coping

---

[1] The legal officer handling the LCC's case at the inquiry noted that: 'One of the reasons the LCC was so vague [on Lots Road] was that it really wasn't until August 1964 that any serious consideration was given to it. I myself wasn't even sure what [the LCC planner] was saying at the inquiry and so I skated around the issue as much as possible.'

with these difficulties and this was more important than other concerns. In fact, the borough argued, the LCC had been willing to be flexible in this regard and this suggested that they saw the importance of dealing with the housing dilemma. Moreover, the generally agreed upon architectural merit of the proposed development ought to make easier the acceptance of a high density approach.

The LCC argued in its turn that, in fact, the *Plan* considered the housing shortage carefully and in it was set down the appropriate standards of judgement for trying to alleviate the problem in light of attempts to maintain and promote decent standards of amenity. The same point applied to open space standards, against which the borough had argued. Indeed, the LCC lawyer said, the borough had approved the latter standards (as well as the former) when the *Plan* was drawn up so why were they being truculent now?

Aside from the borough and the LCC, the other major participant in the inquiry was the counsel for the group of objectors mentioned earlier. There is no evidence that between the end of 1962, when the borough decided not to go ahead with its intention to appeal, and January 1965, the time of the inquiry, the objectors did more than hold some meetings among themselves. Their attention was focused on the inquiry, assuming there was to be one, at which point they could make their views known to the Minister. The objectors were composed of a small number (12) of residents of the area which was to be demolished to make way for the proposed development.[1] They argued through their lawyer that in fact the area under consideration was really two distinct areas in terms of the conditions of the residences. Approximately one-half of the area contained a considerable number of residences in which modernization and conversion had either been completed or was well on its way. This area was the one lived in by the objectors. The other half consisted of run-down property, which although not slums under the housing law, was in poor shape, i.e. no fixed baths, no hot water, and so on. The objectors noted that much of Chelsea had been renewed by private owners in the same way as in this area. If the process was allowed to continue in World's End, then it too would become quite attractive. They admitted, however, that the people who had renewed the rest of Chelsea were the better-off and if this was the case in World's End, its working-class population, the only sizeable concentration in the borough, would be edged out. The objectors contended that some of the people who renewed their houses in the World's End area were not of the type brought to mind by the name Chelsea, i.e., they were working-class people who

---

[1] Groups of this type are the most common objectors at inquiries, i.e., local residents who band together on an *ad hoc* basis to object to a local authority or private proposal. Sometimes they appear without counsel; the better-off usually hire counsel so as to face on equal terms the planning authority which is usually so represented, and in order to deal with the complexities of the law of town planning.

wanted to have pretty houses just like the rest of us.[1] The objectors proposed redeveloping the one-half that clearly needed it and leaving the other half standing. They pointed out that their section of the area housed people at a rate of 169 p.p.a. and in conditions of good amenity.[2] This approach would be good town planning, they said.

Other groups

The other local group that might have been expected to turn up at the inquiry was the Chelsea Society, the local civic and amenity association.[3] The Society is probably best described as a civic society with a preservationist bent, although not Neanderthal in its outlook. Issues of a wider impact than preservation of historical buildings tend to confuse and divide it, and so public stands on these issues are avoided.[4] In the case of the World's End project, such a division was present, but the matter was also complicated by the death of the leading member of the Society, who had been opposed to the development. The Alderman (he was a member of the Borough Council) felt that the whole area should not be redeveloped as it contained many useful residences and some of real merit.

Much of the Society's activity had, in fact, been carried on by the Alderman and his death left the Society, for the moment, without leadership. He had had contacts at all levels of local government in London and apparently in the Ministry as well, and was on occasion able to prevent an historical building being torn down without the matter even coming to inquiry. His ability to get advance information, i.e. before a project became public knowledge, which was often not until an inquiry or until the sound of bulldozers was heard, gave the Society some advantage in conducting its architectural fights. The Alderman's death left the Society divided on the World's End issue and, for the moment, left it unable to make its views known on

---

[1] No figures are available on this point, but there is no reason to assume that the contention is not accurate. However, it is clear that as demand for houses in the area grows, working-class people would slowly be bought out, and few would be able to afford to move in.

[2] It is well to note here that to follow such a procedure and cut the area in half might make an attractive development impossible for the area left over and this indeed was the feeling of the LCC. On the face of it, it might be said that the objectors were really arguing in terms of social class, i.e., they preferred not to have working-class neighbors. This does happen on occasion when council housing is proposed, but in this particular case, given the fact that the area is generally working class, and that there is a nearby council housing estate already, it is unlikely. See Chapter 5.

[3] Bodies of this type have generally been devoted to seeing that architecture of merit or buildings of historical interest are not torn down at all, or at least only under duress. Some of the organizations tend to be rather negative and spend their time proving that every piece of mid-Victorian pattern building is of architectural interest. In recent years this has changed somewhat as many have broadened their interest to include a wider range of land use matters. See generally Chapter 5.

[4] On a case just preceding the one under discussion, the Society was faced with the problem of what stand to take on a parking garage to be built under one of the garden squares of the borough. It was clear that some members would benefit by increased parking whilst others objected on amenity grounds; the gardens would be ripped up and some trees would have to be felled.

the project. It is possible that had he lived, the Society would have appeared at the inquiry but as it was, no public statements were made.

Another candidate for participation in the World's End decision was the local tenants' association, which was composed mostly of tenants in Borough Council buildings. It might be expected that the association would favor more council housing since it would mean a greater membership and presumably more influence. Also, insofar as the tenants were committed to furthering working-class interests in some general way, council housing which would help workers should be supported. However, the association was unable to decide whether the redevelopment merited their support.

In relation to the West Chelsea Redevelopment Scheme a Resolution was passed by my Association last year on this matter. Whilst supporting the scheme in principle it was doubted that the rents charged for council rehousing would be within the means of prospective working-class tenants. My Committee arrived at this conclusion on the basis of the high council rents prevailing in Chelsea at the time.[1]

As a result of this, the association took no public stand.[2]

A third possible participant would be a ratepayers' group who might well be concerned about the impact of the development on local rates. However, they most often become active at the time of property revaluation and then recede back into the woodwork of everyday concerns. In Chelsea, there were no such groups active at the time of the case.

Finally, there was the local Chamber of Commerce. Its activity, or lack of it, must be seen in the broader context of the limited role of businessmen in planning. (See Chapter 5.) Here it is enough to say that for local reasons, the Chamber, which is a group of retail merchants, was largely moribund. Insofar as it was active, its concerns were specifically retailing problems such as Christmas decorations for the shopping street.

---

[1] Personal communication from the Chairman of the Association.

[2] See also Chapter 5.

The level of rents is tied to the initial cost of the development; this is especially true when council rents are computed on the basis of an economic rent which is scaled down according to means. (The other method commonly used, most conspicuously by the LCC, is to charge a flat subsidized rent. Conservative councils tend to favor the former, Labour councils the latter.) If the base figure is high, the result, even scaled down according to means, is likely to be high. This is by way of saying that the cost of the project was an important piece of data which was necessary in order for observers to come to an evaluation of the proposal. However, this data was not presented because it was not and could not be computed. The cost of the project was of no concern to the LCC, and the borough was only at the stage of doing outline thinking. However, outline approval, for all intents and purposes, is final approval as far as the public is concerned. Objections as to high cost will be too late, if not made at the time of the outline application when they are not likely to be given much weight anyway. This applies to the cost of the building, but not necessarily to the cost of the land itself which might well be examined at an inquiry into the compulsory purchase of the land. This type of inquiry is often held simultaneously with the inquiry into the outline application. This case is unusual in that the two inquiries were to be held separately. The borough felt that it must get permission to build above a certain density before it could commit itself to buying more land.

THE DECISION

The inquiry was conducted during the month of January; the Minister's decision was issued in August. Along with the Minister's letter of decision was issued the inspector's report to the Minister which provided the latter's basis for understanding the facts of the case.[1] The inspector's report consisted, in general, of a presentation of the views of the various participants, findings of fact, conclusions and a recommendation as to whether the application be approved or refused. The interesting points are the inspector's conclusions and recommendation, of which some sections are quoted here.

I am of the opinion:

That there is an urgent need for additional housing in the borough.

That to alleviate this problem any redevelopment should, in principle, increase the number of units of accommodation, and not add to the waiting list.

That the fact that the present proposals would rehouse considerably more persons than they would displace is one of the most important planning advantages, provided always that such would be achieved in company with an acceptable residential environment.

That such an environment would be secured by either of the present schemes.

The inspector went on to note that he did not see the pollution problem as an unacceptable risk. He also found that he preferred some elements of the first scheme and some elements of the second.

That in summary, therefore, although I would accept the proposed density and maximum building height, I must give credence to the fact that further investigation of the problem with a view to combining the best features of both proposals might well provide the most satisfactory scheme, and this factor, coupled with the unacceptable details of the plans now before the Minister...leave me no alternative but to recommend refusal.

The Minister followed closely the recommendation of his inspector and stated that he was refusing the application, but did so 'without prejudice to the consideration of any revised application' on the lines of combining the best features of both schemes. The borough, of course, was pleased with the Minister's decision, even though the decision was ostensibly negative. The borough gained its point on just about every count: density, open space, air pollution. All that was required was to have the architect redesign the development to take into account the best features of both proposals and submit the new plans to the Minister. By June 1966, the borough's architect had completed a revised scheme which in May 1967 received approval from the Minister. Because of the metropolitan area reorganization that had intervened in 1965, the new scheme was submitted by the borough's

---

[1] Until the recommendations in the *Report of the Committee on Administrative Tribunals and Enquiries* (Cmnd. 218, 1957) were put into effect (1958) the inspector's report was confidential.

successor, the Kensington and Chelsea Borough Council. In principle, as a planning authority under the governmental set up for the metropolitan area, the new borough could have given approval to the development, but as the Minister had called in the application, the development was in his hands. Building began in late 1969, some eight years after the borough first began to give redevelopment in World's End serious consideration.

4. OFFICES AND CONGESTION IN THE CENTRAL AREA: CENTRE POINT AND ST GILES CIRCUS

CENTRAL AREA PLANNING

Town planning in post-war London was not immediately concerned with the central area.[1] The main effort at first was directed towards the provision of housing, especially in the blitzed areas; somewhat later, efforts shifted to replacing obsolescent dwellings. The great pieces of urban redevelopment in the East End, completed under comprehensive development area powers, were on the periphery of the central core. Moreover, the Town and Country Planning Act of 1947 was not designed to deal with the center but was aimed mostly at residential reconstruction.

This lack of concern with the central area can be traced back to before World War II to at least the Barlow Commission *Report*, the first key document for London planning. While the Commission clearly was interested in dispersing industrial employment from the central area and from the County in general, it had very little to say about office employment.[2] Similarly, while manufacturing firms after the war had to obtain licenses from the Board of Trade if they wished to build or extend premises in excess of five thousand square feet, these rules were not applied to office building. Also, the Local Employment Act of 1960 enabled manufacturing concerns which moved to depressed areas to receive assistance but denied it to offices.[3]

The Abercrombie plans and the *Development Plan* of the LCC also tended to neglect the central area. Like the Barlow Commission *Report*, these plans concentrated on the dispersal of industrial employment,[4] and in the 1951

---

[1] The LCC defined this area to include the City, the boroughs of Holborn and Westminster and parts of the surrounding boroughs. Definitions of the central area vary slightly depending on who is using them, but broadly it is taken to mean the area bounded by the mainline railroad terminals. It is roughly 10½ square miles in dimension and contains most of the offices, larger shops and entertainment facilities of London. There are also some residential uses. The area is roughly the equivalent of what Americans call the 'downtown' or central business district.

[2] And office employment would soon become the largest single source of jobs in the central area.

[3] Town and Country Planning Association, *The Paper Metropolis* (London, 1962), p. 25. The following relies heavily on this pamphlet. The Association is one of the major private organizations concerned with planning in England.

[4] The fact that neither the Barlow Commission nor the various London plans distinguished between industrial and commercial employment probably was a result of poor data. The 1931 Census, which was the only comprehensive data available, was not adequate in this regard. Hall, *London 2000*, pp. 46–7.

Development Plan the LCC in fact said that the general trend in the County was favorable in terms of the goals of the *Plan*. However, after the Council had submitted the *Plan* to the Minister for approval, several events took place which increased the extent of office building in the County. Under the first post-war Conservative government, building licences were ended (1954) and the supply of building materials increased. Moreover, the 1947 Act was changed in 1954 making the planning authority liable to compensate owners for revocation of planning permissions up to their full hypothetical development value. Under the old law it had only to compensate for abortive expenditures undertaken under the terms of permission. This meant that the Council was less willing to revoke any existing permissions for office development.

A further and probably the most important change was the abolition of development charges in 1953. Under the 1947 Act the state had taken over all 'development rights' of the nation's land. The state did not own the land itself, only the right to develop it. Those who could successfully show that their land had some development value on the 'appointed day' (1 July 1948) would be compensated once and for all by the government. The other side of this coin was that when permission to develop was granted, the developer had to purchase back the development rights from the state by paying a development charge. This charge was 100 per cent, i.e. the full increase in the value of the land due to planning permission. Clearly, this reduced the incentive to develop. The abolition of the charges made re-development more profitable and thus increased the extent of office building.[1]

The lack of serious attention to the problems of the central core, the change in the conditions of building and the pent-up demand for offices in London[2] combined to promote an office boom in the central area starting in the middle fifties[3] and also contributed to an increase in central area employment. Before this time, the Council was apparently granting permission without realizing the full implication of doing so.[4] The realization of what had been happening prompted efforts by central and local authorities to frame a policy to deal with the new state of affairs.

In 1954 the Ministry of Housing asked the LCC to obtain more precise data on the central area and in 1955 reduced the amount of the area zoned industrial and commercial in the *Development Plan* and rezoned what was excluded as residential. In the Minister's letter to the LCC in which this and related changes were explained and the *Plan* approved, he referred to

---

[1] Also relevant here is the Third Schedule provision of the 1947 Act which was repealed in 1963. This allowed owners to increase the cubic content of existing buildings when they were rebuilt, often allowing up to a 40 per cent increase in floor space, since the old buildings had higher ceilings than the new.

[2] Marriott, *Property Boom*, p. 5.

[3] For an account of the boom, see Marriott, *Property Boom*, especially Chapter 1.

[4] Town and Country Planning Association, *Paper Metropolis*, p. 26.

54

'the evil of congestion'. It was this statement that marked the beginnings of a clear policy to combat office growth and congestion in the central area. After completing a central area survey, the LCC published, in 1957, its *Plan to Combat Congestion in Central London* in which the Council reduced the plot ratios (see below) in some parts of the central area. The 1960 *Review* devoted a large number of pages to delineating the problems of the central area, particularly the increase in office employment and congestion, and made some proposals to deal with it. By the latter part of the 1950s the Council's policy was clearly 'to restrain [the development of offices] at the center'.[1]

Closely related to the increase in office building and office employment in the mind of the LCC was the increasing traffic congestion in the central area.[2] In a city as built-up as London this presented a particularly difficult problem, further compounded by the shortage of funds available for road improvements prior to the early sixties.[3] The Council tended to favor road improvements of the less costly variety and was reluctant to embark on long-range schemes which required safeguarding of the appropriate land by purchase as it came on the market. In fact, in the post-war period, no major improvement scheme was completed until 1962,[4] and improvements largely consisted of attempts to widen streets and alter traffic flows at critical intersections.[5]

The actual facts of the employment and congestion situation were somewhat different than the LCC thought. The Council, and apparently everybody else concerned with employment and congestion in London, seemed to be working on the assumption that increased office space in the County was resulting in an increase in employment in the central area of about 15,000 jobs per year, mostly in offices. Office space did in fact increase from an estimated 85 million square feet in 1939 in the central area to about 111 million in 1962.[6] However, the increase in employment turned out to

[1] *Review*, p. vi.   [2] *Review*, p. 139.

[3] Money for roads got entangled in the regular financial crises of the period. Either it wasn't available due to continuing shortages of funds following the war, or it was cut back in order to hold down inflationary pressures. See for example, Hall, *London 2000*, Chapter 5.

[4] Hall, *London 2000*, p. 106.

[5] In the original Abercrombie plans for London and the surrounding areas, proposals were made for a ring road system. These gradually fell away under financial pressure, but were resurrected in another form under the GLC.

The Ministry of Transport was, with the London and Home Counties Traffic Advisory Committee on which an LCC representative sat, the traffic authority for London County and the surrounding areas. Alterations in traffic plans, for example, come from these authorities. The LCC was, however, the authority which dealt with major roads within the County. After the period of this case study (in 1960), there was a separate Road Committee which dealt with the latter, but before this time, i.e. during this case, both road engineers and planners were responsible to the Town Planning Committee. Under the metropolitan area reorganization, the GLC has become the traffic authority for London.

[6] Town and Country Planning Association, *Paper Metropolis*, p. 30. This takes into account replacement and losses due to World War II.

be considerably less than expected. Instead of an increase of 150,000 jobs from 1951 to 1961, the increase was only 55,000, the overwhelming amount of which took place in the City.[1] What was not appreciated was the fact that newer buildings provided more spacious accommodation.[2] Furthermore, the largest increase in office workers took place in the category of 'professional services'. Within this subheading, the largest increases took place in 'education' and 'other professional and business services', the latter including such professional organizations as architects, planners, etc. As Hall comments: 'It is ironic, but the literal truth, that the sort of people who called most insistently for a halt of office growth have been among its main causes.'[3] Regardless of the actual figures, however, by the late 1950s, the LCC was determined to limit the growth of office employment in the central area by curbing office building.

ST GILES CIRCUS[4]

St Giles Circus is the intersection of several of the main roads of London and is located in the borough of Westminster. Running east and west from the Circus is Oxford Street, the western arm of which shortly becomes the main shopping street of metropolitan London. In the north is Tottenham Court Road, which on the south side of the Circus becomes Charing Cross Road, leading into the heart of the West End, the main entertainment area. (See map on page 57.)

When the road program was prepared for the 1951 *Development Plan*, the St Giles Circus intersection was programmed for the period 1962–71; the improvement was to be in the form of a roundabout (traffic circle). This was how the LCC itself saw the priority of the project.[5] However, while the draft *Development Plan* was being considered for approval by the Ministry of Housing, a report was published by a Ministry of Transport agency entitled *London Traffic Congestion*. The report stated that the improvement of the St Giles intersection was of great importance and should be

[1] In 1962, there were over 1,400,000 people working in the central area.

[2] Marriott, *Property Boom*, pp. 183–4. The reduced figure for employment increases is also from Marriott, *ibid*. His discussion is based on a report by the Standing Conference on London Regional Planning in which data from the 1961 Census are analyzed.

[3] Hall, *London 2000*, pp. 58–9.

[4] As will become apparent, the events making up this case study are rather complex and only some of them need to be dealt with here. In general the financial aspect of the case has been de-emphasized. On the economics of property development in London see Marriott, *Property Boom*, which is an engrossing study of property developers in London and England generally. One of the chapters in Marriott's book (Chapter 8) is an examination of Centre Point (St Giles Circus) and the developers and land speculators involved in its construction. The foci of his study and the present one are, however, different. Marriott is concerned with planning mostly from the developer's side. Taken together, the studies form a complete narrative of the whole project.

[5] The *Development Plan* listed St Giles as number 6 on a list of intersections with greatest traffic delays, behind places such as Hyde Park Corner and Piccadilly Circus. This was still true by 1958 when the data for the *Review* was compiled.

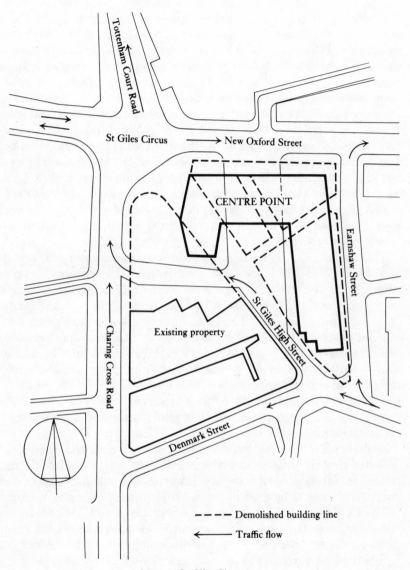

Map 3   St Giles Circus

carried out at an early date. The Ministry adopted this view and so informed the LCC. The County Council now found itself in a position of great difficulty. Completion of the proposed road scheme depended in the final analysis on the Ministry of Transport, since it was to contribute up to 75 per cent of the cost. The LCC was therefore anxious to receive assurances that grant money would be forthcoming within the earlier programming period of 1952–61[1] if it was to go ahead with the scheme. Its need for such assurances was further increased by the fact that it had received several applications for development in the area of the proposed road scheme. If planning permission were granted, the subsequent cost of the land to the LCC was likely to rise owing to the increased value of the property, and it would thus be foolish to grant permission if in fact the roadworks were to be built in the earlier period. However, permission for very limited development would be useful if the road works were not to begin until the later period fifteen to twenty years hence, as was indicated in the original *Development Plan*. Not to allow any redevelopment would leave the land in its present unattractive state.

There followed a series of contacts between the Ministry of Transport and the LCC in which the latter tried to gain the necessary assurances. Although the Ministry's attitude was not considered positive owing to government policy at the time of cutting back on the road program, the necessary grant was finally promised. The LCC, however, was forced to drop a wider road improvement which had included St Giles Circus as one section; the Ministry was not willing to commit itself to this extent. After some additional discussion (this was in the period 1954–6) a minimum road scheme was agreed on which the Ministry would help finance. At one point, the Ministry had some doubts as to whether the minimum scheme would be adequate, fearing that the proposed 40 feet wide traffic circle might not stand up to future traffic needs. The officers of the LCC Engineer's Department, which was concerned with street improvements, did not agree and convinced the Ministry that the scheme was adequate for the present and could be expanded for future needs if necessary. It was decided to build a 40-foot roundabout which would be sited in the south-east quadrant of the intersection.

The LCC now set about acquiring the necessary land for the road scheme. Instead of using the usual compulsory purchase powers under the Planning Acts, the Council decided to use two nineteenth-century laws which would enable the land purchases to be made more cheaply.[2] This was not the first

[1] One of the things that annoyed the LCC most about the reluctance of the Ministry to commit itself financially very far in the future was that it (the Council) ended up financing the Ministry's share of costs for a period of time without even a guarantee that compensation would be forthcoming at a later date.

[2] At the time it was decided to use the old legislation the idea of declaring the site a comprehensive development area was briefly raised by some planning officers, but was discarded as too expensive. A CDA would have involved much more extensive land purchases than would be

time such action had been taken. Although acquiring land under these acts was cheaper, litigation often resulted as owners felt that they were not receiving full compensation.[1] If litigation could be avoided or be of short duration, then the gain in time and money would be considerable.

In 1956, the LCC served a Notice to Treat under the nineteenth-century road acts. There were two main results: litigation and some second thoughts about the whole approach.[2] The complications of the litigation are not of importance here except as it became apparent that it would drag on for some time.[3] Of concern here is the fact that soon after the LCC started action it realized that a minimum scheme under the acts would be quite ugly. The problem with them was that they enabled the local authority to purchase only land to be used for the road and not any of the surrounding area. This meant that after the road had been completed, the frontages of all the surrounding buildings would be left as they were, since the LCC had no authority to purchase them and make alterations. The price of the cheap road would be an ugly roadside.

The Council's second thoughts came in the form of possible comprehensive development of the area concerned; the traffic circle would be a part of a general redevelopment of the site. Discussions were held with Ministry of Housing and Local Government officials in January 1957, since Ministry approval would be required on two counts if the area was to be designated for comprehensive development. First, an alteration in the *Development Plan* would be necessary and second, a CDA would require a compulsory purchase order which would probably result in a public inquiry before a Ministry inspector. Ministry officials counseled caution, noting that any attempt to define the area as a CDA was fraught with difficulties. There were a number of problems about timing and the justification for comprehensive development, quite apart from the fact that the area might be too small to qualify for designation as a CDA. A CDA was not out of the question, the Ministry officials said, but it would be difficult to obscure the fact that it was the LCC's original action that had precipitated the problem.

needed for road improvement. It was unlikely that the Ministry of Transport would have compensated the LCC for the purchase of land around the road, and assistance from the Ministry of Housing also seemed unlikely.

[1] Briefly, the saving to the local authority was based on two points. In one Act, compensation was based on the use of the land for the road, not its development value in general. In the other Act, compensation was paid on the basis not of the frontage of the property being taken (if the frontage was concerned) but on the square yards needed. No consideration was given to the fact that the frontage was the more valuable part of the property. The other main advantage of the Act, in contrast to purchase under the Planning Acts, was that no public hearing was required. Purchase could be carried out by the public authority's declaration of intent and need. The laws have since been repealed.

[2] It should be clear that the participation of the courts in local government in England is considerably less common than in the United States. Administrative hearings held by the central government handle some of the objections that would become tax-payers' suits in the latter.

[3] See Marriott, *Property Boom*, pp. 112–13, for part of the story of the legal complications.

59

The LCC was aware then that even in the unlikely event of a rapid solution to the litigation problem, the situation would still be difficult. It would be awkward to switch to a CDA and it would be unsatisfactory to disrupt the area with the road and leave it that way. Throughout 1957 officers and members discussed possible ways to meet the problem. One method that appeared very promising was to enlist the services of a private developer who would not be hindered from purchasing the surrounding area. The LCC could carry out its road works and the private developer could take care of the surrounding areas. Conversations with developers who indicated interest in the scheme suggested that if the LCC had a firm proposal in mind, then it might be able to interest one in doing a satisfactory comprehensive development on the site.

The planning officers started work on a scheme which could be used either for a possible LCC development when and if the area was designated a CDA or as a basis for negotiation with private developers. However, a difference of opinion arose between the comptroller's office and the planners on the manner in which the central island, i.e. the land within the roundabout, should be treated if the LCC developed the site. The planners felt that in any comprehensive development, office use should be restricted in accordance with the LCC's then developing policy. Where possible, they indicated office space in a new development should not exceed that in the existing buildings; also residential accommodation should be encouraged. The planners' report, submitted in March 1957 to the relevant sub-committee of the Planning Committee, said of their proposed scheme.

[it] is based on the principle of leaving clear the central island of the proposed roundabout which would be of great advantage from the traffic point of view. In view of the Council's policy to restrict office use, consideration should be given in any suggested comprehensive development to the provision of residential accommodation.[1]

The planners went on to note that the Council would have to allow some increase in office space, however, if the area were developed privately. A provision in the 1947 Planning Act allowed applicants a 10 per cent increase in the bulk of existing office use on a given site.[2] Any attempt to hold the increase to less than 10 per cent would invite the serving of a purchase notice by the owner and this might require the LCC to purchase an expensive property.[3]

[1] In design terms the planners felt that this was not a site for a tall building. Also, a building on the central island would obscure the view of an adjoining church.
[2] See footnote 1, p. 54.
[3] An owner can serve a purchase notice if a refusal of planning permission or the conditions attached prevent him from obtaining 'reasonably beneficial use' of the land. This is meant to apply to what Cullingworth (*Town and Country Planning*, p. 87) calls 'serious cases'. It does not, of course, apply for all refusals or conditional acceptances.

But the officers commented,

[it] is not considered that this. . .additional office space [i.e. a 10% increase in bulk] will result in any appreciable increase in congestion in the Central Area of London and, in any case, it may be that some alternative to office use can be found on subsequent consideration.

A similar viewpoint was also voiced by the engineers, but the comptrollers, the Council's financial officers, thought differently. If the central island were left clear and the Council itself undertook development, they were concerned that the cost of the road and the surrounding land would fall on the Council's rates. The best approach for the Council, they said, would be to build offices and shops to the maximum allowable under the *Development Plan*. This would maximize the return from rents and help offset the cost of land and road works. Furthermore, the comptrollers continued, it was 'by no means certain' that a grant from the Ministry of Housing would be forthcoming if the Council decided to do a CDA. The Council's resources 'were already full stretched and likely to remain so'.

The comptrollers pressed these views on both the relevant sub-committee of the Planning Committee and on the Finance Committee which would have to approve any expenditure made by the Council for comprehensive site development. The Planning sub-committee, faced with these divergent views from its officers, found itself in a difficult position. It still felt that 'on planning grounds it [was] essential to secure comprehensive development of the area'. However, realizing that the planners' ideas for a scheme might not be acceptable in financial terms, they indicated that comprehensive development by the LCC would not have to follow such lines. They reported their views to the Finance Committee who agreed that a CDA could be done only if maximum use for offices and shops, i.e. revenue-producing use, was made of the central island. The issue finally came to the full Planning Committee who had to decide on the relative merits of these different viewpoints. Their decision favored comprehensive development thereby committing the Council in March 1957 to developing the area surrounding the road. The financial and physical planning difficulties which would be encountered led the Committee to discuss once again the possibility of private development. It was decided that the Council would take the first steps toward comprehensive development on its own, while leaving the door open for offers from private developers.

One of the initial steps required for a CDA was an amendment to the *Development Plan* designating the area for compulsory purchase. The amendment would require another set of discussions with the Ministry to obtain the necessary approval. The appropriate time to do this, it was decided, was at the forthcoming review of the *Development Plan*. Meanwhile, the problem of the litigation remained and might well make the Ministry reluctant to become immediately involved in a CDA procedure. In January 1959, the LCC officers called on the Ministry. The Ministry adopted much the same cautious line that it had presented at the previous meetings concerning the matter. Ministry officials again noted that there was 'a contradiction in terms between the two types of powers [i.e. between the nineteenth-century acts and the Planning Acts] affecting the rights of owners'. The Ministry now advised that the roadworks be completed and *then* the idea of comprehensive development raised again. The LCC would have to carry through with its original, and now disagreeable, approach and clean up the mess afterwards. Unless the LCC could solve its legal problems it could not act on its commitment to develop the area surrounding the proposed road. However, as a report describing the meeting with the Ministry noted 'the result of [the legal] difficulties is that the execution of [the] scheme is largely at a standstill'. Even the minimum road scheme was in danger, no less comprehensive development.

In addition to the legal problems, it had now become clear that the LCC itself would not be able to afford to do any redevelopment of property surrounding the proposed road in the period originally contemplated. The point was made during the first review of the *Development Plan* in a report (dated June 1959) to the relevant planning sub-committee by the planning officers, the comptroller and the valuer.

In view of the financial resources no areas, other than the two mentioned...are now proposed. On 26 March 1957 the Town Planning (Redevelopment and Road Improvements) sub-committee approved in principle an area of comprehensive development of St Giles Circus (involving a capital outlay of about 1,500,000 pounds) and asked for the area to be included in the revision of the *Development Plan*, but with the proviso that comprehensive development by agreement with private developers should not be ruled out. In the light of all the other commitments, provisions cannot be made for this area in the program for 1960–72 but it is thought likely that in this district redevelopment in cooperation with private developers will be possible.

It was apparent now that the LCC must depend on private development if it was to keep to its commitment of more than a minimum road scheme, i.e. if it was to have any redevelopment of the properties surrounding the road.

Private development

By mid-1959, the LCC's legal difficulties had not yet been overcome; in fact it seemed that they were about to expand. Even if the Council won its point in the lower court, the case seemed likely to travel the whole legal route. And the Council might well suffer some embarrassment in a court appearance since it had originally used what one planning officer called 'cumbersome legislation'. Moreover, the central government was now committed to administrative procedures which gave citizens increased rights.[1] Legislation which took land by declaration, i.e. without public hearing, was likely to be regarded as infringing these rights.

A private developer would be the only immediate solution to a problem growing steadily more difficult. Not only would a private developer be able to deal with the area surrounding the road, but he would be able to extricate the LCC by buying out the litigants on the proposed road site with offers of market prices, or above if necessary. Clearly, the LCC itself was in no position to do this, having originally committed its energies to acquiring the road land at less than market value. A developer moreover could arrange to transfer this purchased road land to the LCC. He could also apply for planning permission on land surrounding the proposed road and possibly be compensated for his efforts in obtaining the road land.

In the autumn of 1958, a private developer interested in the St Giles site appeared on the scene. The Chairman of the Planning Committee at that time described his meeting with the developer.

I received a call from my solicitor who asked to see me about something or other and when I got there I was introduced to [the developer]. I thought his solution was a clever one. I knew that we should be giving away quite a bit but I really couldn't see waiting another five years until we got the road. I was quite pleased by the idea and thought it a good way out of the mess.

The developer chose not to represent himself in making application to the LCC but delegated the job to the architect who would in fact design the building if permission were received. The man chosen for the job was a well-known London architect,[2] who was described by one of the planning officers as being

quite good about nosing out these kinds of [i.e. difficult] deals. He's not really an architect but a middleman who works on cases that other more orthodox architects wouldn't touch. Another architect might not be able to get all the land together; he wouldn't threaten or cajole. We knew that [he] was the man for the job.[3]

[1] See the *Report of the Committee on Administrative Tribunals*.

[2] Marriott in *Property Boom*, p. 27, notes that the architect chosen to represent the developer (who, as Marriott says in Chapter 8, was and is probably the most successful property developer in London) was the head of one of ten architectural firms who between them designed between half and three-quarters of the speculative office blocks in the greater London area out of a total of 4,750 architects in private practice in the area. He was to become the leading speculative architect by the middle sixties in terms of quantity (and perhaps quality) of work done. Using architects as negotiators with the LCC was not uncommon practice for property developers.

[3] Marriott, *Property Boom*, p. 32, quotes a member of the LCC's Planning Committee as follows: 'The trouble with [the architect] was that he knew some of the regulations far better than the LCC itself. Every now and then we had to bring in clauses to stop up the loopholes exposed by [him].'

In July 1959, the architect appeared at the LCC and spoke with the appropriate officers. The conversations with the Valuer's Department[1] concerned the possibility of the developer being able to assemble the needed land. The architect produced correspondence showing that his employer was already in contact with some of the owners who were engaged in litigation with the LCC and had some promises to sell from some of the more troublesome. Other conversations concerned the proposed road route which had to be specified before any designs could be attempted. At the behest of one of the planning officers a somewhat reluctant engineer produced a sketch of the proposed roundabout. His reluctance to commit his department before more was known about the development, and before they had had time to think through the possibilities, becomes understandable in light of the department's subsequent actions (see below). The meeting revealed that the architect was in a great hurry to get matters moving; the longer negotiations took, the greater chance the news of the proposed development would leak out and land prices then rise.[2] The meeting also established that officers in all departments were interested in the developer's scheme.

The basis of the development scheme to be submitted was an exchange of land for a liberal planning permission. The developer, in the course of buying land for his development, would also buy the land necessary for the road and cede the latter to the LCC. In return, he would be allowed to calculate his plot ratio[3] on the basis of the *total* land concerned, not just the land remaining after the road was built.[4] As the architect put the exchange,

our clients will not claim compensation for that part of the property affected by the formation of the new road or road widening as envisaged. This undertaking is given conditional upon the benefit of the plot ratio for the land required for the new road widening.

[1] The job of the Valuer's Department is to assess property for a local authority. It is also involved in negotiations with developers over rentals on local authority property, where such property is to be used in a development. Under the land tenure system in effect in England, it is not uncommon for the local authority to own the property itself and to grant very long leases (99 years, e.g.) to developers who will build on it. The developers then pay a ground rent to the local authority for the property.

[2] Also, the 1959 *Town and Country Planning Act* would come into force on 16 August 1959. Under the terms of the *Act*, an applicant for planning permission had to show that owners of the property for which he was seeking permission (if he didn't own it himself) knew of the application. Before this date, it was possible to buy up property from owners who did not know its true value.

[3] Plot ratio is a measure of the relationship between the bulk of the building expressed in floorspace and the amount of land it is built on. The ratio is designed as a tool to control the height and mass of building; for example, even London's largest ratio, if enforced, would prohibit the building of just about all the major skyscrapers in New York as the plot they are built on would be too small to 'support' the height of the building. Aside from the overall plot ratio, allocations of floor space for various uses are also subject to control.

[4] The exchange in the case of St Giles must be considered somewhat different than was usual in this period insofar as the LCC already owned a good deal of the land necessary for the road.

64

The idea of an exchange was not a new one, having been used in several major developments in central London. It arose out of the shortage of funds to purchase land for road improvements in the central area. By allowing developers liberal planning permission for office buildings, the best commercial investment, developers could be persuaded to cede some of the land they had purchased for road improvements. One of the planning officers commented that

this might be stretching the rules a bit, but until the time just around the St Giles development there was really little doubt about the procedure. There was a demand for offices and we couldn't afford road space.

However, with the easing of financial conditions, the shift of attention to urban motorways and the restrictions on office permissions, such exchanges were halted on the advice of the legal department.

The proposals and subsequent negotiations

The development scheme which the architect submitted consisted of two buildings, one 24 stories high and a lower elongated building alongside. The taller building was to be built on the island of the roundabout with the lower building to the east. In order to provide for the necessary building sites, some of the original streets would be closed and built on.[1] The office space in the original submission was to be about 140,000 square feet.[2] The total plot ratio for all uses was 5 to 1, the maximum allowable for the area under the *Development Plan*. As noted above, the ratio in this case used the total site area, i.e. the road land as well. The office space was to constitute about one-half of the total square footage.[3] The roundabout was to include 40-foot carriageways, which conformed to the engineers' minimum scheme as presented in the sketch given to the architect earlier in the summer.

The application was submitted in mid-August 1959, but by the end of August modifications were already afoot, caused by some rethinking on the part of both the engineers and the architect. At a meeting between the architect and the planners in late August, the former raised the possibility of

It had already invested over half a million pounds, i.e. roughly two-thirds of the investment that would have been required, to purchase the road land. After the various legal problems, the developer in fact paid about 1.5 million for the land he purchased. This last figure is Marriott's; see *Property Boom*, p. 110. It is not clear whether he means the total cost of the land the developer bought or just the cost of the land ceded to the LCC. The former seems more likely.

[1] The closing of the streets enabled the development to be financially feasible and it eased the problems of land acquisition.

[2] This is a very rough figure as the original sketches are no longer available.

[3] The site for the development was approximately 5/8 of the one originally considered by the LCC for comprehensive development. In terms of office space, the planners' suggestion had called for 112,200 square feet. The developer's original submission included then more office space on less land than the planners had contemplated.

increasing the amount of office space and argued for an additional six floors in the main building. A planning officer suggested that the architect write a letter to the Council explaining his proposals and indicating why it might be to the Council's advantage to allow such an increase. The architect did as suggested and argued in support of his request that

the cost of acquisition is found to be very considerably in excess of earlier appraisals. For the purpose of making the development financially feasible it is essential that the scheme shall include the maximum proportion of offices.

In addition he noted his proposal would dissolve the Council's legal problems and allow the Council an early realization of its road scheme.

At more or less the same time the engineers made known some additional thinking on the width of the roundabout. At the time of the earliest discussions with the Ministry of Transport, the Chief Engineer had stated that 40-foot carriageways would be sufficient for a minimum road scheme. But he had also noted that should comprehensive development come, 50-foot roadways might be preferable. This last point, however, was not emphasized in conversations with other officers. Now with the application for redevelopment of the area, the engineers told the planning officers that in order for them to give a favorable report to the Planning Committee on the development, the roadways would have to be widened to 50 feet all round. One of the engineers working on the case noted that, 'when we saw [the architect] coming, we saw the possibility of getting more road width'.

In a subsequent discussion with the architect, planning officers made known the engineers' views. As a result of the ensuing negotiations, the architect agreed to cede additional land, but only for the east and west side of the roundabout. Provisions for the widening on the north and south side, it was decided, were to depend on future development to the north and south of the proposed development. It was assumed by all concerned, planners, engineers and the architect, that acquisition of such future land would be possible. It was also agreed that the architect would submit an application for a 30-story building on the roundabout instead of the original 24 stories. Suitable provision, it now appeared, had been made for the required road widening.[1]

In October, the revised application came to the Planning Committee for approval and was introduced with some enthusiasm by the planning officers. The application called for two buildings, a 30-story block and a considerably lower building, which together contained 196,000 square feet of office space. Also included were provisions for 46,000 square feet for shops and 39,500

[1] It is not possible to document from the records whether the acceptance of revisions by the planning authority and the developer was a question of mutual inducement. Nor are the memories of the participants very clear on the question. The best that can be said is that the revisions coincided and were presented together in the application that finally came before the Committee for consideration.

square feet for residential accommodation. This kept the plot ratio for the whole site including the road land to just about 5 to 1. The buildings were sited in such a way as to allow for the 50-foot carriageways on the east and west part of the roundabout. The large building was to be placed in the center of the roundabout, with the small one to the east of the tall block, separated by the eastern arm of the roundabout. The report asked that the Committee give approval to the height of the building (about 300 feet) and the plot ratio, i.e. to give outline permission.

'The Committee wasn't awfully happy about the proposal', was the way the then Chairman described his Committee's reaction. In fact a motion was proposed to have the height of the building reduced and it was only narrowly defeated, with the Chairman casting the deciding vote. At a subsequent meeting early in the next month the Committee voted on the application itself and gave its approval.[1]

Events then became somewhat confused. The Committee had given approval to the basic outline of the project, presumably including the widths for the roundabout which were shown as 50 feet on only the east and west arms. As noted, throughout these negotiations leading to approval, it had apparently been assumed that increased road widths on the north and south side of the roundabout would be taken care of by future development. In the middle of October, however, after the enthusiastic presentation of the application to the Committee and before its approval in November, the engineers expressed their doubts about the advisability of relying on future development on the north and south sides of the roundabout to provide additional road space. They noted that wider roadways could be obtained by reducing the size of walkways around the main building.

It is not clear why these doubts went unheeded, but the Committee did give approval to the application in the form just noted above. The engineers, however, decided to press their point again after conversations with the valuers. In these conversations the engineers discovered that it might prove very difficult for any development to take place on the north side of the north arm. Some of the property was extremely expensive and early development by the LCC or anybody else could not be counted on. It was now a question of (1) letting the development go ahead as shown in the sketches on which the permission had been granted, with the possibility that road widening on the north at least would take some time,[2] or (2) pressing to see that the developer was forced into making provisions for 50-foot roadways all around, or (3) getting the Council to commit itself to the necessary

---

[1] It should be noted that in both cases the voting was not along party lines. See the discussion of political parties in Chapter 5.

[2] The problem of land for the south side of the roundabout never seemed to have received as much attention as that for the north. In part this was because the LCC already owned some of the land required, making it more likely that it could control the course of future development than in the north where it had no holdings.

purchases. What the engineers desired was firm assurance that indeed there would be an additional widening of the roundabout and they were now further strengthened in their doubts that this would come about by future development.

By February 1960, the architect had become apprised of the engineers' doubts and of the possible need for reworking the scheme. He set out his views on this in a letter to the LCC.

We understand that discussions have...taken place between the Chief Engineer and the Valuer as a result of which further intimation has been made that New Oxford Street [the north arm] should be widened to 50 feet and that the widening should extend on the land covered by our proposed development. This is an entire reversal of the agreement previously reached and would, in effect, make the proposed development impracticable. We understand that your planning officers entirely concur with this point and will not support any counter-proposal which would intrude upon the plan already approved.

The architect was clearly worried that any proposal to increase road widths would result in a reduction of square footage in the tall building.

The whole issue was presented to the Town Planning Committee on 24 March in a report by all the officers concerned except the comptrollers who made a separate presentation. The report stated first that the southern arm would present no problem. On the more difficult problem of the north side, several alternatives were broached, aside from the LCC itself purchasing any additional land that might be required to effect widening. If the engineers insisted on 50-feet road widths all around, and it proved impossible for the LCC to purchase the necessary land on the north of New Oxford Street, then it would be necessary to have recourse to one of the other alternatives presented. The first alternative was to simply reduce the base of the taller building, which would allow an increase in the size of New Oxford Street with the additional land coming from the south side (the developer's site), rather than from redevelopment on the north side. As noted, the architect found this unacceptable and the report noted his views that the consequence of such a change would be that the scheme 'could not be proceeded with'.

The second alternative was to reduce the size of the island in the same manner as in the first alternative, but leave the dimensions of the building as originally proposed. Planners, however, noted that they 'could not recommend the Committee to accept a proposition which would result in a 330-foot building rising virtually sheer from the curb edge'.[1] Basically the alternatives, then, were either to convince the architect to make provisions or commit the Council to buy the additional land required. Some planning officers felt that the matter should remain as it was before the engineers

[1] Why the building was reported as being 330 feet is not clear. The various reports were not consistent on the height.

decided to press their case; however, this position seemed no longer tenable as the engineers were insistent. Others hoped that the Committee could be persuaded to commit the Council to purchasing the necessary land on the north side of New Oxford Street. In general, planners were reluctant to push the architect. They had devoted so much time to reaching agreement and were afraid that the architect might drop the project. The Council would then lose the chance for comprehensive redevelopment in the area.

The view of some of the planners that the LCC itself should purchase the additional land was resisted by the Comptroller's Department and the Valuer's Department. In a report presented to the Committee also on 24 March 1960, the Comptroller's office made it clear that funds were not available to purchase additional land. The comptrollers noted that at the time of granting permission there was 'no suggestion...that further capital expenditure would be required to secure a 50-foot width on the northern and southern arms'. The Valuer's Department's objections were on the grounds that any purchase of land on the north side of New Oxford Street would involve compensation to one of the nation's major clothing chains who had one of their best shops located on the site.

The result of all this was that on March 28 1960, the Planning Committee, at the insistence of the engineers, committed itself to 50-foot road widths all around and to seeing that the developer relinquished the necessary land for the increased widths. A meeting between officers, the Planning Committee Chairman and the architect was arranged for 4 April to persuade the latter to make desired changes.[1] The major consequence of the discussions was that arrangements were made for a series of meetings between planners and the architect at which the major alternatives could be evaluated.

The various meetings produced a compromise whereby the developer would cede the additional land necessary for the increased road width and would redesign the buildings to accommodate the lost office space, i.e. build higher. The planning officers were quite adamant that the office block should not exceed 350 feet, and so some of the lost office space would have to be put in the lower building. The architect attempted to allow for more office space in his new designs, but he was told that he must keep to the original floor space. In the end, he did get about 5,000 additional square feet. The final proposal for the development contained a 34-story office tower, a total of 313,500 square feet, of which 201,000 was office space, all on a site area of 57,000 square feet including the land on which the round-

---

[1] By this time, the LCC knew that a committee appointed by the Ministry of Transport (Committee on London Roads, also known as the Nugent Committee) had recommended that St Giles Circus definitely be improved in the immediately succeeding years. This increased the pressure on the Council to extricate itself from its difficulties and move ahead with the project. This is in addition to the earlier Ministry of Transport report and the resultant reprogramming of the road for an earlier period.

about was built. This made for a plot ratio of approximately 5.5 to 1, or somewhat over the Council's allowable maximum.[1]

The scheme agreed on by the planners and the architect was shown to the Clerk of the Council who gave his approval and called in the Chairman. Under the standing orders of the Council, it was possible for the Chairman to give his approval of the alteration as still being within the terms of the outline permission. However, to insure that there would be no difficulty, the Chairman called in the Opposition Leader on the Committee and got his consent to the alterations. An alternative approach would have been for the architect to submit a new application, but working with the original permission had the merit of speed as the architect was pressing matters along. His employer had options on some of the property on the site and felt that a definite agreement must be reached before any additional purchases could be made. If the purchases of the litigants' property were not accomplished within the next three months the LCC might still have to appear in court.[2]

The final stages

The final shape of the building was settled by April 1960, four years after the original attempt was made to get a roundabout. During all this time the only mention of the development in the newspapers was a small article which merely noted the proposed development without offering any details. At the same time as this decision was reached, the impact of the development on the underground station beneath it was also settled. This involved making an arrangement with the London Transport Executive which ran the public transportation system, and once again the developer proved useful. After the Council had approved the application for St Giles, the developer's architect was brought into the discussions with the LTE. After prolonged negotiation, it was agreed that the developer would provide the shells for new underground pedestrian subways, while the Transport Executive would handle the rest of the expenses. In the architect's mind the provision of the subways was related to another aspect of the case which can only be touched on, i.e. the financial arrangements between the County Council and the developer. The architect felt that the seemingly favorable financial arrange-

---

[1] This, of course, made the plot ratio on the actual building site considerably greater. Marriott, *Property Boom*, p. 114, thinks that the plot ratio on the building site is 10 : 1. It is rather difficult to be precise in this regard because as one planner put it, 'in those days the LCC wasn't too careful about these things'.

[2] In the period when the road widths were being discussed, the Royal Fine Arts Commission expressed some doubts on the aesthetics of the proposed buildings. The function of the body, which is composed of well-known architects, is to review major applications but it has no legal authority to halt building, nor does it generally publicize its views. In the end it dropped its objections due to the fine designs submitted.

ments (see below) were in return for the provision of the shell for the pedestrian subway. He felt that this would have fallen on the LCC, and the provision by the developer was a bonus for the Council. It must be noted that aside from the question of the financial arrangements, the developer did not go unrewarded for his efforts as he was given permission to build spaces for shops in the subway.

The financial arrangements consisted of the developer ceding all the land he had purchased for the development in return for a building lease of 150 years. The arrangement was certainly no burden on the developer as it would not prevent him from selling the building. This part of the arrangement was quite straightforward,[1] but there was also the question of the ground rent the developer was to pay the LCC for the properties it had already purchased under the 1956 Notice to Treat. From one point of view these properties were not very valuable to the LCC; what was left over from any road development (on the assumption that the litigation was cleared up) would likely be too small and fragmented to be very useful. On the other hand, it is clear that the LCC ownership of a share of the property made the developer's job easier and indeed, given the location, they did have some value. In addition to this, the Council had closed a road on which the developer was to build and had allowed him air-rights over the east arm of the roundabout where the two buildings were to be connected. In the actual agreement, the ground rent was based only on those pieces of land which the LCC owned and which were not used for the road works. All other rights in land or airspace were waived. The rent was a flat figure of £18,500 per year for the period of the leasehold. There was no provision for revision of the rent in future years.[2]

Reaching agreement between the LCC and the developer was one thing; trying to get the tenants to sell out their freeholds or leases was quite a different matter. It was for this problem that LCC officers felt the architect was the right man; this was a particularly difficult job of land assembly.[3] The United Kingdom has no equivalent of American urban renewal laws which allow public purchase in certain cases for private development. This means that a developer may have a planning permission for a site and most

[1] A planner concerned with the case explained that the LCC was, 'reluctant to give up any freehold [ownership of land] at all. I've never known the LCC to do this. The whip we use, if necessary, is to say to the developer "if you don't do this, we will issue a compulsory purchase order not only on the land needed for the road but for the whole plot, and, if this happens, you won't get any land at all".' The planner went on to say that developers were not usually reluctant because they were getting 'a good commercial deal' and they were 'not interested in the land itself but only in a big rate of return which they could get from rental space'.

[2] Marriott, *Property Boom*, p. 115, estimates that because of no provision for rent revisions, the LCC lost upwards of 10 million pounds.

[3] A planning officer commented on the problem of land assembly that 'we (the LCC) needed someone who would do all the dirty work of assembling the land without having any compulsory purchase powers available for much of the site. This was not something any architect would have taken on.'

of the necessary land and still be unable to complete his development because of reluctant owners. Even if the planning authority strongly favors the development, or is heavily committed to its success because of its own involvement, it is not possible to issue compulsory purchase orders unless the land will be used for public development of some type.

However, a resourceful developer is not always hindered by such difficulties. One of the engineers working on the case described the procedure the architect used in dealing with some of the more tenacious occupants as follows.

A developer comes to the LCC and says, 'look I have all but a few properties and the last few won't get out. Use a CPO [compulsory purchase order].' The LCC says they'll think about it. The developer goes back and says, 'look, if you don't get out, the LCC will use a CPO, and you'll get less money. Settle with me.' Most of them do. However, there was one fellow who stuck it out to the bitter end and finally [the architect] had to pay him a big price on top of trying to scare him off by pulling the buildings down around him. The LCC could never have done that.[1]

In many cases, the threat (which is finally a bluff) produces the desired result. It is only when owners know the law that they can hold out, as was the case at St Giles.

The final important decision affecting the development at St Giles was made late in 1960, casting doubt on the value of the whole enterprise. The roundabout on which so much effort had been expended was made useless by a change in the traffic system of the surrounding area. In December 1960, the Ministry of Transport wrote to the LCC saying that, as a temporary measure, it was making Tottenham Court Road into a one-way northbound street, thus making Charing Cross Road and Tottenham Court Road into a one-way system.[2] This was part of the Ministry's continuing interest in one-way traffic schemes as a method of moving traffic more rapidly. The change made the roundabout quite unnecessary; there was no longer a need for a street pattern to send traffic off in four different directions. The problem of northbound and southbound traffic blocking each other's attempts to turn onto east or west routes was eliminated, and this was the problem the roundabout was designed to meet. For a short period the change in traffic plans left the LCC in some doubt as to whether the Ministry would now be forthcoming with the promised grant. If the roundabout were unnecessary,

---

[1] Confirmation of this less than tender treatment of some of the occupants is provided by a letter from a chartered surveyor acting for one of the occupants who wrote to the LCC protesting the treatment of his clients. The surveyor contended that the developer had been belligerent and their attitude has been 'if you do not agree to our terms the LCC will make a CPO and you will not do very well out of that'.

[2] An adjoining street, which ran through the London University precinct, was also made one-way in the opposite direction. The stream of traffic which presumably would be drawn into the University area made the conversion doubly distasteful to the LCC.

so might the grant be, at least in the Ministry's eyes. However, the grant was given as promised; the Ministry saw the one-way scheme as only temporary until Tottenham Court Road was widened. This last depended on London engineers committing funds which, at last report, they were not anxious to do until they got assurances from the Ministry that their efforts would be rewarded by a return to a two-way system. Such assurance would not be forthcoming until the widening was started.[1]

By 1967, the development was completed and named Centre Point. The low building was then rented but the main block remained unrented.[2] It was generally agreed that the development was more than usually attractive. Its value from the developer's viewpoint, however, was not aesthetic, but financial. It is not possible to give the profit margin with any accuracy, but one estimate by a reputable financial editor runs as high as £11.7 millions.[3]

The reaction of many of the LCC officers and members was summed up by one planning officer who said,

I wasn't in favour of it, but if you wanted the road this was probably what you had to give. We might have gotten away with less if we had bargained harder. It all hinged on how badly you wanted the road.

The LCC had clearly saved money over its original minimum scheme. It had to purchase less land to get the necessary (and in fact, larger) road widths. And it had indeed got the road somewhat quicker than would otherwise have been possible under the circumstances. The costs are much more difficult to measure. They include: a big dent in the policy of restricting office building, a loss in aesthetic value,[4] at least if the planners' original contentions about the site are accepted, and a financial loss due to the provisions of the rent scheme. One planner summed up the costs this way.

The site is too small. It's in the middle of a heavily trafficked area and would generate more traffic. It is in the middle of a traditional shopping area and not an office area.

[1] At present (1973), the roundabout is still not in use.

[2] With rents going up, this is probably by choice. The developer has said publicly that he wants to rent the whole building to one client and in fact there have been several negotiations, none of which have succeeded. In 1972, both the local planning authority (Camden Council under the metropolitan government) and the Minister responsible for planning have made public criticisms about unlet office buildings. The Minister has moved to prevent this from occurring, while Camden has indicated it would like to purchase Centre Point, if it can raise the money.

[3] Marriott, *Property Boom*, p. 116. Marriott contends that Centre Point 'will probably be in absolute terms the most profitable single building ever promoted in [the United Kingdom]' (p. 110).

[4] This refers to a loss of the views of surrounding buildings. Moreover, a planner who worked on the case said that the building 'did not measure up to the LCC's high building policy of the time. It missed on several points.'

5. THE POLITICAL ENVIRONMENT OF COUNCILORS

The preceding case studies give substance to the descriptive characteristics of land use politics in London outlined in the first chapter. Most generally, the studies show that the citizenry in whatever guise had very limited involvement in the making of development control decisions. The planning authority (and most importantly its elected representatives) was under very little pressure from citizens to choose any particular course of action. For example, in the World's End case, while there was controversy between the two authorities the public did not really become involved until the case came before an inquiry. The consequences of the decision in terms of who would live in the buildings and whether the people whom it was designed to serve could afford to live there, consequences which might be thought to generate some citizen activity, went undiscussed publicly. Indeed the whole question of whether public housing should be built at all was not raised by any citizen spokesman. Similarly, in the St Giles case there was no organized group arguing that the development would add to the congestion of an already crowded area. Closely related to the low level of citizen pressure was the limited attention elected representatives gave to determining how decisions they reached might be received by their constituents. In contrast to representatives in American cities, when members in London became involved in planning choices they did not seem to be very interested in trying to gauge the views and interests of their constituents as a guide to their own actions.

The small number of participants actively engaged in making land use decisions followed not only from the limited activity by citizens but also from the lack of strong interest by most elected representatives. Rather than bargaining and competition among many participants being the principal means by which large-scale land use decisions were reached, they tended to be the product of a cooperative search among a limited number of planning officers and members. Effective authority was delegated to these officers and representatives and it was their interpretation of planning policy that constituted the principal component of decisions reached by the authority. Of particular interest was the important place given to planning officers. In both the World's End and St Giles cases it was the planners who generally decided what was at issue in the decision, carried the principal burden in

74

the negotiations with applicants and guided the final choices made. Members of the Planning Committee, and the other representatives who occasionally became involved, generally acted to review and modify planners' recommendations. Contrary to American experience, there were few laments by professionals about political interference. The terms of the discussion in the World's End case on the extent of open space to be required, for example, were set by professional values concerning acceptable standards rather than 'political' considerations of what might be acceptable to various groups of concerned citizens.

In spite of the concentration of influence in relatively few hands and the limited need by officers and members to shape decisions to accord with citizen pressures, the case studies reveal that the planning authority had difficulty in defining and serving its ends. Indeed, applicants were successful in getting permission for aspects of development that the authority did not in fact approve, even though the planning agency could by law prevent any development it wished or approve development subject to certain conditions being met. In the St Giles decision, while the planning authority made certain concessions to the applicants because of its legal difficulties, it went beyond what was likely necessary to insure continuation of the developer's interest. This was particularly the case when the authority allowed the developer to include additional office space after it was agreed that the project should be redesigned to take account of the problems with the road. If the case studies are an adequate indication, while the authority had numerous advantages in its negotiations with developers it was not a highly successful bargainer.

These are the principal features of land use politics that are highlighted in the cases; the remainder of the study will analyze each of them in some detail. The present chapter analyzes political cleavages and organization among the citizenry, which were the principal facets of the political environment London members faced, and examines some important characteristics of the latter's behaviour. An understanding of the characteristics of the political environment which members faced is crucial for comprehension of the features of land use politics that have just been described. Subsequent chapters will explore the remaining themes.

AUTONOMY AND ENVIRONMENT

The central feature of the relationship between the elected representatives of the County Council in London and the citizenry was autonomy. As noted, members generally had limited contact with constituents, except for dealing with the problems of particular individuals. They were neither very often approached by organized groups interested in having the Council pursue some particular action nor did they often seek such groups out.

Moreover, when groups did approach members they were in a position to, and did, rebuff them. The extent of contact was summed up by one member who noted quite simply, 'I really operated in a kind of vacuum.' A second member commented in a similar vein, 'the attitude seems to be, "we elect you and you get on with the job – unless we have a grumble and then we'll talk".'[1] A similar attitude was prevalent within the local political parties.

Did the local party ask me to vote a certain way? Well, they were very generous about this. I would explain and they would be quite decent about it. They never asked me to vote one way or another. Very little came up through the party really. On reform of local government, for example, they and I were at odds but this was thought to be my business. I gave the LCC line to the Herbert Commission [investigating metropolitan area reform for London]. The party took the line that 'we know old [name of member]; we sent him to the LCC and let him get on with it'.

Something of the norms underlying citizen/representative relations comes out in the comment of a member who described the process of recruitment of candidates for Council seats. He noted that the party organization established a list of candidates who were available and from this list constituency parties invited three or four candidates (if that number was available) to appear before a selection meeting. He continued:

One needs to live in the County for County Council elections but one does not need to live in the constituency for which one stands. In fact, many constituency parties think that one ought not to live in the local area, that you should be above local events and not susceptible to local pressure. That way there wouldn't be any rows over how you voted.

In general, members did not often shape their conduct of Council business in direct response to the expressed views or interests of constituents nor in direct response to the broad sources of political division among their constituents. In contrast to elected representatives in American cities, there were relatively few constraints on their behavior that stemmed directly from constituents' expectations or expressed views, or members' perceptions of these. The related divisions in the electorate of class and party did set some constraints but these tended to be rather loose or to be seen by members as not important for the matter at hand.[2]

The extent to which constituents were organized and the extent of cleavages among the citizenry were closely associated with the degree of

[1] Margaret Cole, an ex-alderman of the LCC commented: 'As to what happens in London generally, I think it scarcely an exaggeration to say that nobody who is not actually connected with it takes the slightest interest.' (*Servant of the County*, p. 5.)

[2] See Chapter 6.

autonomy of representatives. The latter may be defined as the degree to which the actions of elected representatives in setting policy and translating that policy into particular decisions are directly shaped by the views and interests of constituents.[1] Behavior is shaped as representatives are faced with a series of incentives and disincentives to perform certain actions which arise from the views and interests of the citizenry, i.e. from the actors constituting their (representatives') political environment. The link between degree of autonomy and the characteristics of the political environment is treated here as a simple deduction. In the case of London, the description of representatives as party men, as against political entrepreneurs, is the deductive link. London representatives did not need to invest in regular monitoring or molding of citizen preferences and so were autonomous.[2]

The extent of autonomy of representatives is related to factors other than the nature of the political environment and the perception of it.[3] It also depends at least on the member's conception of his job as an elected representative.[4] For example, citizens may pressure a representative to support a certain course of action but the content of the representative's role may imply that he pay little attention to certain kinds of demands. The latter is a principal concern of the succeeding chapter. Here the characteristics of the political environment and, to some extent the representatives' perception of them, are of major interest and for these purposes the simplified analysis of representatives' behavior utilized here is helpful. London representatives faced a political environment that was comparatively certain compared to that in which their American counterparts operated; and this

[1] Attempts to transform the definition into an operational concept will present formidable problems of observation and measurement; it will not be easy to observe the extent to which actions are shaped in the fashion described. A start might be made by a survey of members of an organization in order to elicit the sources they perceive as providing important behavioral cues. This approach raises the problem, however, that what the organizational member perceives may not be an accurate rendering of the situation. See the comment below in footnote 3.

[2] The behavioral assumption made here is that candidates want to get elected and representatives stay in office. For more elaborate examples of this deductive mode of analysis, see John C. Harsanyi, 'Rational Choice Models of Political Behavior vs. Functionalist and Conformist Theories', *World Politics*, 21 (1969), 513–38; and Michael Shapiro, 'Rational Political Man: A Synthesis of Social and Psychological Perspectives,' *American Political Science Review*, 63 (1969), 1106–19.

Of course, the analysis here does not apply to aldermen who did not stand for election. It may reasonably be argued, however, that on the basis of this fact they too were autonomous.

[3] It is difficult to clearly distinguish between these two phenomena. However, for some purposes it would be a grave disadvantage not to be able to discuss the fact that the behavior of a member of an organization is shaped by environmental factors in ways he cannot either articulate or perceive. This is a classic tension in social science, viz. that between analysis from the point of view of the observer and perceptions of the subject as to how the world operates. Cf. Dill, 'Environment and Autonomy,' p. 411.

[4] The member's conception itself can be linked to environmental variables. See Chapter 6.

A more complete analysis of the behavior of representatives would take into account incentives arising from the 'internal environment' or 'climate' of the organization. See, for example, the papers in Renato Taguiri and George H. Litwin, *Organizational Climate* (Boston, 1968). Clearly, the implication of the present discussion is that for the problems addressed in this study, such variables are of limited interest.

level of certainty depended principally on the pattern of political cleavages and the level of political organization of the citizenry.

POLITICAL CLEAVAGES

The constituency and the general electorate which faced a London representative differed from that which his American counterpart sees. Where a city councilman in a large American city, particularly in the Northeast and the older cities of the Midwest, sees a heterogeneous electorate most of whose major social and economic differences are politically relevant, the London representative saw an electorate which was relatively homogeneous with only one important political cleavage.

Political cleavages may be thought of as relatively enduring points of division among citizens which operate across particular issues and more broadly defined issue areas. The basis for a cleavage may be an attribute of citizens, such as race or place of residence, or it may be an attitude, for example the proper function for city government.[1] Here we are interested in both types. In addition, we are interested in, among several properties of any cleavage of a given type, the properties of: extent of crystallization, intensity of fragmentation, and extent of cross-cutting.[2] In other terms, the problems we are concerned with are: of the total community, how many people are conscious of there being cleavages which divide them from fellow citizens, how intense are such divisions, and to what extent do the same citizens regularly find themselves on the same side of a cleavage.

In London, political conflict insofar as it revolved around cleavages in the electorate was rooted in social class and principally expressed through the two main political parties. Other possible cleavages – such as ethnicity, race and neighborhood – were absent or insignificant.[3]

Figures for London show the high level of ethnic homogeneity.[4] Roughly

[1] Douglas W. Rae and Michael Taylor, *The Analysis of Political Cleavages* (New Haven, 1970), Chapter 1. Rae and Taylor distinguish a third basis for cleavage, viz. that by activity or organizational membership. But as we are concerned here with differences which cut across particular issues and issue areas, and organized groups tend to specialize in particular issue areas, this kind of 'cleavage' is best treated separately under political organization. Distinguishing between attitude and attribute cleavages on the one hand and organizational activity rooted in them on the other is not always possible or even desirable.

[2] Rae and Taylor, *Political Cleavages*, Chapter 1.

[3] The basic point of reference for the discussion of American cities is provided by Banfield and Wilson, *City Politics*.

[4] For a discussion of the relations between ethnicity and urban politics in American cities see the following: Banfield and Wilson, *City Politics*, pp. 38–44; Nathan Glazer and Daniel Patrick Moynihan, *Beyond the Melting Pot*, 2nd ed. (Cambridge, Mass., 1970); Raymond Wolfinger, 'The Development and Persistence of Ethnic Voting,' *American Political Science Review*, 57 (1965) 896–908; and Michael Parenti, 'Ethnic Politics and the Persistence of Ethnic Identification,' *American Political Science Review*, 61 (1967) 717–26. Banfield and Wilson on p. 38 provide a list of American cities with population over 500,000 ranked according to number of foreign born or with at least one parent foreign born. Eleven such large cities have more than 30 per cent of their population in this category.

15 per cent of the population of the Administrative County was born outside of England, Scotland or Wales. Of this a substantial (but unknown) portion did not participate in politics, being citizens still of their home countries.[1] The two biggest ethnic groups were the Jews and the Irish (and the colored population increasingly), but they were not present in great numbers in comparison with most large American cities. Large numbers of foreigners did not come to London and pose a threat to the existing inhabitants; the self-awareness of the immigrants was not heightened by the reactions of the indigenous population to their numbers.[2] Furthermore, they had a place in the society into which to move – the society was stratified and these social class differences were beginning to be reflected in organizational terms at the political level. The tendency was for ethnicity to be submerged at both the social and political level by overarching class differences in contrast to American cities where, if anything, the former overshadowed the latter.[3] The suggestion is that whether ethnicity is politically salient has a great deal to do with the nature of the ongoing political system which greets immigrants. Specifically, are they bid for as immigrants with emphasis on their country of origin, or do local politicians emphasize some other characteristic, for example, social class?

The colored population of London was small in numbers.[4] Moreover, it was not composed of people of the same national origin but principally of three different nationality groups (West Indian, Indian and Pakistani), each of which was further subdivided into language and cultural groups. This reduced an already small section of the population into even smaller

---

[1] *Census 1961, County Report, London.* Of the total number of Irishmen in London (approximately 160,000) something between 1/3 and 1/2 were citizens of the Irish Republic, who, although they could vote in London elections, probably did not do so in great numbers. The wide latitude in the indicated percent of Irish citizens is necessitated by inadequate census categories.

[2] See John A. Jackson, 'The Irish', in Centre for Urban Studies, *London: Aspects of Change.*

[3] Also relevant here is the question of whether there *are* politicians concerned with the local electorate or whether political organizations are very much tied to politics at the capital. See the following for comments on the interaction between class, ethnicity and types of political systems in England: Stephen L. Elkin, 'Immigrants and Local Politics in Three English Cities' (unpublished paper, University of Pennsylvania, 1969); E. P. Thompson, *The Making of the English Working Class* (London, 1963); John Rex and Robin Moore, *Race, Community and Conflict* (London, 1967), pp. 154–5; David Butler and Donald Stokes *Political Change in Britain* (London, 1969), Chapter 6; Robert Alford, *Party and Society* (Chicago, 1963), Chapter 6; and Richard Rose, 'Class and Party Divisions: Britain as a Test Case' (University of Strathclyde, Survey Research Centre, Occasional Papers #1, n.d.). In general, on the political salience of various attribute cleavages, see Seymour Lipset and Stein Rokkan, 'Cleavage Structures, Party Systems and Voter Alignments: An Introduction' in Lipset and Rokkan, *Party Systems and Voter Alignments: Cross National Perspectives* (New York, 1967); Marc Howard Ross, 'Class and Ethnic Bases of Political Mobilization in African,' Cities American Political Science Association, Washington D.C., 1972; and Raymond Wolfinger, 'Some Consequences of Ethnic Politics' in Kent Jennings and Harmon Zeigler (eds.), *The Electoral Process* (Englewood Cliffs, N.J., 1966).

[4] Colored people made up 4 per cent of the total LCC population. *Census, 1961, County Report, London.* However, this is almost certainly an undercount. See E. J. B. Rose *et al., Colour and Citizenship: A Report on British Race Relations* (London, 1969), Chapters 9 and 10.

fragments who, in fact, had difficulty in finding grounds for cooperative action. As a result of both divergent interests and difficulties in establishing common organization, the already limited electoral importance of the colored group was limited even further.[1] Non-white groups were politically more self-conscious than other ethnic groups, but their attention tended to focus on the national government. While local authorities were seen to be increasingly relevant to their problems, important decisions were still made centrally. In major part, this focus on central government was a consequence of a concern with questions of law, such as discrimination and admission to the country, rather than distributive problems such as housing and education in which local governments played an important part.[2] In London, it is clear that local officials did not find it necessary to make any distinction between white and colored communities. For example, when housing decisions were made, little if any notice was taken of color. One planning officer put it this way.

Colored people as such don't exist as a factor in making decisions. All are treated equal as a matter of policy. Nobody wants to know about this as a planning factor. Non-whites are a new problem and the system is not ready to deal with them yet and so far nobody sees them or wants to see them as a special problem.

Another common political division in American cities is by neighborhood. Much of intense concern in American city politics revolves around the question of which area of the city will or will not have a particular building or facility. In general, neighborhood interests, which are often ethnically grounded, are one of the divisions to which elected officials pay great attention and many urban politicians build a career on serving the interests of such a constituency. In London, however, neighborhood divisions were not politically important. In the Chelsea case, for example, while LCC members from the borough did take some interest in the decision, this was not done in a public fashion so that political credit might be gained. Nor in fact did the interest go much beyond keeping an eye on events. Deliberations about planning policy in the Council did not involve the logrolling behavior common to American city councils and in fact on some decisions representatives from the particular area were not even consulted. The reason is not hard to find: members' political fortunes did not depend on pleasing their particular constituents. They were not elected to serve neighborhood interests but rather gained election as party men (see below).

[1] For an extended discussion of the colored population in England generally, see Rose *et al.*, *Colour and Citizenship*.

[2] By 1970, decisions made by local governments were in fact seen by colored groups to be important and as a result organization at the local level was greater than in the period under discussion. This reflected in part an increase in the size of the colored group. Unfortunately, reliable data on changing size is unavailable, but see Rose, *et al.*, *Colour and Citizenship*, Parts II and III.

Service to one's own constituents isn't really the level which makes any difference. It matters least... There is virtually no sense of this kind of relationship... Voting is strictly on party lines and it is mainly the party faithful who vote. There isn't much campaigning and very few meetings. One's only real activity was canvassing. One would say 'I'm (member's name) and I'm standing for the Labour Party. I hope you will support me.' My party identification was really the only badge of identification.[1]

The extent to which representatives from an area affected by a decision would be involved in the discussions of the appropriate committee was the subject of some disagreement among members. What is clear is that such representatives did not play a crucial role in the decision-making process, as is often the case in American cities; when they did appear their views played a limited part in the discussion. One member of long experience on the Council put it this way.

They generally didn't contact me as a local member. I had to watch out for it. I'd keep an eye on the agenda papers and then just blow in. I wasn't really invited, although I usually got some warnings. My appearing before the committee didn't happen all that often. I was there to plead the case for a sectional interest and this was always a small part of the total discussion.

There is some additional evidence of the small importance attached to serving neighborhood interests. The figures for home residence and constituency for candidates in the 1961 London election (the last LCC election) show that Conservatives had 64 per cent of their candidates living outside their home constituency; Labour had 46 per cent living outside; and the Liberals, who put up fewer candidates, had 29 per cent living outside. Even when one looks at the borough (which is a larger unit than the constituency) *over 40 per cent of the candidates lived outside the borough which contained their constituency.*[2]

The operation of the rating (taxing) system for London also suggests the low level of neighborhood and area conflict. Briefly, the rating authorities were the boroughs, while the LCC issued 'precepts' each year on the former for a certain percentage of the revenue collected by them. Built into this system was an equalization scheme by which the better-off boroughs subsi-

---

[1] On the more general question of gaining special treatment for constituents, one member suggested that this practice, which is common in American cities and is used to build political followings, was not accepted in London. 'There have been occasions when housing lists have been slanted, but... it has not been popular to serve one's constituents through getting them on the housing list [for public housing]. Quite the reverse actually. Here it is not good to tell your electorate that one has done this.'

See also the comment by the member in Chapter 6 where she remarks that members *ought not* to give much weight to neighborhood interests. By way of contrast, see the comment, by Meade Esposito, Chairman of the Brooklyn Democratic organization, on the value of favors for constituents in maintaining an organization. *New York Times*, 7 March 1971.

[2] Figures are from L. J. Sharpe, *A Metropolis Votes: The London County Council Election of 1961*, Greater London Papers, No. 8 (London, 1962), pp. 36–7.

Table 1. *Rateable value, equalization payments and expenditure – Metropolitan Borough Councils – 1964–65**

District	Area in acres[a]	Resident population[b]	Rateable value, 1 April 1964		Rates raised for Borough Council services	London Equalization Scheme: Receipts (−) or Payments (+)
			Amount	Per head of population		
			£	£	£	£
City of London	677	4,580	[c]44,426,187	9,700.0	6,196,925	+ 1,416,744
Battersea	2,164	102,820	4,683,843	45.5	765,527	− 485,403
Bermondsey	1,505	50,340	4,167,736	82.8	640,889	− 437,673
Bethnal Green	759	46,420	2,443,419	52.6	485,932	− 396,695
Camberwell	4,481	175,740	7,409,806	42.2	1,247,031	− 739,240
Chelsea	660	46,200	7,163,001	155.0	768,954	+ 130,334
Deptford	1,565	68,500	2,828,503	41.2	542,699	− 269,657
Finsbury	587	32,070	9,376,607	292.4	984,032	+ 128,184
Fulham	1,703	109,410	6,009,914	54.9	778,264	− 515,968
Greenwich	3,863	83,630	5,122,969	61.3	746,670	− 307,314
Hackney	3,293	164,350	8,208,800	49.9	1,178,047	− 687,205
Hammersmith	2,287	107,530	7,983,555	74.2	947,291	− 164,062
Hampstead	2,266	101,060	7,675,861	75.9	947,983	− 82,869
Holborn	405	20,430	12,097,599	592.1	1,068,371	+ 509,415
Islington	3,092	227,090	10,073,394	44.4	1,644,018	− 470,000
Kensington	2,292	172,990	18,470,368	106.8	1,904,875	+ 443,076
Lambeth	4,090	223,140	13,781,243	61.8	1,888,141	− 385,727
Lewisham	7,017	223,170	8,993,901	40.3	1,719,747	− 420,214
Paddington	1,357	117,050	9,226,823	78.8	1,061,209	− 31,512
Poplar	2,346	68,530	4,650,218	67.9	663,424	− 299,198
St Marylebone	1,472	67,250	24,157,041	359.2	2,333,467	+ 926,891
St Pancras	2,693	121,870	12,828,893	105.3	1,716,529	− 229,506
Shoreditch	658	37,040	4,086,661	110.3	574,695	− 231,359
Southwark	1,131	84,830	6,270,720	73.9	824,383	− 248,514
Stepney	1,770	91,130	7,429,995	81.5	1,028,296	− 392,518
Stoke Newington	864	53,330	2,114,455	39.7	336,674	− 86,842
Wandsworth	9,109	348,450	16,219,533	46.6	2,258,384	− 431,951
Westminster	2,504	85,840	69,840,971	813.6	6,810,145	+ 4,292,910
Woolwich	8,282	149,810	8,161,223	54.5	1,234,560	− 618,378
Total, Administrative County	74,898	3,184,600	345,903,239	108.6	43,297,162[d] −	84,251[e]

(a) As compiled by the Director General of the Ordnance Survey in 1957.
(b) Registrar General's estimated home population, mid 1964.
(c) Including the Inner and Middle Temples.
(d) Total for City and Metropolitan Borough services only.
(e) The net receipts and payments under the London Equalization Scheme do not balance because some authorities have included in their accounts for 1964–65 the original estimate, and others a revised estimate.
* From GLC *London Statistics, 1955–64.*

dized the poorer. Table 1 reveals the extent of redistribution between the boroughs for 1964–5. The data indicate that of the 29 units (boroughs, plus the City), 7 were contributors and the rest recipients. While something similar also takes place in American cities, it is not done within a system of local governments which are more or less independent and which could generate conflict over the apportionment of shares, but through a single city-wide government. And yet in London, where the transfers did take place in the context of a series of local governments, the scheme apparently operated without conflict. The equivalent arrangement for an American city would be one in which neighborhoods raised their own revenues and, to some degree decided on expenditures, or in which there was a metropolitan area government where the constituent units keep their revenue and expenditure powers. In either case it requires no great imagination to conjure up the major conflicts that would likely result.

The above should not be taken to mean that there was no neighborhood activity at all or that members did not act on occasion to serve the interests of their particular constituents. There were local civic and amenity societies which did take an interest in neighborhood affairs, but they had limited impact especially when it came to the electoral fortunes of LCC members. The Chelsea case is instructive in this regard. It will be remembered that the Borough Council did not attempt to start a local campaign designed to persuade the County Council to make a favorable decision. This was because either stirring up neighborhood opinion was not considered to be possible, for by and large people were not concerned as a neighborhood, or, even if activity could be induced, the LCC was unlikely to be impressed.[1]

The extent to which race, ethnicity and neighborhood were points of political cleavage of course rests on a number of historical factors, but as has been implied the existence of a class-based party system also had an impact. The disciplined political parties promoted a comparatively high level of interest aggregation.[2] A similar point can be made concerning the probability that divisions *within* a particular class might become points of cleavage. For example, it is not uncommon in American cities for affluent members of the middle class and the somewhat less affluent members of the same class to be ranged on different sides of several issues nor is it unusual for more affluent and less affluent members of the working class

[1] It is worth emphasizing a possible difference between planning and other services with regard to the extent of neighborhood conflict. It is possible that roadbuilding stirred up more neighborhood interest than other types of land use decisions. However, in other service areas it is likely that neighborhood considerations played an even smaller role than in planning. Whatever the variation between issue areas, the general point is clear: the political fortunes of representatives were not greatly affected by neighborhood considerations.

[2] On parties and interest aggregation, see Gabriel A. Almond and G. Bingham Powell, *Comparative Politics: A Developmental Approach* (Boston, 1966), Chapter 5.

to see their interests being opposed.[1] For London, there are no solid data on the extent of division within classes, but on the basis of impressionistic evidence it would appear that divisions of interest between the upper and lower working class were less likely to become politically important because of the existence of a working-class party. Policy decisions made by the LCC while Labour held a majority tended to favor the more established sections of the working class sometimes at the expense of the less well-off and the newly arrived immigrants. And yet this distribution of public resources, especially in the area of council housing where those who lived in the worst housing often had great difficulty in getting rehoused in Council property, did not generate much political conflict within the working class.[2] The difficulties of establishing an effective organization independent of the Labour Party, already complicated in the case of the lower working class by a lack of resources, were increased by the fact that the Party already existed as an organization committed at least formally to the betterment of all working men. This is aside from the more general impact of there being representatives who had little incentive to pay attention to extra-party electoral considerations. When we turn to the middle class a similar point can be made. Again, impressionistic evidence suggests possible cleavages between less affluent and more affluent members of the middle class concerning issues such as Council subsidization of the poor were muffled by the presence of a party which represented the middle class generally and which was also committed to using governmental authority to aid the poorer sections of the community.

Another cleavage characteristic of large American cities which was largely absent in London is between those who see the city primarily as an economic unit whose health must be guarded and promoted and those who see the central function of the city as a meeting place of many competing groups, especially the poor. For the former, one of the principal tasks of local government is to promote the economic growth of the city by attracting new industry and commerce, or at least preventing economic decline. The latter tend to see the city government as an instrument to ease the plight of the poor and to support their bid for moves up the economic ladder. More generally, a central problem is to guarantee some measure of access to city government for these disadvantaged groups so that they may compete with other interests

[1] For this point to make sense, occupation-based definitions of class will have to be utilized. Sub-cultural or life-style definitions in fact concentrate on such differences within occupationally (or income) defined class distinctions.

[2] Those in the poorest housing often did not benefit from Council housing schemes because, as a former Chairman of the Housing Committee noted, many were transients who were not on a site long enough to come under the rehousing provisions of the Council. More difficult to pin down is whether the Council tended to assign its poorest tenants to its worst housing and the better-off to the nicer estates. On the last question, see Elizabeth Burney, *Housing on Trial* (London, 1967).

for a share in the city's goods and services.[1] These conceptions of the role of cities and the functions of local government in supporting the roles are not mutually exclusive, at least not over the long run; economic growth will ease the plight of the poor. Nor are they simply another manifestation of the class cleavage to be discussed below. Although there are clear class overtones, the major spokesman for each view have tended to be people from middle-class or upper middle-class backgrounds.

The most obvious manifestation of the cleavage in American cities is on the question of land use in the downtown area. Should urban renewal be used primarily to boost the city's commercial position or should it focus on the housing problems of the less well off in the city. In the short run, these tend to be competing as concentrating on the former generally reduces the supply of inexpensive housing.[2] More generally, especially in older American cities, leading businessmen, particularly those in retailing and real estate, and local officials have been concerned about the decline of the central business district and the need to revitalize it. Discussions of many issues in city politics are influenced by the effect which a particular policy will have on the economic health of the downtown area. Increasingly in recent years added to this concern has been a second one, viz., the effects of such policies on the well-being of the central city poor.

In London the situation was quite different. Local businessmen, local officials and articulate citizens were not worried that commerce was slackening and that, in particular, downtown revenues were declining.[3] The consequences of this can be found in two extraordinary (from an American viewpoint) facts about London merchants: they were not organized to deal with local governments;[4] and the merchants apparently did not protest

---

[1] This distinction draws on Oliver Williams and Charles Adrian, *Four Cities* (Philadelphia, 1963), especially Part III. Williams and Adrian distinguish four views that citizens and officials may hold about the functions of local government. These are: caretaker; promoter of life's amenities; arbiter of conflicting interests; instrument of community growth. It is the last two that concern us here.

[2] On controversies in urban renewal, see James Q. Wilson (ed.), *Urban Renewal: The Record and the Controversy* (Cambridge, Mass., 1966), especially the article by Herbert Gans entitled 'The Failure of Urban Renewal'.

[3] See the following on the state of opinion and on the actual situation: D. T. Stevens, 'The Central Area,' in J. T. Coppock and Hugh G. Prince (eds.), *Greater London* (London, 1964) pp. 167–200; Ruth Glass, 'Introduction,' in Centre for Urban Studies, *London: Aspects of Change*, p. xx; and *Review*, p. 13, Table 1.

At the present time (1973), London planners and elected officials have become increasingly concerned with the economic growth of the city. This seems to have originated with them rather than with central city businessmen. On the increasing concern, see Greater London Council, *Tomorrow's London* (London, n.d.) especially Chapter 3. It may be that the limited interest in city growth is not characteristic of other large cities in England. For example, cities such as Birmingham have always been growth conscious. (I am indebted to Peter Hall for this last point.)

[4] The Oxford Street Association, Oxford Street being the main shopping street of central London, was run out of a public relations firm which handled the usual complement of other

when the London *Development Plan* called for overspilling – i.e., reducing the population of London.[1] The observation of a planning officer indicates some of the conditions associated with the lack of concern on the part of downtown merchants and others about any decline in central area commerce.

Merchants on the whole are concerned with their own trading life. And this is seen as a short term proposition, say five or ten years. Where immediate opportunities are golden for the near future, redevelopment may mean, at least temporarily, a competitive loss. There is little incentive to look to the long term when profits are so good for the short.
Competition is lacking here. It's different from the cut-throat scene in New York. There is more laxness. People are more sleepy. Big stores were more or less landmarks. There was no need to compete. Only recently has purchasing power increased to make for more competition. They can't rest on their laurels any more.

Promoting this prosperity were factors such as continuing growth in office employment, excellent public transportation into the downtown area, limited resources to invest in suburban shopping centers and relatively poor roads and few cars (by American standards) with which to reach suburban centers. In addition, because the central government subsidizes local authorities so heavily, the financial viability of the cities is less likely to become a major local concern. The fact of extensive central government support of local finance probably has a particularly strong impact on the political activity of local businessmen since the need to work with local officials to promote a favorable business climate, a favorite pastime in American cities, would be considerably less.

The central business district of London then was still very much alive and even prospering. Merchants thus saw little need for redevelopment to make the central area more attractive nor did they generate a 'booster' or 'let's revitalize our city' psychology. It is likely that in a major American city, if a development of the dimensions of St Giles Circus were caught up

clients. Its main concern was with Christmas decorations for the street. Questions on relations with the LCC drew blank looks. In general, businessmen play a considerably smaller role in English politics than their American counterparts. One consideration here is probably that the latter played a larger part in the origin and early growth of their cities than the former. At any rate, Delbert Miller notes that in the contemporary period the prestige of businessmen is lower in England than in America. See Miller, 'Industry and Community Power Structure: A Comparative Study of an American and an English City', *American Sociological Review*, 23 (1958), 9–15. On the participation of businessmen in American city politics see Banfield and Wilson, *City Politics*, Chapter 18.

[1] It should be clear that after the population was reduced it was supposed to be brought back roughly to its 1961 level. In this sense, over the long run merchants would not have lost out. Also it should be noted that some merchants in local shopping areas appear to have been more active than their central area counterparts. However, the Chelsea Case suggests there was quite a bit of variation. Data to explain such variation are not available.

in difficulties, central city businessmen would become involved in promoting its approval so as to bolster commercial activity in the central core.[1] There was no evidence of such activity or even interest in London. In fact, there was little public articulation of 'a business interest', and in consequence the opposition of business interests and the interests of the less well-off which underlies a good deal of controversy in American cities was largely absent.

Since the mid 1960s there have been several changes that have affected the possibility of continuing prosperity for the central core and which have led to the concern by local officials noted above. Among these are the continuing movement of population out of the London area, the growth of investment in suburban shopping centers, increased congestion in the central area and increased car ownership.[2]

The political division that was important in London was the class cleavage. Class divisions shaped the voting patterns in local elections as well as provided the major basis for controversy over land use, housing and related matters.

Voting behavior in London and in national elections was very similar in its social basis. At both levels, class affiliation was a principal factor influencing the direction of the vote.[3] The continuity in voting patterns is supported by a study of the 1961 London County Council election. L. J. Sharpe, in *A Metropolis Votes*, notes that in comparing the 1959 general election voting of his sample with their votes in the 1961 election there was only a 3 per cent switch in party allegiance between national and local parties.[4] For the constituency which he sampled, Sharpe presents data, shown in Table 2, on the extent of class voting, indicating the class basis of the two parties in London elections.

One of the more important manifestations of class cleavage in American cities, which is often joined to racial differences, is in the area of housing policy. It shows up in such matters as: what shall be the character of a given neighborhood, this being interpreted in both physical and social terms; should local (and central) government build and operate public housing for the poorer sections of the community; and more generally, should either

---

[1] See, for example, the part local businessmen played in the controversy surrounding the Federal Trade Center in New York as reported by *The New York Times*, 7 December 1969.

[2] On increased car ownership and its implications, see Peter Hall, *New Society*, 1 January 1970, p. 26. For a somewhat less sanguine view of the economic health of the central area for the same period as discussed here, which focuses particularly on retailing, see Peter Wilsher, 'The Stores Take Stock,' *The Sunday Times*, 2 October 1966.

[3] For a discussion of the class basis of voting in national elections see Alford, *Party and Society*, Chapter 6 and Butler and Stokes, *Political Change*, especially Chapter 4. Alford and Sharpe (see below) rely on occupational measures of class while Butler and Stokes look at subjective measures as well. Alford provides some evidence to support the assertion that class voting is stronger in England than in the United States.

[4] Sharpe, *A Metropolis Votes*, p. 84.

Table 2.   *Class voting in the 1961 LCC election**

	Upper-middle and middle-middle	Lower-middle	Skilled and non-skilled working class
Conservative	77.5%	51.5%	23.6%
Labour	22.5%	48.5%	76.4%
Number	71	66	254

* Sharpe, *A Metropolis Votes*, p. 86. It should be noted that no party names appear on the ballots in LCC elections. See also Butler and Stokes, *Political Change*, p. 38. Sharpe (p. 3) comments that 'an LCC election is in many ways unique among British local elections, for the two-party system is probably more fully entrenched on the Council and throughout the LCC area than in any other local authority in the country.'

level of government subsidize housing for lower income groups. The impact of class divisions could be found in London in discussions of the first and second questions, although here the extent of controversy was not high by American standards. Division in the third area was largely absent. While social class was the most important source of political controversy, conflict over policy questions which were rooted in class considerations was comparatively limited.[1]

An LCC member with long experience in housing and land use problems indicated the extent of controversy in land use decisions which was rooted in class differences and particularly in the class composition of particular areas. In a comment about the choice of council housing sites, she also suggested that such considerations were not of major importance as far as the Council was concerned and that there was a broad consensus on the need for a public effort in housing.

As to local people, yes they object but it depends on the area. In Battersea [a predominantly working-class area] there is no objection, but when you get to places like Wimbledon [a predominantly middle-class area] there is. People in Wimbledon say it [council housing] will depreciate the area. They do object on

[1] There is a general point about political development, particularly in England, which is relevant to the succeeding discussion. It concerns the relationship between the existence of a single important political cleavage and the intensity of controversy in policy areas in which the cleavage is relevant. Below, certain historical and situational factors which worked to limit the intensity of conflict are touched upon, but this is clearly a problem of general theoretical interest. Eckstein, for example, in his work on the theory of stable democracy analyzes how in certain situations limited conflict develops in association with the existence of a single cleavage. See Harry Eckstein, *Division and Cohesion in Democracy: A Study of Norway* (Princeton, 1966), especially the essay reprinted in it, 'A Theory of Stable Democracy'. Richard Rose, looking at class conflict over time in England, suggests that, in fact, working-class political activity 'has involved ... a pursuit of specific and limited goals...' Rose, 'Class and Party Divisions', p. 10. Rose also argues that class divisions will be associated with *less* intense conflict than other cleavages.

the whole, that is owner occupiers do. Also they usually get overruled. It doesn't matter what the complexion of the Council is. Tories were more gentle perhaps but they knew too that land is needed for council housing. Tories on the Council were more sensitive to the middle-class objectors...All told though, there was a fair agreement to build council houses among the parties.

Although class considerations were more important to Londoners (even though of less importance to their councilors), they were probably not as salient as they are in similar situations in American cities. Part of this undoubtedly stems from the overlapping of class and racial categories in American cities, which means that public housing tends to serve lower-income Negroes. This intensification of class differences and class hostility by racial considerations was largely absent in London. In addition, it is possible that the more clearly differentiated English stratification system may have reduced the intensity of divisions among citizens over housing policy generally and the placing of public housing in particular. Specifically, the proximity of working-class neighborhoods or enclaves to those of the better-off is probably productive of less anxiety in England than in the United States where it might be argued that the demonstration of a superior social status is more difficult and hence productive of more anxiety.[1] While a good deal of evidence would be needed to establish this, it is probably true that where there are visible signs of a person's status at hand, and the signs are varied and persistent over time, then there is less anxiety over having someone lower down the social scale living nearby. The English situation comes a good deal closer to this than the American.[2]

In American cities, discussion of whether government should construct and manage housing and in general provide housing subsidization for low-income groups often revolves around the interests of the different social classes.[3] Recent controversy has probably been less concerned, at least at the public level, with whether government should play a role in providing housing for the poor and more with the means by which this is to be done and the extent of the help. The fact that low-income housing programs have never grown to any great dimensions, except in a few cities, has

[1] It is likely that residential mixing of social classes is on the decline in central London. This would be caused by the relocation of many working-class people outside London and the movement of many middle-class people into the outer reaches of the metropolitan area. It is possible that the lower anxiety in London is a carry-over of habits associated with the necessary propinquity of earlier years. See, Greater London Council, *Tomorrow's London*, pp. 24–5. On the extent of residential mixing see Peter Norman, 'Third Survey of London Life and Labor: A New Typology of London Districts', in Mattei Dogan and Stein Rokkan, *Quantitative Ecological Analysis in the Social Sciences* (Cambridge, Mass., 1966).

[2] Compare for example money as a sign of social status and speech patterns. See Gans, 'The Failure of Urban Renewal', p. 545 for a similar argument. On the English class system see e.g., Josephine Klein, *Samples from English Cultures* (2 volumes, London, 1965), particularly Volume I, Section II.

[3] See for example, Meyerson and Banfield, *Politics, Planning and Public Interest*; Harold Wolman, *The Politics of Federal Housing* (New York, 1971).

probably also worked to reduce the level of controversy over government involvement.

In London, while there was some controversy over the extent of government involvement in the provision and financing of housing for the working class, and this did involve class considerations, the conflict was comparatively limited, especially on the former question.[1] On the financing of council housing there was some argument over whether the Council should subsidize tenants by charging uneconomic rents as the Labour Party preferred or through a rent rebate scheme as favored by Conservatives. This disagreement reflected among other things a traditional distaste on the part of the working-class, rooted in the experiences of the Depression, for a 'means test' which would be required for the rebate scheme.[2] It also reflected a fear by council tenants, who were predominantly working class, that the scheme would increase the cost of housing. For the Conservatives it was a case of getting 'more for your money', i.e., of making sure that Council tenants paid what they could in fact afford.

On the more general question of whether there should be *any* role for government, local or national, there was no public controversy at all in London. The comment of the councilor quoted above is relevant in this regard. The extent of agreement may be inferred from a striking fact from an American perspective – the Council often built housing that did not differ in any significant extent from that occupied by the middle class. An agreement to build public housing did not apparently have to depend on an implied or explicit agreement not to allow the recipients of state aid to live in a manner comparable to those footing the bill, as appears to have been the case in American cities.[3] Public housing programs in England rest on a long-standing state concern with housing and on a considerable history of state involvement with assistance to the poor and the working class.[4] This general acceptance of a government obligation for the provision of public housing reflects a great housing need[5] as well as the existence of attitudes which favor a role for government in the economy aimed at the promotion of social welfare.[6]

[1] In the period under consideration (1964–5) the extent of public provision was not in fact an issue. But when the Tories gained control of the new Greater London Council they did move to reduce the Council's involvement in public housing by instituting a scheme whereby sitting tenants could purchase their homes. This suggests that under the LCC such views were held by the Conservatives but as they were not in a position to do much about them they said little in public.

[2] See for example, Richard Titmuss, *Commitment to Welfare* (London, 1968), pp. 115–18.

[3] See Nathan Glazer, 'Housing'.

[4] See Ashworth, *British Town Planning*, Chapter 3.

[5] Witness the comment of an administrative grade officer in the Ministry of Housing: 'In London, an argument that public housing isn't needed and that private development could do the job wouldn't carry much weight. The housing shortage is simply too great.'

[6] See Samuel H. Beer, *Modern British Politics* (London, 1965), Chapters 7 and 12. Caution needs to be exercised in interpreting the preceding discussion. As evidence on mass attitudes

A final reason for the limited impact of class cleavages in the making of housing policy and land use policy generally concerns the sites which the LCC chose to develop. A senior officer reviewing the course of planning under the LCC and comparing it to that under the GLC commented that 'for the first time we are affecting upper-income groups with things like the motorway box. Before, we only really worked on slums and moving factories.' The LCC of course was involved in some land use changes in middle-class areas. But, by and large, major redevelopment took place in working-class areas. The Council did not often act in such a way as to stimulate an awareness of their interest in existing land use patterns on the part of the middle class. The sources of the LCC's land use policy in this regard are more difficult to disentangle than its effects. One constraint within which it had to operate was clearly the existing use of land. The sections in the central areas of the city which could be redeveloped so as to provide additional housing units over what existed on the site were not in substantial middle-class areas. Nor clearly were slum areas which needed to be rebuilt. The bombed residential areas were also mainly in working-class neighborhoods. Road building was another possible disturbance to middle-class areas, but again the modest improvement schemes of the LCC assured that this would be no more than a minor annoyance.[1]

The lack of complex political cleavages in London meant that representatives faced a political environment which was more certain than that faced by their American counterparts. London councilors were less often confronted with issues which generated intense feelings among diverse sections of the city's population and hence were rarely faced with sudden upsurges in citizen concern. Troublesome problems such as police brutality, dissemination of birth control information and sectarian teaching in the public schools which plague American urban politicians were largely absent.[2] And as noted, even controversies in which class differences were important were relatively

concerning the matters discussed is non-existent, the analysis relies on observation and on extra-polation from elite attitudes which were expressed in the interviews and which are documented in other studies. In England, this last is a dangerous business as governmental elites are quite capable of acting contrary to the views of the majority of the citizens. This indeed is one of the concerns of this study. The recent (1970) decision not to reintroduce hanging is instructive in this regard. It would appear that a majority of the population preferred that hanging be again instituted while a majority of the MP's thought otherwise and so voted.

[1] In addition to the above it should be noted that in the post-war period the authority generally designed its developments to high standards of architecture and amenity. This probably reduced somewhat the intensity of any conflict attendant on a redevelopment proposal.

[2] More recently, the behavior of the police toward colored immigrants has become a matter of public concern. See *The Times*, 11 August 1970. It is also likely the case that color has become more important in housing decisions as housing authorities in London begin to redevelop 'grey zones' where the colored population is concentrated. Under the LCC very little redevelopment was done in such areas principally because the rehousing burden would have been too great given high densities.

limited in intensity. Moreover, shifts in the pattern of opinion as different issues arise which characterize American cities, particularly as manifested in the size and content of coalitions, were not in evidence. On any given issue, there was a higher degree of certainty in London as to how public discussion would be divided (if indeed there was any discussion) and consequently London representatives were, for example, not often faced with the problem of trying to deal with present allies who had previously been antagonists, which is a consequence of the American situation. The structure of political cleavages in London made largely unnecessary the continuing aggregation of opinion which is typical of American cities. High environmental certainty was a function of limited variation and high predictability in the content and intensity of citizen demands and in the size of coalitions that were built on these preferences.

ORGANIZED GROUPS

Societies differ in the extent to which social life is carried on in formally organized groups. Social scientists sometimes refer to this as the level of secondary differentiation.[1] Societies also vary along a dimension which characterizes the degree to which political life revolves around organized groups which attempt to influence the course of government either by promoting new directions or working for the continuance of others. In short, political systems differ as to the extent of interest group activity.[2] The relationship between the level of secondary differentiation and the extent of interest group activity is unclear and serious consideration of the problem would take us beyond the confines of this study. That they are related is suggested by the fact that there are probably no examples of a high level of interest group organization in the context of low secondary differentiation. Yet, that London and large American cities probably do not differ much in the level of secondary differentiation but *do* differ in the extent of interest group organization belies any notion of a straightforward connection.[3] Even if

[1] See for example, Etzioni, *Modern Organizations*, p. 107.

[2] Groups which have contact with government, but do not work to influence its actions are not considered here to be interest groups. In London such groups are common especially in the social welfare field, the contact consisting of receiving guidance from local authorities. The distinction between contact and influence is one of degree and is often not easy to make.

[3] Some social scientists appear to think that the concepts of level of differentiation and extent of interest group activity are virtually interchangeable, at least in an American context. See, for example, Lewis Froman, 'Organization Theory and the Explanation of Important Characteristics of Congress', *American Political Science Review*, 62 (1968), 518–26 and Kenneth Prewitt and Heinz Eulau, 'Political Matrix and Political Representation: Prolegomenon to a New Departure from an Old Problem', *American Political Science Review*, 63 (1969), 427–41. A related issue is the transformation of social differences into political cleavages. See Ralf Dahrendorf, *Class and Class Conflict in Industrial Society* (Stanford, 1959), pp. 180ff. On the former see also Arthur L.

we cannot thoroughly discuss here the more complicated and general problem, we can analyze some of the factors associated with the comparatively limited extent of interest group organization in London. This will extend the discussion of environmental uncertainty with the emphasis now being on its organizational dimensions. Greater interest group organization will increase the level of uncertainty as officials are faced with an increase in possible types and combinations of claims for public action.

Three types of factors, which are not meant to be exhaustive, may be distinguished which help explain the level of interest group activity. First are what may be called background factors, examples being the existence of a communications network and of a leadership group or freedom to organize publicly.[1] Some specified level of these background factors is required before interest group organizations can take place *at all*. They are necessary but not sufficient factors. A second class of factors are those that increase the *probability* that there will be organization, an example being the existence of shared sub-cultural values in a group that is affected in common by actions of another group or by government. The third class of factors are those that affect the *extent* of organization in a political system. It is with the last class of factors that we are concerned here, although those discussed will also likely affect the probability of organization as well. In practice it is often difficult to distinguish between the second and third class of factors.[2] More specifically, we are concerned with what accounts for the extent to which existing 'social' organizations direct their attention to influencing the course of government. Similarly, what factors account for the extent of new organizations whose primary purpose is to influence government?

Under the general heading of factors associated with the extent of interest group organization four concepts are of particular interest for analyzing the situation in London. These are: the number of political cleavages; their intensity; the extent to which it is thought legitimate by members of groups which have been formed for essentially social purposes to engage in political activity (this is related to more general attitudes concerning citizen participation); and the extent to which the political structure, including legal arrangements, 'encourages' or allows for citizen participation. Each of these will be discussed in turn.[3]

Stinchcombe, 'Social Structure and Organization' in James March (ed.), *A Handbook of Organization* (Chicago, 1965) and Banfield, *The Moral Basis of a Backward Society* (New York, 1958). One of the main problems with the existing literature, which mostly deals with aspects of modernization, is that the concepts employed are not particularly useful for comparisons between modern societies although they may be suitable for contrasts between traditional and modern societies.

[1] Cf. Dahrendorf, *Class*, Chapter 5.

[2] It is likely, however, that the factors discussed will not be very powerful variables if we are trying to explain variation in the probability of organization. Dispositional explanations of any kind are in general difficult to handle in an empirically satisfactory manner.

[3] The analysis here, especially that concerned with participative political structures, draws on William A. Gamson, 'Rancorous Conflicts in Community Politics', in Terry N. Clark, *Com-*

Politics and Land Use Planning

Political cleavages

The discussion of political cleavages in London suggests one hypothesis to help explain the low level of interest group organization in the city. It was noted that not only were there fewer major cleavages than in large American cities, but the ones that existed tended to be less intense, again as compared to the American case. In both instances the expectation is that the level of interest group organization would be lower. The relationship between number of cleavages and number of organizations is straightforward: greater heterogeneity means more interests around which organization is likely to take place. The *intensity* of cleavage should affect: (1) the likelihood that existing 'social' organizations rooted in the cleavages will turn to political activity; (2) the likelihood of the formation of organizations rooted in the cleavages whose principal purposes are political. High intensity will likely lead to attempts to use governmental authority to prevent loss and insure gain, i.e., to organization to influence government.[1]

Political culture

In London members of at least some organizations formed for non-political purposes were reluctant to become involved in local politics even when events took place whose resolution required action by local authorities.[2] While adequate data are not available on the relevant attitudes, there is some suggestive evidence in a study of a council housing development in central London. The tenants association of the council estate was active in attempting to influence the Borough Council's housing policies, even going so far as to put up a candidate for a Council election. The authors of the study note that this was by no means usual for such an organization and quote a comment made in the association's bulletin by its editors.[3] The editors' remark suggests by its somewhat defensive tone that at least the

munity Structure and Decision-Making: Comparative Analyses (San Francisco, 1968) and Neil Smelser, *A Theory of Collective Behavior* (New York, 1962). Also relevant are James Coleman, *Community Conflict* (Glencoe, Ill., 1957), Schattschneider, *Semi-Sovereign People* and Dahrendorf, *Class*, especially pp. 180ff. The last three are studies of political conflict and relevant here because of the insight they provide into the interrelationships between conflict and political organization. Gamson in another work, *Power and Discontent* (Homewood, Ill., 1968) mentions two other concepts: liquidity of organizational resources and type of issue being considered.

[1] Cf. Schattschneider, *Semi-Sovereign People*, Chapter 1.

Aside from the succeeding discussion of political culture and political structure, one other factor may be relevant. It is possible that citizens affected by land use decision did not, at least in the early years of planning, understand what was at stake. Hence, they did not organize new groups or make use of existing ones to defend or further their interests. Of course, over time this factor would become progressively less important, and as we are here discussing a period well after the first years of the planning system, this kind of explanation is of little use.

[2] The major exceptions to this were organizations that were formally tied to one of the political parties, e.g., the trade unions. See the discussion below of functional groups.

[3] Centre for Urban Studies, 'Tall Flats in Pimlico', in Centre for Urban Studies, *London: Aspects of Change*, pp. 273–4.

leaders of the association were aware that such political activity was unusual and perhaps might even be thought reprehensible. They commented that 'politics are the proper province of any Community Association...We do not believe politics to be a word of which we need to be ashamed.'[1] A clue as to why such political activity by a community association might be regarded as unacceptable is provided by the remark of one of the council tenants who, feeling that the tenants association should not engage in political activity, commented that, 'it's wrong to put pressure on the Council in that way.'[2] While the authors do not go on to clearly explain why this view might be held, reference to some fairly well-documented citizen attitudes on the way politics should be carried on provides guidance.

Much research on English politics has argued that there are widespread attitudes in the population which legitimize hierarchical political arrangements in which those who are elected are to be free to decide on the course of public policy. There are, it is said, widely diffused attitudes which support a limited role for the public, i.e., which make it 'wrong' to put pressure on the local council. These are generally described as 'political culture attitudes' and we may in this regard talk about more or less participatory political cultures, i.e. cultures which do or do not 'encourage' citizen political activity. English political culture appears to be closer to the non-participatory end of the scale than the American variety.[3]

It is important in discussing political culture to distinguish between public norms, citizen attitudes and the attitudes of political leaders.[4] Citizens and leaders may or may not hold attitudes about the way politics should be carried on which accord with public norms however the latter are defined. The difficulty in maintaining the distinctions stems in part from the type of data generally used, and in fact employed here. Most often, analysis of both attitudes and norms relies on the verbal reports of individuals, whether leader or citizen, and it is difficult to infer what is personal attitude and what public norm. The discussion below of the views held by citizens and leaders is meant to be interpreted as an analysis of norms, the difficulties of so doing being noted.[5]

[1] Quoted in Centre for Urban Studies, 'Tall Flats in Pimlico', p. 274.
[2] Centre for Urban Studies, 'Tall Flats in Pimlico', p. 276.
[3] For a wide-ranging critique of this generally accepted view of English political culture see Lynda Erickson, 'Youth and Political Deference in England', Canadian Political Science Association, Montreal, Quebec, June 1972. As noted elsewhere in the present study, there is evidence of changes in citizen norms (see footnote 2, p. 101) which suggests that the late 1950s and early 1960s were different from the 1970s. The kind of sophisticated survey analysis, particularly the use of complex attitude scales, is not available to settle the questions raised by Erickson.
[4] Cf. Robert R. Alford, *Bureaucracy and Participation: Political Cultures in Four Wisconsin Cities* (Chicago, 1969), p. 5. The discussion that immediately follows draws heavily on Alford, particularly pp. 5–6.
[5] For the difficulties of explaining individual behavior or some structural outcome by reference to norms, see the perceptive discussion by Brian Barry, *Sociologists, Economists and Democracy* (London, 1970), Chapter 4. Barry takes the view, obviously adopted here, that norms *can* have explanatory power, *if* their existence can be adequately established.

One source of data on political culture attitudes for the purposes of this study is a recent investigation by Eric Nordlinger entitled *The Working Class Tories*. Nordlinger's data are drawn from interviews with 473 working-class voters in several different urban areas. The study establishes the importance of what may be called 'political deference' as a major strand in British political culture, i.e., it demonstrates that there are attitudes which legitimize a passive role for the electorate and a predominant role in public policy-making for government officials.[1] This interpretation of deference, with its concern for trust in authority, needs to be carefully distinguished from that which emphasizes citizens preferring that their 'social betters' rule.[2] The latter seems less likely to be important in explaining behavior when the definition of social betters is in disarray.

Taken together, Nordlinger's data indicate that a significant portion of the population holds attitudes which on the one side provide for only a limited representational role for the citizenry, and on the other side provide for an active government which should lead. The data show that even when respondents are told that a majority of citizens does *not* favor a governmental action, substantial numbers of people reply that this should not be sufficient deterrence to government action if the government perceives the policy as being good for the country.[3] Majority opinion is usually considered to be the strongest practical assertion of public views on policy, and if this may be overridden, then the presumption is that the views of the public are not thought to be of great importance. The implication is that the public role in the eyes of many respondents is to be limited to electing a government and not subsequently influencing its course of action.[4]

Nordlinger points out that underlying what he calls these minimal representational norms is a 'diffuse sense of trust' of government.[5] He notes that the 'members of the political class are then viewed neither as men having an inordinate amount of power nor as men willing to sacrifice the public interest for their own private ends'.[6] There is a feeling that those whom one allows substantial independence of action in policy-making will, in fact,

---

[1] Eric Nordlinger, *The Working-Class Tories: Authority, Deference and Stable Democracy* (Berkeley, 1967), particularly Chapters 1 and 3. In Chapter 3, Tables 7, 8, and 10 are particularly relevant. For highly critical comments on the study see the review by Jerrold Rusk, *American Political Science Review* (1970), 1317–19. See also Robert McKenzie and Alan Silver, *Angels in Marble: Working Class Conservatism in Urban England* (Chicago, 1968), and Butler and Stokes, *Political Change*, Chapter 5. R. D. Jessop argues that the discussion of deference and related norms has been quite confused. See 'Civility and Traditionalism in English Political Culture', *British Journal of Political Science*, 1 (1971), 1–24. See also Paul Abramson, 'The Differential Socialization of English Secondary School Students', *Sociology of Education*, 40 (1967), 246–69.

[2] Jessop, 'Civility'.

[3] Nordlinger, *Working-Class Tories*, pp. 84–8.

[4] Cf. Harry Eckstein, 'British Political System', Chapter 4 in Samuel H. Beer and Adam Ulam (eds.), *Patterns of Government* (New York, 1958).

[5] Nordlinger, *Working-Class Tories*, p. 15.

[6] Nordlinger, *Working-Class Tories*, p. 15.

use this independence to serve the public good. He further argues that the result of all these attitudes taken together is to legitimize a 'private decision-making style'.[1] Simply, if the public is to have a limited role in policy-making and government is to have a substantial degree of independence, then it is acceptable for government to make its decisions in private. Good public policy is to be defined less by consulting the wishes of the public and more by what is agreed upon by the government officials privately deliberating.

There is another set of norms which also leads to active government and a limited role for the public. Following Samuel Beer, these may be called 'collectivist'. The difference between the hierarchical attitudes just described and these is that the collectivist attitudes are concerned more directly with strong political parties.[2] Beer's arguments suggest that one of the basic sets of attitudes which underlay politics in London was the legitimation given to strong party organizations and the resulting impetus given to active government. Parties, classes and functional groups[3] were to be the major features in the political universe. The public, except as it worked in the parties outside the Council, was not to be given any important role. Working for the party (or being a member of a functional group) should be the extent of participation. Support for Beer's analysis as applied to London can be found in the remarks of a member with long experience on the Council who commented on the importance accorded to strong party organizations.

Decisions made by the Leader are always endorsed by the whole Party. I don't know how else it could be done in government...There is party loyalty when a decision has been hammered out. The minority within the party accepts the decision; this is democracy not anarchy. You accept the majority decision. We would say that this is the basis of democracy.[4]

For our purposes, while the data and arguments of Beer and Nordlinger are suggestive, they have some shortcomings. Nordlinger's data are not comparative; therefore we do not know how English responses differ from answers respondents would give elsewhere. Also, the data were drawn from an all working-class sample. Beer's study does have a comparative intent, but we have little way of knowing how the attitudes he describes are distributed in the population. There are, however, some data collected by Almond and Verba in their study, *The Civic Culture*, which support the arguments made by Beer and Nordlinger, but do not have the same shortcomings in terms of the present study.

[1] Nordlinger, *Working-Class Tories*, p. 9.
[2] Beer, *British Politics*, especially Chapter 3. This discussion is drawn directly from Beer's book. It should be noted that Beer does not use survey data to support his argument. Rather, he relies on comments of observers and participants, i.e., the attitudes and observations of elites.
[3] See below.
[4] This should not be interpreted as meaning party voting was extensive on the LCC. See Chapter 6.

Almond and Verba asked a sample of populations in five countries whether they had attempted to influence their local governments. Whereas 33 per cent of the American sample answered in the affirmative, only 18 per cent of the British sample did so.[1] Almond and Verba also asked their respondents what they would try to do in order to influence their local government. 56 per cent of the Americans replied that they would try to organize an informal group, a letter-writing campaign or a petition; only 34 per cent of the British gave this response.[2] Of course, care must be taken in inferring attitudes from behavior. The lower participation in England may reflect opportunity as much as norm, for example. However, given the general agreement among observers concerning the nature of English political culture, the risky inference that public participation is not so highly valued is made less so.[3]

Almond and Verba report data on childhood socialization experiences of their cross-national sample of adults which also supports the present analysis. The British respondents report that as children they were much less likely to question the authority of school teachers or participate in school discussions or debates than American children, whose experiences were ascertained in the same manner. The relevant data are presented in Tables 3, 4 and 5. If we assume that socialization experiences in such institutions as schools influence adult political attitudes,[4] then the data suggest that British adults are likely to have less questioning attitudes toward authority and less concern for political participation than American adults. British respondents consistently report a less 'participatory' experience in school.

Several comments about English local politics will summarize the preceding discussion and also lead to a comparison with American norms. The first is by a planner in Coventry who is talking about his local council's relations with the public.

At the same time the public were pleased to be consulted and glad to play a part in helping the Council produce a revised plan which took their views into account.[5]

[1] Gabriel Almond and Sidney Verba, *The Civic Culture: Political Attitudes and Democracy in Five Nations* (Princeton, 1963), p. 188. 21 per cent of the German respondents answered in the affirmative. The corresponding figures for Italy and Mexico are 13 per cent and 9 per cent respectively.

[2] *Ibid.*, p. 191. The figures for Germany, Italy and Mexico are 13 per cent, 7 per cent and 26 per cent respectively. See also the following: Richard Rose, *Politics in England* (Boston, 1964), Chapter 2; Edward Shils, *The Torment of Secrecy* (New York, 1956); Seymour Martin Lipset, 'Value Patterns, Class and the Democratic Polity,' in Reinhard Bendix and Seymour Martin Lipset (eds.), *Class, Status and Power* (Glencoe, Ill., 1953).

[3] See the discussion by Barry referred to in footnote 5, p. 59 for some of the problems involved in such inferences.

[4] See, for example, Richard Dawson and Kenneth Prewitt, *Political Socialization* (Boston, 1964).

[5] Quoted in 'Drawing Citizens into Planning', *Town and Country Planning*, 33 (1964), p. 443.

Table 3.* *Freedom to discuss unfair treatment in school or to disagree with teacher, by nation*

Per cent who remember they felt	U.S.	U.K.
Free	45	35
Uneasy	22	18
Better not to talk to teacher	25	41
Don't know, don't remember and other	8	6
Total per cent	100	100
Total number	969	963

* Gabriel A. Almond and Sidney Verba, *The Civic Culture: Political Attitudes and Democracy in Five Nations* (copyright © 1963 by Princeton University Press), Table 4, p. 32. Reprinted by permission of the Princeton University Press.

Table 4.* *Actual discussion of unfair treatment or disagreement with teacher, by nation*

Per cent who remembered this occurred	U.S.	U.K.
Occasionally or often	46	36
Never	46	57
Don't know, don't remember and other	8	7
Total per cent	100	100
Total number	969	963

* Almond and Verba, *Civic Culture*, p. 333. Reprinted by permission of Princeton University Press.

Table 5.* *Freedom to participate in school discussions and debates, by nation*

Per cent who remember they	U.S.	U.K.
Could and did participate	40	16
Could but did not participate	15	8
Could not participate	34	68
Don't know and other	11	8
Total per cent	100	100
Total number	969	963

* Almond and Verba, *Civic Culture*, p. 333. Reprinted by permission of Princeton University Press.

A second comment is from a newspaper article dealing with British schools which are the responsibility, at least in part, of local authorities.

We should consider one element in American education which is almost totally lacking in both public and grammar-school education in this country: the assumption by parents that the local school is 'their' school, the institution not of an Establishment or a State but of the community on the spot, an institution which can only work properly if the parents accept the responsibility for continuous and constructive interest.[1]

Finally, and back to planning, a distinguished local government official and leading authority on planning commented on citizen participation as follows.

Mr Heap [Desmond Heap, Comptroller and City Solicitor to the City of London Corporation]...said that if electors had to get into the decision-making process after their chosen representatives had been duly elected this could only mean that the current form of representative democracy had broken down.[2]

The underlying theme of these observations is that the local public does not expect to take part in local politics. They might be 'pleased' to be invited to participate, but they are not to be involved as a matter of course. Local parents are somewhat dubious about interfering with the running of local school systems. In general, there is no strong presumption that the public needs to be consulted to legitimize any particular policy. Policy-making is the job of government officials and citizens need do no more than elect their representatives.[3]

American attitudes toward political life, if we can take populist attitudes[4] as an indication, contain a good deal of emphasis on public participation. Rational individuals should band together to influence government; the communality of views itself confers a certain legitimacy. The public is to be more than an electorate, but through a series of devices is to become involved in policy-making. At the least, public policy-making should indeed be public; secrecy and insulation from public surveillance are criticized. Between government and the public, both as possible guardians of the public

---

[1] Quoted in the *Observer*, 16 October 1966, p. 2. Cf. the comment by an observer of a recent conference of the National Association of Head Teachers: 'They [the head teachers] say that mothers and fathers should be "honored" to be invited into schools, but not expect it as a right...' Patsy Kumm, 'What is Going On in Our Children's Schools,' *The Times*, 27 August 1969.

[2] 'Call for Better Law on Planning Blight', *The Times*, 15 October 1969.

[3] This set of norms is taken to its logical conclusion by J. A. G. Griffith, a noted student of English law and public affairs who comments: 'If local services were likely to be improved by scrapping the whole set-up of local government and handing the lot over to central departments, I would do without locally elected members without a shudder.' 'Maud: Off the Target', *New Statesman*, 20 June 1969.

[4] Shils, *Torment of Secrecy*, especially pp. 98–104.

good, however it is to be defined, Americans seem to prefer the public.[1] The English, whether because it is government *per se* or because it is party government, are inclined to give government a much larger role.[2]

Functional groups. The preceding discussion of hierarchical norms is basically an analysis at the mass level with the implication that such views are supported by elites as well. There is some suggestive evidence that finer distinctions were made in London concerning what types of public expression should be accorded a hearing: some views were considered to be more acceptable than others by those in a position to enforce that distinction, in this case officials of the LCC. The distinction they made can be described as one between 'functional' groups and 'pressure' groups. Both of these come under the heading of what we have called interest groups.[3]

In a study of the London *Development Plan* it is noted that a distinction was made by the County Council between the Chamber of Commerce, which was consulted because it had 'expertise' and the civic associations who were invited to a lecture on what the LCC was proposing to do. This was true even though the kinds of views the latter held probably had wider support in the community. Their ability to contribute expertly to the discussion over the *Development Plan* was considered to be minimal.[4] Additional

---

[1] Shils, *Torment of Secrecy*; Lipset, 'Value Patterns'; Beer, *British Politics*, p. 41; and Rose, *Politics in England*, pp. 41 and 44, note that populist attitudes toward political life are stronger in America than in England. See also Louis Hartz, *The Liberal Tradition in America* (New York, 1955).

It may well be that English political culture emphasizes both *privacy* for individuals and *public* purpose. The first is reflected in stringent libel laws (stricter than those in the United States), but does not include strong support for individual participation in political life as we have discussed it here. The second means, for example, that citizens do not have strong property rights when the public good is at stake; hence a well-developed planning system. The values are individualistic but of a particular kind – the individual's life is to be private but his individual views on public policy are to carry less weight than some holistic view of the public good. Americans seem to have the reverse emphasis – little value on the good of the community (and concomitantly great emphasis on individual participation) and comparatively less privacy to be allowed to individuals. Both cultures could be called 'individualistic', but with a difference.

[2] Jack Dennis and his colleagues argue on the basis of a study of the attitudes of a sample of English school children in Colchester that the norms described here are in the process of changing, and particularly, trust in government may be on the decline. See Dennis *et al.*, 'Support for Nation and Government among English Children', *British Journal of Political Science*, 1 (1971), 24–48. See especially Tables 9, 10, 11 and 12. Dennis' data parallel what may be changes at the adult level in extent of participation. Relevant here are the recent growth of consumer associations, more politically active tenants' associations, and neighborhood groups responding to road proposals in Greater London. In general, see Brian Lapping and Giles Radice, *More Power to the People: Young Fabian Essays on Democracy in Britain* (London, 1968). For a critique of Dennis' work see A. Birch, 'Children's Attitudes and British Politics,' *British Journal of Political Science*, 1 (1971), 519–20 and Dennis Kavanaugh, 'Allegiance Among English Children: A Dissent', *British Journal of Political Science*, 2 (1972), 127–31.

[3] Beer, *British Politics*, Chapter 3.

[4] Stephen L. Elkin, 'The Development Plan for the County of London', unpublished manuscript, Harvard University, 1966.

Witness also the comment by a planning officer on the influence of civic societies (e.g. the

evidence that such distinctions were made by LCC officials is provided in the following comments made by senior Council planners. The first, who held the most senior planning post, said:

I think that one can distinguish between an American approach to planning where they try to involve the community and the one in England where one emphasizes the role of elected representatives and what you call 'vested interests'. You can judge the state of citizen participation in England by the state of the rights of third parties. They are heard but their status certainly isn't high, and no government would recommend that it be fully recognized.

He went on,

one feels quite happy with elected representatives and the organized interests. As long as we consult these people that is enough. You know that if you belong to the Chamber of Commerce you will be represented by this body.
When you think of how to consult the public, there is a real problem...In some American cities planners take the plan around from neighborhood to neighborhood and discuss it and so forth. We're not interested in *ad hoc* groups. We feel quite happy in putting our faith in organized interests.

The second planner commented:

if the public fails to organize itself so that it can be heard, and what is more, be heard as responsible, then their views are not of sufficient importance to be considered. It is probably true that short of having a set of professional advisors, the noises that they [the public] make will not be taken seriously.

Taken together these comments suggest that there was little feeling that active public involvement was to be encouraged; in other words, populist attitudes were weak. The emphasis was on groups that could contribute knowledge, or who already were involved in making the society function in some sense. In practice, populist attitudes mean giving a hearing to people who have banded together to present a common view – in effect, giving legitimacy to groups because they are *there* and part of the legitimate social fabric. We can call these pressure groups. Functional groups are either groups which support the two broad economic classes[1] (who certainly

Chelsea Society) which, relative to other participants outside the government, were among the most active participants in planning. The officer noted that on occasion these local societies got to see the Chairman of the Planning Committee: 'The Chairman, when he saw the various societies, would generally take our advice as to whether the particular group had anything to offer. He would explain what we were doing. These societies really have little influence.'

[1] Beer, *British Politics*, Chapter 3. John Rex and Robin Moore, in a study of race relations and local politics in Birmingham indicate that a similar distinction is made by officials in that city. See *Race, Community and Conflict*, Chapters 8–9.

Another example of a functional group, in this case a class-supporting group, is the London Trades Council. Through its close relationship with the Labour Party, both in the Council and in the electoral organization outside of the Council, it was able to make its views known on a variety of subjects relevant to local government affairs in London. The L.T.C. sponsored candidates for Labour Party seats, helped with the campaigning and had frequent consultations with the Labour Party leaders on the Council. According to its chief permanent official, it probably had less influence in planning matters than in other areas.

contribute to the health of the society), or groups which have expertise, the modern contribution to social health. It was the latter kind of group that LCC officials preferred.

Participative political structure

The structure of government for London paralleled the content of the norms concerning how political life should be organized. Neither gave much encouragement to the participation of the citizenry organized or otherwise. The political structure gave little opportunity for citizens to influence the course of governmental affairs in London nor did it provide much incentive for new groups to organize whose major aim would be to influence local government.[1] The already difficult job of organization was made more difficult by lack of information about policy-making and by lack of opportunities to influence government; and these are likely to be necessary to convince possible members of the value of supporting an organization. The particular characteristics of governmental structure that are of interest here are: the extent of legal opportunities for participation; the extent to which information about the activities of government is available; the extent to which aspects of any decision are diffused or separated to diverse parts of government; the pattern of central/local relations, particularly the extent of a national orientation among central government officials.

Legal structure. In London, there were no referenda on policy matters or financial questions and there was limited possiblity of recourse to the courts to prevent local government action.[2] In addition, there were no public hearings to which the public was invited,[3] and most business was carried out in committee and sub-committee meetings which were not open to the press or the public and whose agenda told only the barest details of what was discussed. Accounts of what was said were not available, the decisions of the committee, under circumstances defined by the Standing Orders, being reported to the full Council.[4]

The town planning machinery reflected this general bias against public participation. Provision for public participation was made only upon *refusal* of planning permission by the authority. There was no regular provision for public participation if approval was forthcoming. Therefore, in the case

---

[1] Gamson, 'Rancorous Conflict', p. 198, defines a participative political structure as one that 'permits or encourages widespread citizen participation'.

[2] See Daniel Mandelker, *Green Belts and Urban Growth: English Town and Country Planning in Action* (Madison, 1962), p. 141. For an American contrast, see Altshuler, *City Planning*, pp. 371–2.

[3] On American cities in this regard see Banfield and Wilson, *City Politics*, Chapter 6.

[4] In some areas of England the press is even excluded from the meetings of the full Council. See Evelyn Sharp, *The Ministry of Housing and Local Government* (London, 1969), pp. 60–1.

of applications by private developers, as in the St Giles case, or application by borough councils, as in the Chelsea case, it was quite possible for a major development to be approved without the general public, in whatever guise, having knowledge of the development or any legal means to force the local authority to hold a hearing on its desirability.[1]

The same attitude toward public participation can be seen in the case of a public hearing upon refusal of planning permission.[2] The contrast with the public hearings characteristic of American cities makes the point. While public hearings in America operate on the principle that whoever has a view on a particular matter has a presumptive right to be heard, in English town planning inquiries the only people who are guaranteed standing by law are those who are making the application.[3] Public hearings are thus often unsettling and also occasions for histrionic displays; planning inquiries tend to be much quieter affairs with arguments between the planning authority and the applicant consuming the major portion of time. A clear indication of the status of public participation in planning inquiries is given in the following statement by an officer in the administrative class of the Ministry of Housing and Local Government.

Third party status is pretty low unless they can prove some real and direct interest [in the matter at hand]. It is very rare that they will produce any decent suggestions. Their objections are generally discounted.[4]

The same point is even more relevant when the developer was the LCC itself. When a housing authority in an American city decides to construct housing, there are often public hearings or public debate by the city council, whereas in London the Housing Committee and its officers, in consultation with planning officers and the Planning Committee, largely decided upon development. There might not even have been any discussion of the project before the full Council. Except in cases when the LCC decided to consult with local residents (which generally appears to have been after plans had

---

[1] It is, however, possible to get the Minister to take the application out of the hands of the local authority by a call-in.

[2] In the case of a private hearing held by the Minister, public participation is, of course, eliminated. In practice, this is rarely done.

[3] The position of third parties, i.e., roughly any part of the public outside the applicant himself, is not quite so clear-cut as this discussion suggests. At most inquiries the inspector for the Ministry does allow interested (or third) parties to make brief statements. This was the case in the Chelsea inquiry. On this, see Mandelker, *Green Belts*, pp. 108–9. Also, under a call-in third parties are given more weight in discussion. Inquiries for development plans also allow greater public participation. The question of who may participate in planning is complicated by a widespread feeling that the control of development is not an exercise in the consideration of alternatives and thus an invitation to contention. Rather, it is to be regulation for the prevention of abuse. In addition to attitudes which limit the participation of the public, there are, therefore, attitudes specific to town planning which do not place a high value on 'outside' views. See R. E. Wraith, 'Planning Inquiries and the Public Interest', *New Society*, 22 July 1971, pp. 145–7 and Chapter 7 below.

[4] Cf. Sharp, *The Ministry*, p. 37.

already been drawn up and land purchased or made available), interested parties were shut out.[1]

The shortage of information. It is possible to follow politics in most cities of the United States by reading a local newspaper. While the information gathered is unlikely to be comprehensive, a fair idea can be gained of the participants, the issues, the stakes, and the alliances. In reading a newspaper in London one by and large got news about Parliament, the cricket matches, and the Queen's functions, but little if anything about local government. The news that appeared was generally of the kind that simply announced a new local authority project. For example, in the World's End case the Chelsea Labour Party was ignorant of important decisions taken by the LCC Planning Committee. This suggests the difficulty even strongly interested parties had in discovering the course of events.

One of the LCC members talked at length about some of the reasons for the lack of any significant information in the newspapers about London politics, and her remarks are worth giving at length. The comment also supports the analysis above of a private decision-making style.

Publicity does handicap one in making decisions. We were very frightened that councilors would not realize the implications of what they were talking about. Discussions about development might for example raise prices of property in the area. Also one mustn't criticize officers. One employs them and they are defenseless. To do so could cause a lot of trouble. Officers never talked to the press. For example, the Council deliberately never gave its case concerning the Risinghill School. [A case involving a controversial headmaster at the school.] To do so would have meant saying bad things about officers, so out of loyalty we said nothing. Municipal employees have always had that kind of relationship with their members. They do not give away the secrets of the Council, they remain silent. In return councilors on the whole have stayed quiet about the staff. If one wants to really discuss major changes, for example in education, it's very much better to do this in a calm atmosphere where one can reasonably discuss what is going on. Everybody can talk in confidence without fear that what they are saying is going into the newspapers. One wants to feel free to discuss and if one felt it would go into the newspapers one wouldn't discuss it. As well, great harm might be done if there was publicity. For example, Risinghill was a mixed racial area and it was very difficult to talk; it wouldn't have helped. Perhaps it is wicked and Victorian to keep quiet like this but it does avoid community hostilities. On roads for example there may be lots of alternative routes. Supposing we allowed discussion in the press on this there would be lots of people who would be very anxious about the choice. This would do the most appalling amount of harm and quite unnecessarily if the route they were worried about was not chosen. One needs to be able to investigate quietly.

[1] In cases where high buildings were to be constructed or questions of amenity were involved, it was the Council's policy 'to give notice' to surrounding residents and local residents' societies. Their views were 'taken into account before any decisions were arrived at'. *Review*, p. 225.

This view was echoed by officers. One planner put it this way.

There is a long tradition of local government officers: they are not supposed to speak to the press. We have a privileged position and if we want to keep our job if there is a party change we shouldn't stick our neck out by talking to the press. This is an important problem. It [publicity] is all quite irrelevant if one does not have to be well known. In America, to be well known as a civil servant is very important. We don't have to be well known because we have the law on our side.

The officer's remark besides pointing to the agreement between officers and members concerning speaking to the press, suggests one reason why the agreement was possible. The Council had sufficient legal authority to carry out its policies and thus it was unnecessary for officers to build public support in order to induce cooperation among various holders of legal authority. Unlike their American counterparts, officers could (and had to) direct virtually all their efforts at persuasion inside the Council. As for the reticence of members, aside from the reasons suggested by the councilor, additional, and more important, factors are indicated in the following comment. Again, it is a member speaking, this time pointing to the importance of the rules of the Council for restricting contact with the press.

Partly it's because one is tied by restrictions of confidentiality. A document is confidential until it goes to the committee, but by the time the committees have dealt with it, in effect the decision has already been made. There is no point in moaning about it. It's not profitable.

It might be asked why the confidentiality rule was respected by members. If it were necessary for a representative to court the favor of his particular constituents presumably, at least on occasion, this rule would be broken. The political price of *not* doing so would likely be too costly to incur. In London there was little incentive for members to break the rules or to publicly moan because their concern was less with maintaining and building an independent electoral base than with maintaining amicable relations with other members, particularly party leaders. This last point requires some expansion.

Much of the local political news that appears in American papers is the result of the fact that the political fate of the major participants rests on electoral approval of them as individuals. These elected officials show regular concern for the sentiments of their constituents, and their ability to resist promptings of other participants rests, in part at least, on this independent electoral base. As a result, the public arena is often used to promote favorable action, penalize an enemy of the moment or settle disputes which cannot be managed internally.[1] In London, however, as has been noted, members

[1] See Morris Davis and Marvin Weinbaum, *Metropolitan Decision Processes* (Chicago, 1969), Chapter 5.

did not have individual electoral bases and as a result, energizing the public by feeding it information was at a minimum.[1] Election to the County Council depended little on personal reputation, and steps up the Council hierarchy did not significantly depend on popularity either. Length of service and ability were more important factors. Similarly, election as a parliamentary candidate was more likely to be a reward for service at the local level and ability displayed than popularity with the local electorate. This becomes more obvious when it is noted that a man will most often not stand for Parliament in the area in which he lives. In general, members' concern for building up support for their actions was directed inside the Council rather than outside to the citizenry. We shall return to this point in Chapter 6.

Party discipline also militated against the giving out of information to the public. When the parties faced the public they did so as united bodies. In private committee deliberations, party lines were less important, but when it came to the full Council – i.e., to public appearance – the party made every effort to appear united.[2] Any public discussion of party business raised the specter of disunity and was frowned upon and might have been disciplined. The premium was on an united front which would present an image of responsibility and strength; the result was to limit public discussion of party business and differences within the party.

One consequence of the various factors noted was that, for at least some members, not talking to the newspapers about local politics was felt to be quite natural; coverage of Council business by newsmen having extensive contact with various Council officials was not thought of as an alternative to the existing situation. When it was suggested to one member that one of the reasons there was so little news about London politics in the papers was because members and officers had no incentive to talk to newsmen, he replied,

if you had asked simply 'why was there not more interest' I would have said 'ask the newspapers'. One felt the newspapers were not appreciative of local concerns. The point you bring up is a new angle. I hadn't thought of that. I guess it was an

---

[1] While it might be argued that the analysis here is circular – lack of information helps explain limited organization and limited organization helps explain lack of information – a more useful characteristic of it is an example of mutual reinforcement, which is a quite common form of interaction.

[2] See Chapter 7.

On 20 January 1959, the LCC leadership tabled the following motion which was passed in the party caucus. 'No member shall write to the press or make public statements either orally or in writing attacking the policy of the party or decision of the group [Labour Group on the LCC]. In the event of any violation of this rule, a member or members render themselves liable to the whip being withdrawn.' Quoted in Young, 'Party Political Organization'. This attitude on the part of the Labour Party may also reflect experiences with a press hostile to socialist movements.

innate feeling about things, that is we ought to keep things quiet...I've just taken the whole thing for granted before. I've never thought about it.[1]

The lack of information about London politics is reflected in and reinforced by the national focus of the news media. A newspaper devoted to London life and politics might be able to write about the 'life' but would be at a loss when it came to political news. The newspapers published in London are national dailies devoted to national news.[2] The two possible exceptions are the London evening papers which devote some space to London affairs, but even their coverage, in comparison with American reporting, is still very sketchy. The fact that London is the capital city may divert attention away from local politics and make it unprofitable for newspapers to print news about local politics (if they had any). The lack of a London paper reinforces the lack of news about London politics.

Planning administration. Mainly because of its substantial legal authority and to a lesser extent because of wide-spread agreement by those actively concerned with the content of planning, the LCC was in a position to restrict the terms of the discussion of planning decisions. In practice this meant separating the consideration of 'planning' concerns from other aspects of land use; this reduced the likelihood of citizen political organization because it would be at the time of greatest interest, viz. the decision whether to allow development, that citizens with related concerns such as the scale of rents or the impact of a redevelopment on taxes would most likely to be able to engage the attentions of their fellows. Having to wait until discussion of such matters was permissible would reduce enthusiasm.

The World's End housing case is relevant here. It was noted by one of the senior officers dealing with the case that the costs of construction would very likely mean that the rents for the council housing would be too high

[1] Just how far this norm of not speaking to the press can be taken, aside from the LCC leadership's action just noted, is illustrated by an incident in the new London Borough of Redbridge. A borough councilor was brought before a disciplinary committee, which had the authority to ban him from all Council committees, on a charge of speaking to the press about a Council decision. The Council had, in fact, issued a statement on the matter later the same morning on which the councilor had spoken. According to the councilor, he said nothing that was not said in the Council statement. *Evening Standard*, 5 September 1969.

[2] There was a practical difficulty faced by newspapers in gathering news about London politics. The London newspapers went to press at the time the LCC was beginning to meet. However, if London officials were prone to speak to the press this would clearly be a minor impediment.

Political reporting of local politics seems to vary in depth of coverage if one looks at the London borough newspapers. The borough newspapers do seem to get more news about politics in the boroughs concerned. They do not do any better than the national dailies on London news generally, however. Their greater comparative coverage of borough affairs, and this does not appear to be true for all papers, seems to be partly due to the fact that there *is* a paper to cater to the local community and so there are reporters who attend council sessions and track down news about property development in the borough, for example. The presence of these borough newspapers may be a function of a greater sense of community in some of the boroughs (some are simply administrative creations rather than 'natural areas') and thus a greater interest in local affairs.

for many working-class people. He said, however, that this was not the concern of the planners and, furthermore, he could not remember any case in his considerable years of service that turned on the issue of rents. What was at issue in the case were factors such as density and open space, not who would benefit by the public housing. Citizens concerned about such matters as rents would have had to wait until some future time to make their arguments at which point interest in the whole project would doubtless have waned.

The roots of the separation of planning from other aspects of land use may be found in the agreement among those actively concerned with planning that it was, or at least ought to be, concerned with physical matters not with social and economic dimensions.[1] From an American viewpoint, this distinction put to one side some of the more controversial issues surrounding land use decisions. For example, questions of the social class of people moving into new developments and their racial composition were not considered relevant planning concerns. Some comments on the proper content of planning decisions by members who dealt with land use provide additional evidence.

One of the important reasons we don't deal with social planning is that we don't like losing appeals. We've got to issue decisions which will stand on appeal, and planning legislation is only concerned with physical planning, not social and economic planning. Knowledge or fear of appeal is a very real sanction that prevents us from dealing in social or political or economic factors.

Town planning has nothing to do with issues like race and class. The Planning Committee can't deal with them. A housing committee can make such policy as well as the Council. This isn't the concern of town planning.

As the remarks suggest, this narrow definition of planning at the local level was paralleled by the attitudes on planning held by the Ministry. The Committee and the planners, even if they were inclined to go beyond physical planning, were inhibited by fear that decisions made on other grounds would not be upheld by the Ministry if the matter should come to appeal.

The pattern of central/local relations. The pattern of central/local government relationships in England[2] has the consequences that many decisions made by local/state units in the United States are in effect made at the central level. By itself this may limit the incentives for citizens in the local areas to organize, as they would then have to compete in a larger arena which would encompass other local organizations. This would in turn reduce their impact, except as locally based groups could join together for some common purpose. In general, the ability of any given local group to promote

[1] See Chapter 7.
[2] The pattern varies somewhat throughout the rest of the U.K., with Wales being the closest to the English pattern.

particular local interests would not be great in the national arena. However, American experience suggests that the drift of effective decision-making authority to the central government is not by itself determinate. If those who decide on and administer national policy are open to local influence, and indeed are even the product of local political coalitions whose interests they feel obliged to represent, then the difficulties of local organizations seeking to serve their interests in the larger arena may not be tangibly increased. In the United States this is especially so as national administrators very much need to court the favor of representatives who have such local ties, principally because of the decentralized, non-programmatic nature of American political parties.[1] The crucial consideration in England is precisely that, in comparison to the American situation, representatives in the national legislature and central government civil servants tend much more to have a national orientation in the setting of policy. Decisions are less the product of bargains struck between locally-based interests but reflect rather the views of officials who look to the country as a whole and the views of organized groups who take a similar view. Insofar as local citizens wish to gain some end that has local significance and insofar as many of the important aspects of the relevant policy are settled at the central level where local views will carry little weight, the incentive to organize around local interests will be limited. In consequence, local representatives will less likely face organizations which take an interest in aspects of a policy that *are* settled at the local level.[2] The implication of the present analysis is that where national authorities *can* be persuaded to view policy choices as a problem of aggregating local interests, or in fact already view the matter in this fashion, then locally-oriented interests will find it useful to organize. More importantly, they will not only pursue their interests at the national (and state) level, but also in the local arena. Where the incentives for local interests to organize are reduced, representatives at any level of government will be spared their attentions.[3]

[1] See, for example, Morton Grodzins, 'The Federal System' in *Goals for Americans*. The Report of the President's Commission on National Goals. (Englewood Cliffs, N.J., 1960).

[2] While much work needs to be done on central/local relations, particularly the extent to which M.P.'s and civil servants are receptive to local interests and the extent to which locally oriented groups pursue their activities at central government level, some clues may be found in the following: J. A. G. Griffith, *Central Departments and Local Authorities* (London, 1966), particularly Chapters 1 and 8; Samuel Huntington, 'Political Modernization: America vs. Europe', *World Politics*, 18 (1966), 378–414, in which the national orientation of M.P.'s is discussed; and Eckstein, 'The English Political System' where the views of civil servants are considered. Also see Howard Scarrow, 'Policy Pressures by British Local Government', *Comparative Politics*, 4 (1971), 1–28 and Paul Peterson, 'The Politics of Educational Reform in England and the United States', American Political Science Association, 1972, Washington, D.C.

[3] A related point about central/local relations is worth mentioning here. In the United States, the increasing role of the central government in local affairs, particularly in large cities, seems to have increased the number of participants and the intensity of conflict in city politics. One of the likely reasons is that the question of which local (or state) agency will administer the federal funds is often open to negotiation. This appears to have been particularly true in the administration

In England, a particularly impressive illustration of the preceding analysis is in the area of education policy. By law, central government officials are charged with securing

the effective execution by local authorities under their control and direction, of the national policy for providing a varied and comprehensive educational service in every area.[1]

In practice this means that local educational practice is very much the product of central finance. The organization of schools, their examination system, teacher salaries, etc. are set in at least broad outline by central authorities. Citizens at the local level who have preferences for particular approaches within their own area are faced with local authorities who most often have little leeway to alter existing arrangements and with central authorities who are reluctant to consider variation of national policy for particular towns or cities. The possibility of having any impact on policy, which is one important incentive offered to prospective organizational members, is thus in short supply.[2]

Having said all this it must be emphasized that local authorities are not simply administrative arms of the central government. There is a rather complex relationship with local authorities having some measure of autonomy. This can be seen from the case studies: the LCC had a great deal of leeway in setting density and open space standards and in designing the road system. There were important choices to be made and conflicts to be resolved.[3] However, in the determination of the basic features of public policy, decisions made in the Parliament and the central department are much the most important.[4] Some measure of the complexity of the relationship can be seen in the following comments by the former senior civil servant of the Ministry of Housing.

But primarily the reason for the Ministry's belief that authorities should, largely, be allowed to go their own way has been that the services for which it is responsible have been seen as essentially local services. Authorities are independent, responsible only to their electorate, and every officer of the Ministry is bred to respect this independence. It is true that the Ministry exercises a series of controls, controls which, in practice, severely limit the independence of authorities. In practice statutory provisions...are less important than they seem. Whatever may be in-

of the poverty program. In England, however, the increasing role of the central government as might be expected has had no such effect. The analysis above is of course relevant in this regard as is the greater apparent reluctance in England to set up special agencies at the local level to administer central government funds, particularly agencies that are at least partially run by local citizens.

[1] From the Education Act of 1944 quoted in Griffith, *Central Departments*, p. 50.

[2] See, e.g., Griffith, *Central Departments*, Chapter 2 and Peterson, 'British Interest Group Theory Reexamined: The Politics of Comprehensive Education in Three British Cities', *Comparative Politics*, 3 (1971), 381–402.

[3] See L. J. Sharpe (ed.), *Voting in Cities* (London, 1967), Chapter 1.

[4] Griffith, *Central Departments*, p. 515.

scribed on the legislative tablets, it is the tradition of British local authorities by and large to do what the Government of the day asks them to do, though they will do it at their own pace and in their own way.[1]

Central ministries and the Government of the day may employ a series of devices to see that policies are properly executed. These range from the more powerful controls of grants-in-aid, sanction over local authority borrowing and auditing of local accounts to the less powerful tools of information circulars and general guidance through consultation.[2] The District Auditors are particularly interesting officials in this regard. They are employed by the central authority to audit the accounts of many local authorities and have the authority to disallow expenditures which are *ultra vires*. In general, like the courts and the Parliament, District Auditors have taken a strict view of local authority powers. More importantly, they are in a position to disallow expenditures not only for 'bad faith' but because of 'honest stupidity' on the part of councilors or officers or because of 'unpractical idealism'. In short, the Auditors' powers are sweeping. The District Auditor plays an equivalent role to that played by American courts in tax-payers' suits; at specified times during the year (for one week) people of the local authority may look at certain council records and lodge complaints with the Auditor, who will then investigate.[3] Against these controls and tools must be laid the fact that a recalcitrant local authority is sufficiently autonomous to stymie a Ministry. In general, as long as a local authority does not require by law some specific permission from a ministry and/or is willing to use revenue raised from its own rates rather than borrowing, it may do as it pleases. Except of course, the government may decide to introduce legislation to stop the particular practice.[4] The relationship between central government and local authorities is multi-faceted and cannot be measured on any simple scale of dependence/independence. Local authorities do vary in terms of what they attempt and what in fact is accomplished. But on balance the pattern of central/local relationships has the consequence of reducing local political organization.[5]

[1] Sharp, *The Ministry*, pp. 25, 26, and 28–9.

[2] See Griffith, *Central Departments*, Chapter 1. For a breakdown of central government grants to the LCC for the period 1955–6 to 1964–5, see GLC, *London Statistics, 1955–64*, p. 224. For this period they constituted roughly 20 per cent of the LCC's income.

[3] On the District Auditor, see L. M. Helmore, *The District Auditor* (London, 1961), and Sharp, *The Ministry*, p. 54. The LCC was not subject to the usual method of controlling local government borrowing, which was through central approval for each instance of borrowing for capital investment. Rather, each year it negotiated a money bill with the Treasury for its borrowing for that year. This then had to pass through Parliament.

[4] See the brief review of a dispute between the new London Borough of Haringey and the Ministry of Housing where the comment is made that the latter is 'impotent' to enforce its views. 'Haringey Again', *New Society*, 4 December 1969, p. 902.

[5] The formulation of an appropriate indicator(s) for the central/local aspect of participative political structures while of great importance will undoubtedly prove difficult. At issue is not only the multi-dimensionality of the distribution of influence between the two levels of govern-

An analysis parallel to that concerning the impact of central government can be made in the policy areas of transportation, hospitals, police and public utilities, all of which in London were administered by special district authorities. These authorities were run by officials, who if they did not have national orientations did have viewpoints which were not local in nature. Somewhat loosely, the organizations might be characterized as regional. As well, being special districts who had independent grants of authority and a membership many of whose appointments were made by other than the local authority, they were not vulnerable to local political pressures. The consequence, as with the impact of central government, was to limit the kind and extent of incentives that might be offered to prospective members of organizations concerned with these policy areas at the local level.

CONCLUSION

London representatives faced the electorate not as popular political figures who were offering their own particular brand of services but as members of a political party. The disciplined party system resulted in relatively 'faceless' candidates.[1] An individual member was not a coalition builder and had no need nor was there much basis for him to become a popularly known political figure. His career did not depend on it; rather getting and staying elected depended on his party's appeal to the citizenry. Moreover, although members were elected principally on the basis of party label this did not mean that party considerations as they related to electoral success determined their activities on the Council. As noted earlier, the constituency parties did not act to monitor behavior of members, nor were citizens deeply concerned about the record of *local* parties. The policies and performance of national parties were of considerably greater importance in shaping electoral choice.[2] Finally, insofar as party differences reflected and appealed to class differences, the fact that class cleavages were not intense left the parties with scope for discretionary behavior. Neither directly through constituency parties nor indirectly through the party in the Council shaping members' behavior in response to electoral considerations were members sharply constrained. Their autonomy was relatively high and party organization, which

ment, but also a measure of the extent to which central authorities have a national orientation. All of this would then have to be somehow summated and then combined with other indicators of 'participativeness' for a total score. For an attempt to measure the extent of local autonomy across various nations see Paulo Reis Vieira, 'Toward a Theory of Decentralization: A Comparative View of Forty-Five Countries', unpublished Ph.D. dissertation, University of Southern California, 1957. Cited in Frank P. Sherwood, 'Devolution as a Problem of Organization Strategy', in Robert T. Daland (ed.), *Comparative Urban Research* (Beverly Hills, 1969). See also Elkin, 'A Note on Comparative Urban Inquiry'.

[1] Cf. Sharpe, *Metropolis Votes*, p. 57. On party discipline see Eckstein, 'The British Political System', Chapter 4. See also the discussion in Chapter 6 below.

[2] Cf. Sharpe, *Metropolis Votes*, p. 7.

in the abstract might be thought to have resulted in members' attention being closely drawn to the electorate and particularly to its class divisions, in fact did not have that result.

Councilors in London were not political entrepreneurs.[1] They did not have to engage in a continuous dialogue with their market, the public, to see what would sell and, compared to their American counterparts, had little incentive to invest any significant amount of resources in trying to monitor and mold citizen opinion. The high degree of autonomy of London elected officials was associated with a political environment in which the content of demands, their intensity, and the coalitions built out of them varied relatively little and were highly predictable. This in turn depended on the pattern of cleavages and the level of political organization among the citizenry.[2]

The political environment of LCC councilors also included the central government, particularly the Ministry of Housing and Local Government, the boroughs and the special districts. Insofar as they could withhold authority necessary for Council actions or in other ways control resources that were required for the LCC to act, then they were also possible sources of uncertainty. This is suggested by the St Giles case where the authority's handling of the whole development problem depended in part on whether the Ministry was likely to approve treating the land as a Comprehensive Development Area. The boroughs and the special districts were of less importance in this regard because in the case of the former there was almost no legal authority in question while in the case of the latter involvement with the LCC was intermittent. However, while for the authority as a whole the actions of central departments were of considerable importance, individual members did not need to deliver to their constituents services, projects and the like which the central government was in a position to withhold. Again, they were not political entrepreneurs and the actions of the central department were of little moment for their political fortunes.

The analysis here should not be construed as showing that the political environment was completely certain. There were some organized groups and some cleavages of course. However, not only was certainty high compared to American cities but in the latter it is probably the case that local officials operate in an atmosphere in which the existing high level of organization and the associated environmental uncertainty leads to more of both.

---

[1] See Banfield, *Political Influence*, pp. 240ff. for an extended discussion of this concept.

[2] While the whole analytical focus of the study to this point has been on elected representatives, the conclusions about autonomy apply equally to other members of the organization, viz., aldermen and officers. If nothing else, as noted, the autonomy of aldermen is established by the fact that they did not need to stand for election. As for officers, a parallel analysis could be done, but as this would rely on the same concepts and relationships no more need be done than to mention their autonomy. There was little incentive for them to carefully monitor and mold citizen opinion: a relatively certain political environment directed their attention inside the Council as well. See also the discussion in Chapter 6.

This is so for several reasons. Given a variety of groups interested in the same policies, as is often the case in American cities, there will be competition for supporters and resources even though there may be shared views. In this competition, the ability to gain concessions from governmental authorities is an important inducement for prospective members and consequently the incentive for organizational leaders to invest a high level of resources to gain results is great. Moreover, attempts by one group to influence the course of government will more than likely activate other groups who are now being presented with issues on which to build organizational followings. More generally, in this competitive and interactive situation, insofar as groups rely on issues as organization incentives, as is increasingly the case in American cities, then the level of environmental uncertainty could increase. This is because organizational maintenance requires that governmental authorities be induced to perform as demanded relatively frequently; other types of incentives do not imply any particular kind of governmental performance to anything like the same extent.[1] There may well be a threshold of environmental uncertainty, construed at least as a function of interest group behavior, which once passed is in some sense self-generating. Large American cities seem to have passed it whereas London seems to have been some distance away. This suggests that the distance between London and, for example, New York or Chicago in terms of the autonomy of local officials is associated with more than simply the number of interest groups and the pattern of political cleavages. American local representatives operate in an inherently more uncertain situation than their English counterparts.

[1] On the shift to issues as incentives in American cities, see Banfield and Wilson, *City Politics*.

6. DELIBERATION AND THE DELEGATION OF AUTHORITY

The St Giles and the World's End cases indicate that by American standards there were surprisingly few officials of the planning authority (elected or appointed) who were involved in making large-scale land use decisions. Also striking, again by contrast to American cities, was the composition of those who were actively involved. The explanation of these two features, numbers and composition, provides the principal focus for the succeeding discussion.

Some additional comments are necessary concerning the composition of those who were active. Local representatives whose constituents were to be markedly affected by the redevelopments played little or no part in the procedures whereby the authority reached its decisions. This is aside from any other representatives whose political interests might be thought to have been affected by a major public housing or downtown commercial development. They were not in evidence either. Consequently the composition of those who actively participated in land use decisions did not vary a great deal. In large American cities the cast of characters varies at least to the extent that the elected officials who are actively involved reflect the variation in those whose political interests are affected. By contrast in London, those who were actively concerned with planning decisions were largely those who had functional responsibilities for land use. When, for example, members outside the Planning Committee became involved, as in the St Giles case, it was rarely because their political interests were being touched but because they sat on a committee whose involvement was required in the particular case. Similarly, when the Leader of the Council became involved in a decision, again St Giles is an example, although this was most often in response to the possibly controversial nature of the case, it was not controversial because individual members were incurring or might incur political costs and thus engage in public controversy. Rather, it was the possibility that the LCC as a body might suffer embarrassment that made the issue controversial. Indeed, the Leader's involvement in particular cases did not reflect concern for his *own* political fortunes.[1] In general, the major partici-

[1] The other important occasion when the Leader might take an interest in a development control decision was when a particular party stand would generate large political credits; this did not happen often for reasons that are apparent from the analysis in Chapter 5. In the most

pants were the officers working on the case (this might include non-planning officers), the Chairman of the Committee and a few other Committee members. The latter were generally councilors who had some special competence or general concern with the class of matters at hand and who might be drawn from the ranks of the minority party; it was not just leading members of the majority party who took an active part.[1]

Perhaps even more unexpected than the limited interest of most members in land use control decisions to those acquainted with the American situation was the very active part played by planners and other officers. This was the case whether party considerations were seen to be relevant or not. Some comments by several LCC officials will give added substance to what is suggested by the case studies. One member, a former Committee Chairman with long experience of member–officer relations on the LCC, described the position of the latter as follows.

The London tradition was partnership between members and officers. Each had a job to do. There was a great deal of respect and discussion. Supposing one wanted to start something new one could send for the chief officer and say I have decided to do thus and thus and go to the Committee and get it passed. But we in London always had long talks with our officers until agreement was reached. The amount of suspicion and transgressing was low on the whole. Members didn't persist in what officers didn't like. This reduced the friction and officers didn't persist when members really wanted something. The officers were the active types and the Committee was to review. The average member was a lay member. The officers were to put forward suggestions, the members were to see that the public would accept these suggestions.

Another member indicated some additional aspects of the position of officers.

We tried to get the various officers involved to agree with each other before they came to the Committee. The Committee didn't like to be faced with disagreement. When we did get it we generally sent the officers back to seek agreement.

In short, officers were to work out the major problems and present the Committee with recommendations it could accept, rather than providing essentially technical help to representatives who were trying to shape developments in terms of their perception of constituency interests. One member summed it all up, perhaps a bit glibly, when he noted that 'to a large extent it's a question of the tail wagging the dog'. Planners clearly did not win every battle but they rarely lost because members insisted on

---

controversial decisions, the majority party leadership, institutionalized in a policy committee, which included all committee chairmen, would become involved. See the discussion below of the relationship between the political parties and planning.

[1] On the more routine cases the three members forming the panel of the development control sub-committee for that particular occasion, along with the planning officer concerned, would make the decision themselves.

some frame of reference that was unacceptable to them as professionals. Not only were planners generally the active agents in reaching decisions, but the concerns which dominated the discussion gave greater play to their skills as professionals rather than the 'political' skills and concerns of elected representatives.[1]

The LCC, at least among councilors, was an organization composed of more or less formal equals.[2] Clearly then coordination of effort in reaching land use decisions could not take place through procedures laid down in a table of organization designating those in authority. What has been described above is an organization in which such coordination took place principally through the delegation of effective authority by organizational members to a small subset of their number, including, in some instances, nominal subordinates. In contrast we may distinguish organizations where members reach decisions through bargaining, which may take place within the confines of the organization or involve actors in the organization's environment.[3] We may also point to organizations in which coordination takes place through leaders of the organization having a stock of inducements, such as jobs, which are dispensed to gain the acquiescence of other organizational members (the leaders of such organizations may be defined as such because they hold the inducements).[4] These incentives must not be concessions over the issue or problem under discussion, otherwise bargaining would be taking place. Within the group to whom effective authority is delegated in an organization there still remains the question of how effort is coordinated in reaching decisions. Empirically, it is likely that there is a high degree of association between extensive delegation and decisions reached by deliberation which revolves around trying to find common principles and drawing inferences for the particular case, or doing the last from already established principles. Our principal task is to analyze the factors which help account for the dominance of these analytical modes, i.e. delegation and deliberation, in the LCC. Of special concern is how the environmental features analyzed in the preceding chapter shaped and interacted with the norms and values of representatives.

---

[1] Witness the comments made by a private architect with long experience as a consultant to local authorities in London. The remarks were made at a public inquiry into the refusal of permission for one of his schemes.

Architect This is a new experience for me to find a Committee actually making a decision contrary to its officers. I really find it difficult to see how it would go about it.

Legal Officer Then you must realize there is a possibility of the Committee overriding the officer's recommendations?

Architect I will consider that point from now on; I have never considered it before because it never happened.

[2] The Leader and committee chairmen did have some small additional legal authority.

[3] See March and Simon, *Organizations*, Chapter 5. Organizations will vary between those in which one mode dominates to those that have a mixture of modes.

[4] See e.g. Meyerson and Banfield, *Politics*, for a discussion of such an organization.

POLITICAL PARTIES

The place to begin investigation of delegation within the LCC is with the political parties, particularly the majority party. Some part of the delegation of effective authority can be explained by reference to the willingness of party members to acquiesce in the decisions of party leaders. The existence of disciplined and hierarchical parties is clearly part of the explanation of the active role played by the Chairman of the Planning Committee and the occasional part played by the Leader of the Council.

The political party organizations between them organized the County Council.[1] The important posts in the Council were all party posts with the Leader of the majority party carrying the principal leadership burden in over-all Council affairs. The members and committee chairmen were chosen in party councils. Before a committee meeting the chairman, who was the party leader on the committee, and the leader of the opposition party on the committee read through the agenda papers and consulted with their respective party leaders and/or policy committees on possibly controversial matters. As the case studies suggest, the chairman was much the most important figure on the committees. He had the only regular contact with officers, helped to prepare the agenda and ran the committee meetings, often by simply giving the sense of the committee and asking if there were any objections. The chairman was the main link between ordinary members and officers. If a matter was likely to come before the public, where the presentation of a united party was deemed to be essential, a full party meeting might be called where a party stand would be enforced. Party meetings were also held by members of the committees to work out stands if they were thought relevant. On budgetary matters the situation was much the same; if there was a dispute between service committees the matter was settled in the majority party leader's office.[2]

Any satisfactory hypothesis aimed at explaining the existence of hierarchical parties in London would involve an examination of the nature of British political parties generally and ultimately an excursion into British political development and would thus require a discussion beyond the confines of this study. Some relevant points do however emerge from the evidence gathered for this study. First, from what has been said in the preceding chapter, it is clear that candidates for the Council had virtually no other way to gain election or retain a seat except by maintaining an identification with one or another of the major parties. This enabled party leaders to enforce their decisions through the threat of withdrawal of the party label.

[1] For an extended discussion of party organization within the LCC see Morrison, *London*, Chapter 8.

[2] Witness the comment by Herbert Morrison, a former Leader of the Council, on the importance of the position he held: 'but in all matters of importance or where difficulties arise, they (the chairmen) must bring their troubles to the Leader of the Council.' Morrison, *London*, p. 65.

However, this was not often done and so would seem to have limited explanatory value, although the impact of the *threat* of withdrawal cannot be discounted. Again, there is some evidence that party leaders were able to gain the support of party members through distribution of patronage. In contrast to party leaders in at least some American cities,[1] majority party leaders in London certainly had fewer jobs to dispense. At the least, all jobs in the public bureaucracy were distributed in accordance with the regulations of the local government civil service. However, leaders of both parties did have the major voice in who was to sit on various committees and who was to lead the party contingents in these committees. As well, the leader of the majority party also had the authority to fill non-paying jobs on various local boards and authorities, such as those for hospitals and local cultural institutions. The extent to which these various appointments were used to enforce the decisions of the party leadership however is not clear. Several members when discussing the problem commented in a fashion similar to one representative who noted that, 'one was certainly not promised jobs. This certainly was never expressly understood. I can't even think it would be implicit or implied in anything that was said.' In general, as Chapter 5 suggests, insofar as councilors were interested in advancement within the Council or to positions in regional or national authorities, this could be pursued most efficaciously through the parties; thus, rendering effective and lengthy party service was desirable.[2] Party leaders were the beneficiaries of this state of affairs.

Regardless of the extent to which appointments were used to enforce leadership wishes or of the impact of possible withdrawal of the party label, the question remains of why the leaders were in a position to wield such authority in the first place. A useful point is suggested by Beer in his analysis of 'collectivist' politics, some of the highlights of which have been presented in the preceding chapter. As noted, Beer argues that, at least at the elite level, there are widely dispersed norms which see well-organized parties as crucial to the existence of effective government. Political parties which are hierarchically organized[3] and in which one of the primary jobs of the ordinary members is to support leadership decisions are seen as necessary for making governmental policy in a complex age. It seems reasonable to assert that such collectivist norms were at work at all levels of government, not just the national level with which Beer is particularly concerned. The remarks made by various members provide support here, particularly with regard to the value of disciplined parties. The first is the

[1] The Democratic Party in Chicago would be the preeminent example. In general see Banfield and Wilson, *City Politics*, Chapter 9.

[2] See the discussion below of the pattern of incentives for councilors.

[3] It should be noted that Beer thinks that there are differences between Labour and Conservatives in this respect with the former placing more emphasis on internal democracy. In general see Beer, *British Politics*, Chapter 5.

response of a representative to a question concerning the basis for the existence of hierarchical parties.

The most important thing though I think is the tradition of working as a team. An appeal to party loyalty will generally produce the results. It is not necessary to do any more. If somebody is very much upset he might make a fuss. If he does so, then it is usually accepted because we know he's very upset. One's attitude is that one ought not to have fights on the team. One wouldn't go to the press; that would be very unusual. Mostly you find party members will stick together. If a man is really upset...he takes his grouse to the Leader, the Chief Whip or the Policy Committee.

For this member, party discipline and the existence of party leadership are closely joined. The party leadership was able to maintain itself because party loyalty was widespread.[1] A second member made a similar observation.

One should have a disciplined party. Looking at it through the eyes of the Leader, if he has a new policy to introduce...he takes it to the party. If they approve it is binding. Otherwise, how can you govern?

While the conception of how government should be organized held by London representatives can help account for the important part played by party leaders in planning decisions, it does not help explain the willingness of most members to defer to officers, both for decisions taken within their own party[2] or in committee, and to minority party members or members who did not hold formal leadership positions in the majority party. As has been noted, development control decisions while generally made by a relatively few members of the authority were not simply made by party leaders. Indeed, probably more than half were not party decisions at all.[3] What is required is a more general understanding of how members conceived of their jobs and concomitantly how they reacted to the political environment in which they operated, an analysis which goes beyond considerations specific to party. This more general analysis can then be used to supplement discussion of party related factors. When decisions were taken on party lines, members in supporting their party leaders were not somehow abstracted from the political setting in which they functioned and from other attitudes which shaped their actions. We can more fully comprehend the basis of the influence of party leaders if we can isolate these general

[1] It is logically possible to have party loyalty and discipline and not have hierarchical parties. Empirically the two seem to go together and party leaderships use the psychological incentive of loyalty to maintain their positions.

[2] This would of course only apply to the majority party.

[3] A former Chairman of the Committee commented that 'party votes were not very frequent. It was not my practice to dictate the party line.' Another member of the Committee noted that 'in a lot of matters party was simply not relevant'. For example, in the St Giles case, party considerations were absent as they were in the earlier stages of the World's End case.

features as well as gain some understanding of the delegation of effective authority when party considerations were not relevant.

DELIBERATORS AND DELEGATION: ROLE

A central fact in understanding the behavior of London councilors is the legislative role which they typically occupied. By directing our attention 'backward' to what factors were associated with their conception of their legislative job and 'forward' to other factors aside from the legislative role which also shaped their behavior, some understanding of why councilors delegated effective authority may be gained as well as clues providing for a more general comprehension of their actions. While the set of factors can be isolated and analyzed in their relation to delegation, the complex interactions between them can only be touched upon.

The behavior thought to be appropriate for LCC councilors is suggested in two comments by members with long experience on the Council. Both are concerned to point out the unacceptability of bargaining and compromise as a way of reaching decisions, and by implication the merits of deliberating on the best way to reach some end or ends.

In order to help the general pattern one has to put the community first. A compromise approach might work in small units but the County Council is dealing with matters of such large import that one cannot take the view of compromising with local neighborhoods.

In town planning...you don't get bargains and compromises. It depends on the integrity of the council doesn't it? There are great dangers in town planning and you need great integrity. You don't get the sort of thing in which neighborhoods bargain. Here it is done much more as a planning exercise...We are pretty good in this country in this regard.

Another long-experienced member summed up the above in his remark: 'it would be frowned upon if there were anything like bargaining.' In a more positive vein, Herbert Morrison, long-time Leader of the Council, commented that

while I was on the Council, I saw that over a wide field both parties have been willing to consider many questions on the facts and the merits, irrespective of party views[1]

While the case studies cannot tell us anything directly about how members thought they *ought* to behave, since for the most part they describe actual behavior, they are suggestive especially if we contrast the behavior of representatives as it is portrayed with that of American representatives in urban land use decision-making. A useful comparison is between the behavior of

[1] Morrison, *London*, pp. 67–8.

representatives in Chicago with reference to a public housing project, as described by Meyerson and Banfield, and the behavior of the Committee members in the World's End case. In the former, the major concern of the representatives was not incurring large political costs; in consequence they engaged in a good deal of bargaining and compromise with each other and with the various organizations and individuals concerned.[1] In the World's End case, although the concerns of the Committee, and particularly of the Chairman, were not altogether clear, one thing deemed important was to see that the project was in accord with general standards of what constituted a satisfactory environment. A decision on how to treat the borough's application which was reached by bargaining would have been at variance with this concern to enforce environmental standards.

The deliberator role, as we shall call the above prescriptions, was (as presumably most roles are) procedural in focus.[2] The prescriptions were concerned with how representatives ought to behave in making decisions about planning matters or in Council activities generally. Aside from the prescription to discuss the merits of the case was an implication that representatives should not see themselves as spokesmen for particular constituencies. In the standard terminology of the analysis of representation they were to be trustees not delegates; if they were to deliberate they must be free of the constraints of promoting the interests of their own constituents.[3] This is likely one embodiment of the trust in authority discussed in the preceding chapter. Another implication of the injunction to deliberate was that there was something to deliberate about, i.e. that there either were or could be some standards, procedural or substantive, which could be used to decide a particular case.[4]

The fact that members were aware of the deliberator role as being the central set of prescriptions guiding their behavior says nothing directly about the extent to which they identified with the role, i.e. what might be called the affective dimension of their role conception. No direct evidence on the matter can be provided here, but some inferences may be drawn from an exploration of some salient political and normative features of the

---

[1] Meyerson and Banfield, *Politics*.

[2] For a general discussion of roles see Bruce J. Biddle and Edwin J. Thomas (eds.), *Role Theory: Concepts and Research* (New York, 1966) especially Chapters 1–4.

[3] See e.g. Heinz Eulau, *et al.*, 'The Roles of Legislators in the Legislative Process', in Biddle and Thomas, *Role Theory*. Eulau, *et al.* discuss a 'system of roles' (p. 247). The finer distinctions they draw are useful (orientation to constituents, area, and pressure group) but given the kind of evidence presented here it would be presumptuous to do more than point to general orientation.

[4] To accept this description of the councilors' role as valid, a great deal more evidence would be required. At the least, an analysis of interview data from the universe of councilors would be needed. The discussion here rests on observation of councilors, the case studies and, most importantly, open-minded interviewing. More systematic analysis would undoubtedly reveal variation in the extent of awareness of role prescriptions and identification with the role (see below). On the question of the expectations of significant others, and their ability to enforce these, no evidence aside from the general discussion of citizen norms is presented.

situation in which members operated. If the role prescriptions described were inconsistent with other major norms relevant to the representative's political behavior or with the political realities they faced, particularly what was required to get and stay elected and to promote policies, we would expect those who occupied the role to experience uneasiness, particularly some reduced degree of satisfaction in fulfilling the demands of the role than they otherwise would have felt. 'Inconsistency' is meant simply to stipulate the extent to which political realities or other norms imply or prescribe behavior which is at variance with the role prescriptions. Conversely, if it can be demonstrated that important norms and the political realities are consonant with role prescriptions then we would expect high identification. In London, both the political realities and other political norms were highly congruent with the deliberator role.

When representatives in London attempted to articulate their conception of the public interest they defined a view which was unitary or holistic, which emphasized trying to serve the good of the community conceived as a single whole. The relevant contrast is to representatives in large American urban areas who, at least implicitly, most often conceive of the public interest in pluralistic terms, i.e. as resulting from the interplay of various community interests.[1] The implication of this last view is for a representative to conceive of his job as being one of many bargainers in the political process. The implication of the former is that representatives should devote their efforts to defining or discovering the good of the community, in short, to deliberation.[2] A major exception in American cities to this analysis are reformers, old and new style, who tend to take a more holistic view.[3] They probably experience the kind of uneasiness with legislative roles just noted since their conception of the public interest is at variance with expectations of how city councilors ought to behave, at least the expectations of many constituents and of other politicians but to some degree their own expectations as well.[4]

The holistic view of London representatives is captured in the remarks of one representative who commented on the difference between trying to help individual constituents and making decisions for the city as a unit.

There is a real contrast on questions of individual welfare and considerations of policy. One makes great efforts to help individuals. But in matters of development and reorganization, for example, it is the good of the community that counts first above that of any particular neighborhood...One must have an overall plan for

---

[1] See Banfield, 'Note on a Conceptual Scheme', pp. 322–9 in Meyerson and Banfield, *Politics*.

[2] See, for example, Banfield, *Political Influence*, and more generally Banfield and Wilson, *City Politics*, Chapter 15 and Conclusion.

[3] Banfield and Wilson, *City Politics*, Chapter 11.

[4] See James Q. Wilson, *The Amateur Democrats* (Chicago, 1962), particularly Chapters 5, 10 and 12.

highways, sewage, refuse disposal and the like. One can't organize services to suit one area and not another.

Another member commented in a similar vein, this time contrasting a concern for ethnicity as a factor in making city policy with a concern for the community as a whole.

The constant preoccupation in the United States with ethnic groups is not the case here. The emphasis here is on general principles. It is possible to look at London overall because it hasn't been so mixed.

A planner with long experience in dealing with and observing the Planning Committee at work made a parallel observation when he noted what happened when a member of the Committee pushed for 'particular' interests.

Members were able to take a global view. If a member was too subjective the Chairman would say 'we know your view', you need to take a more global view.

Finally, the view of a student of English local politics is highly pertinent to the discussion. He notes that

if pluralism is present [in England] it is not connected in any clear and practical way with minor *territorial* units. What has been present since the late nineteeth century is what two Americans...have called the 'Anglo-Saxon Protestant middle-class ethos'. [Banfield and Wilson in *City Politics*.] With such an ethos, the emphasis is on 'good government' and 'administration' not 'politics' and on 'business-like' attitudes. The ideal decision-making process is based on 'common agreement'; divisions in the community must be glossed over.

In short, the prevailing norms are holistic; city government is to be concerned with administering for the whole community not with mediating differences within it.[1]

It is likely that this conception of the public interest was thought to be relevant by members not only when decisions were made on a non-partisan basis but also when decisions were taken on party lines. Party decisions were not principally thought of as occasions in which some section of the community would gain, sometimes at the expense of another, although this was clearly at issue in some cases, but rather as the enforcement of one of at least two competing views of the community's good. It was a question of assignment of different weights to different sections of the community

---

[1] James G. Bulpitt, *Party Politics in English Local Government* (London, 1967).

The discussion below of the recruitment process to the Council with its middle class emphasis provides clues to the persistence and the extensiveness of the holistic view. While the relationship between class and conception of the public interest is complex, Banfield and Wilson suggest that (upper) middle-class people are more likely to adopt a holistic view. See *City Politics*, Chapter 3 and 'Public-Regardingness as a Value Premise in Voting Behavior', *American Political Science Review*, 58 (1964), 876–87. Clues to the origin of the holistic conception can be found in Stanley Rothman, 'Tradition vs. Modernity in Britain', in Richard Rose, *Studies in British Politics* (New York, 1966).

and to different aspects of community well-being, and this was certainly the occasion for conflict, but there was a concern for the city taken as a whole.[1] The relation between this community-regarding view and the interests of the parties is suggested in the following comment by a Council member. If we discount the attempt to put an acceptable varnish on the notion of party advantage, there is still the suggestion of concern with the community as a whole.

In the LCC, the dialogue on the committees was between the Chairman and the Minority Leader of the committee. The Minority Leader would start off the discussion by saying what he and his colleagues thought was the right thing to do trimmed by party expediency. In a lot of matters party simply was not relevant. Often we tried to ask ourselves 'what is the best thing to do here'. The concern was with the good of the community, but on occasion we had to trim back for the sake of our constituents.

The same member was quite concerned to point out that though the party had to 'trim a decision' for the sake of its party supporters, 'one was trying to lead. I mean this, we were genuinely trying to lead them.' The remarks taken together suggest a party at the same time trying to satisfy the 'narrow' interests of its supporters as well as trying to direct the latter's attention to a broader idea of the appropriate basis for public policy.

The interrelations between the hierarchical norms dispersed in the citizenry, the deliberator role, and the conception of the public interest should be noted. These would all seem to be various aspects of the normative dimension of a political system in which the governors govern vigorously and the rest of the population by and large thinks that's the way it ought to be. In return the governors pledge to behave themselves and also justify their freedom from citizen constraint by saying that they are serving the whole community. This last suggests a strong element of ideological self-justification. However, in London as the citizenry was apparently not unresponsive to such justifications, and in fact to some degree promoted them, and the governors were not generally dishonest or corrupt, there is clearly more to be said than just noting that it was in their (the governors') interest to define their legislative role as one of deliberation and their conception of the public interest as holistic. This theme will be raised again in the concluding chapter.

If we turn to what has been loosely called the political realities of the representative's situation, the congruency argument may be extended. In the World's End case the behavior of the member from Chelsea (who was also Leader of the Opposition on the Council) is particularly instructive for our purposes. Given the opportunity to advance his political interests

---

[1] Beer in his analysis of elite norms at the national level makes a similar observation. See *British Politics*, Chapter 3.

with his constituents by taking the whole matter to the press, or looking for possible allies, or in general by using some of the repertoire of the American urban politician, he confined himself largely to checking on the extent of support from the borough among councilors. Of course, in doing so he may have made some attempts at persuading them to support the borough, but certainly his efforts did not go beyond conversation. The discussion of the autonomy of representatives, and of the political environment of members presented in the preceding chapter provides a framework with which to analyze this incident. Briefly, representatives had little need to promote policies or decisions which reflected the interests of their constituents or organized groups within the community in order to maintain their political fortunes. Some members did of course seek to see certain policies or decisions adopted but this largely stemmed from their personal evaluation of policy problems built upon their experiences with such matters and filtered through party viewpoints or widely agreed upon policies (see below). Representatives had little incentive to speak for particular sections of the community and thus engage in bargaining with any other representatives engaged in a similar task. As a consequence, London councilors did not need to devote political resources to seeking allies, punishing enemies and the like and thus *could* devote their attention to a consideration of the merits of the matter at hand.

Furthermore, should London representatives have wished to engage in extensive bargaining they would have found it difficult because some of the essential ingredients of a successful legislative bargaining system were absent. For such a system to operate to any great extent, it is likely necessary that there be other valued 'items' to trade besides votes. This is because any given legislator whose cooperation is needed may not have on his agenda at the particular moment an issue about which he feels strongly enough to prompt him to trade his vote on a present issue in return for that of another legislator on this succeeding one. If there is nothing else to offer him besides a vote on a succeeding issue no bargain will be struck. However, in many political systems some astute publicity may raise the political costs sufficiently so that the legislator is inclined to enter the bargain; public reputation would be a highly valued resource in such a case. Similarly, side payments could be offered, i.e. inducements not directly related to the matter at hand. If such inducements, e.g. support for a political friend of the legislator whose cooperation is required, are irrelevant or hard to manufacture, again bargaining becomes difficult because what can be offered is limited. In London, the fact that members were highly autonomous meant in fact that the repertoire of inducements *was* limited and bargaining therefore difficult.

Overall, the political realities of London, particularly the interrelations between the political environment and the behavior of representatives that have been analyzed here in terms of certainty and autonomy, provided few incentives for actions which were at variance with the deliberator role. The autonomy of representatives was consonant not only with the role of deliberator but also with the holistic conception of the public interest. The general norms of the public interest conception, the more specific norms of the role and the autonomy of members were mutually consistent and thus mutually supportive.

DELEGATION AND DELIBERATION AS BEHAVIOR

We are interested in the role councilors typically played as it was associated with their behavior. In the particular case, the latter was most often not that expressly delineated (deliberation) but that which was implied, viz., delegation. For most members most of the time, the role was, given the presence of certain other factors to be discussed, associated with delegation. On occasion, for these members, when they did become actively involved in Council business it did in fact produce deliberative behavior. For other members, those to whom effective authority was delegated, along with the officers involved, the role was generally associated with deliberative behavior What is required then is an examination of the interaction between the deliberator role, delegation and deliberative behavior.

A role might be thought of as providing its occupant with an incentive to pursue the behavior prescribed. Satisfaction would be gained by fulfilling the role demands as they are internalized by the individual and as he perceives they are shared by the wider society. For the relevant behavior to actually accord with role prescriptions it is presumably necessary that the balance of incentives in the environment of the actor point in the same direction as these prescriptions. If they do not, behavior at variance with the role prescriptions is likely.[1] In London the balance of incentives that issued from the environment of the organization did in fact point to behavior for members that differed from the prescriptions but *not* in a normative sense. The behavior 'indicated' by these incentives was an extension of the deliberator role,[2] and thus the normative and objective factors shaping the representatives' behavior were mutually supporting.

The balance of incentives for most representations pointed to delegating effective authority to those who had the time, interest and competence in planning matters. This is suggested by the World's End case for example, in which the Chairman and the senior planners, all of whom had experience, time and interest, acted to interpret Council policy in the matter and carried on the negotiations; other members, on the Committee or outside, played a considerably smaller part or no part at all. The balance of incentives may

[1] Or at least possible, depending on the strength of environmental incentives. Withdrawal is another possibility.

[2] From the point of view of an observer *and* that of members. Some of the comments of members presented below support the last.

be clearly seen by looking at the cost and benefits associated with the two alternatives facing representatives, viz. whether to delegate or exercise authority. This calculus is meant only to highlight the kinds of factors that impinged on members and not to reflect actual thought processes; clearly members did not go through elaborate cost–benefit calculations (although in fact the considerations noted here are few) in choosing their course of action, but it is not implausible to argue that members were aware of the factors to be noted and that these shaped their actions. In this sense it may be said that they acted 'as if' they did go through the calculations. The discussion here extends the analysis in the preceding chapter on the relationship between certainty and autonomy; specifically, it draws out the appropriate inferences from these concepts as they related to delegation.[1]

The principal benefits to be gained by exercising the authority inherent in the councilors' position can be considered under the following headings: intrinsic, policy, prestige and public service benefits. Intrinsic benefits are those that accrue simply by the act of being responsible and exercising choice, quite apart from the ends to which such authority may be used. While members did undoubtedly get some satisfactions of this kind, this must be seen in the context of the fact that for many of them serving on the Council was at best of marginal importance. Many did not initially even wish to stand for office, but were asked to do so by constituency parties. Many served out of civic duty, or for the very modest social prestige of office or perhaps even to end the pressure being put on them by local party officials. All of these motives could be served by simply either standing for office or by the fact of election and did not require actual exercise of authority.[2]

Policy benefits are those which accrue from promoting some particular policy or decision within the Council as a consequence of which one's political standing is improved with constituents. As should be clear, given the comparative certainty of the political environment, such actions were largely unnecessary. As long as a member maintained some minimum attendance record (and even the impact of not attending is unclear) little else mattered except party label. More importantly, it was generally the case, given the very limited information available about local politics, that constituents would not even be aware of attempts to promote particular Council actions.

---

[1] The discussion here encompasses what above has been called the 'political realities' facing members. In that context, the analysis aimed at showing that the incentives arising from the councilors' environment were consonant with the deliberator role. There was no discussion of the specific behaviors associated with these incentives, only a concern to show that representatives were not likely to find it difficult to accept the role. Here the concern is with actual behavior.

[2] For data which support this characterization of councilors' motives see Sharpe, *Metropolis Votes*, p. 36.

Prestige benefits result from simply being visible to the citizenry, i.e. roughly the benefits of being recognized. Again, councilors operated largely without publicity and thus being active in Council affairs would not improve visibility. Public service benefits are those associated with promoting policies or decisions which are felt to be of community benefit: the rewards of working for a better community. Aside from the points made concerning the motivations of members under the heading of intrinsic benefits, the fact that councilors were unpaid is pertinent. This last meant that most members had to continue with their regular jobs and thus had limited time to devote to Council affairs even if they had the interest.[1] Given the nature of London politics, the only major benefits gained by exercising authority were of the intrinsic and public service kind. And for most members even these did not count heavily.

The major costs of exercising authority were what may be termed decision and information costs. The former refers to the resources invested by a member in being involved in reaching a decision. The latter refers to the costs of acquiring information about the matter at hand. Although it is difficult to estimate these costs, it is clear that even if they were rather modest the low level of benefits for most members would mean an unfavorable ratio of costs to benefits for the alternative of exercising authority. There were of course some members who derived substantial enough benefits to outweigh the costs and who consequently preferred an active role in planning matters and Council affairs more generally: for them, intrinsic and public service benefits were greater than for other members. For the latter, there was then the alternative of delegating effective authority to these members who had the time, interest and the increased competence which came with the first two. In addition, effective authority could be delegated to officers, who also had these qualities, to work in concert with the activist members.

The major possible costs of delegation to officers and to those members who had the propensity to be active were largely political. They may be characterized as: losing support from constituents because of not playing an active role in Council business and losing support because the decisions and policies of those to whom authority was delegated were unacceptable to constituents. The former has already been dealt with under the heading of prestige benefits. The latter has been discussed as well but it would be useful to expand the point especially as it applies to officers. The contrast to American cities where delegation to officers is fraught with political costs is worth emphasizing. Being a political entrepreneur in these cities means that rather than delegation being common, bureaucrats are often sought as allies in the promotion of policies and in the protection of representatives' political positions. One planner with some direct acquaintance of American planning talked about the matter at some length.

[1] See the discussion below concerning recruitment.

The game is played in this country according to rules. My impression is that in the United States you haven't got any rules. You start with conflict. It's all politics. There are various influences, political and financial, that you have to contend with. Here if you have a planning application, differences between officers and members are one of degree.

We [the LCC] are not under immediate pressures like in America...It's different here than with American representatives. Our representatives don't have to explain themselves to their constituents. Their constituents vote on party tickets. You don't have to talk to Mrs. Smith and then come and tell me that Mrs. Smith is unhappy. They [the members] are elected to serve London and I think they see their jobs that way.

The planner moreover commented by way of introduction to this comparison that he 'never even knew where [which local area] the members came from'.

An additional comparison to American cities will be useful. In these cities representatives are reluctant to allow either other representatives or planners to zone the city's land without their being able to change the zoning should political circumstances require it.[1] In London, the zoning of usage in the *Development Plan* reflected the views of senior planners and several important members.[2] Most members were not involved in setting the original zones nor were they subsequently very active in pressing for variances. Applications were generally considered within the framework of the zones defined, and the constant efforts to introduce exceptions characteristic of many American cities was largely absent.

On the benefit side of delegation, the principal gain was that resources which otherwise would have to be devoted to decision-making could be freed for other uses, perhaps outside of politics altogether, from which satisfactions could be gained.[3] For most representatives, the ratio of costs to benefits was favorable as costs were likely to be very low and not outweigh even limited benefits. In comparison to the alternative of exercising authority, the incentives for representatives which derived from their political environment clearly indicated delegation. A member long active in Council affairs summed up the matter this way.

There tends to be only a few members who can spend the time required to be Leader or a chairman. Most ordinary members give only two or three hours a week. They tend to be passengers frankly. They have confidence in people who have gone into the problem and who have the time, unless they see something outrageous and then they get upset.

[1] See Meyerson and Banfield, *Politics*; Richard Babcock, *The Zoning Game* (Madison, Wisc., 1966); and S. J. Makielski, *The Politics of Zoning : The New York Experience* (New York, 1966).

[2] See Elkin, 'Development Plan'. The zones also reflected the views of the Ministry, as the *Plan* required its approval, and was in fact altered somewhat in the process as a result of this requirement. As noted, the zones also tended to follow existing usage.

[3] This is generally handled on the cost side of the equation under the heading of opportunity cost. For the purposes of discussing in effect 'doing little or nothing' as an alternative, it is useful to treat it on the benefit side.

Competence and the deliberator role

One of the implications of the deliberator role is that those who have the greater competence on the subject matter under discussion should play the dominant part. If the aim is to decide what is the best thing to do, those who know the most should have the major voice. This is in contrast to a situation in which knowledge of the matter at hand would be less important because the aim of policy-making is to serve the interests of diverse sections of the community as the latter defines them. Some American cities, particularly with regard to land use decisions, conform to this description. As the comment of the member just quoted suggests, in London members did perceive some measure of differential competence on planning affairs which was based at least in part on the ability of a few representatives to devote substantial resources to dealing with applications and land use matters generally. By extension this perception of differential competence would apply to planners as well. Therefore, given the role which they occupied, members in general would be willing to delegate effective authority: the role prescriptions and the balance of incentives pointed then to the same behavior.

An additional point concerning the role prescriptions must be made. Representatives would be unlikely to delegate effective authority to those thought to be competent unless the latter held ends similar to their own in land use policy and a similar orientation to the broader aims of Council policy, i.e. a conception of the public interest. Some discussion of the extent to which such shared ends and orientations were present is therefore required. Nothing needs to be added to the analysis above concerning the extent to which elected members shared a conception of the public interest. However some comments are required on the degree to which *officers* and members shared a view of the public interest and also on the extent of agreement among members and between officers and members on the ends of land use planning.

In American cities planners apparently hold a holistic conception of the public interest,[1] while elected representatives, at least implicitly, hold a pluralistic view.[2] The result is a divergence concerning how local government should operate with the planners relying on professional values and techniques and the representatives being concerned with the political benefits and costs of land use decisions. London planners like their American counterparts held a holistic conception. The job of the planning authority was to decide what was best for the city as a whole. This was implicit for them in the very nature of planning – an attempt to define how the city as a whole should look on the basis of principles of land use developed by plan-

[1] Altshuler, *City Planning*, Chapters 5–8; and Banfield and Wilson, *City Politics*, pp. 221–3.
[2] See the discussion above, pp. 123–4.

ners like Abercrombie and others interested in planning. One planner put it this way.

If you employ experts, professional men, they shouldn't be manipulated by little areas or neighborhoods. What is good for the city is *good*; that's it. If professional men recommend something that is in the framework of Council policy you shouldn't swerve because an area of the city does not like it.

Another commented that

the planner is the custodian of the community. He can speak as the guardian of the public interest because he is a detached and disinterested party. His choices are not motivated out of self-interest.

Moreover, members recognized the similarity of orientation between themselves and planners and the consequences for delegation, at least at an implicit level of understanding. For example, one member when presented with two broad conceptions of the public interest, pluralistic and holistic, in the context of a question about relations between officers and members commented: 'officers are so trusted because they share our way of looking at the public good. I felt I could always trust them.'[1]

When we turn to policy ends in planning, similar conclusions to those reached concerning the conception of the public interest obtain. There was a consensus on policy ends which included members as well as planners and this contributed to the delegation of effective authority to interested members and planners. London planners were the principal executors of a tradition in planning ideas which was rooted in a concern for civic amenity and a dislike of highly urbanized environments. It was this tradition which informed the discussions of development control within the planning authority and was generally shared by those concerned with land use for the city.[2]

Observers and practitioners of planning for London made a distinction between town planning on the one side and social and economic planning on the other. These distinctions were by no means clear-cut, especially as the original formulation of proposals for London did involve a consideration of economic and social goals.[3] However, the distinction seems to have been as follows: town planning works with the physical environment of bricks and mortar and the like, while other forms of planning work with other

---

[1] It is likely that the oft-noted feeling present in England of trust in civil servants, the willingness to allow them a great deal of discretion, is to be explained at least partly by the above points. For a discussion of the trust put in local government civil servants see Peter Self, 'Town Planning in Britain and the United States', *Town Planning Review*, 25 (1954), 67–81.

[2] For a discussion of the roots of planning thought for London and England generally, see the following: Ashworth, *British Town Planning*; Donald Foley, 'British Planning: One Ideology or Three', *British Journal of Sociology*, 11 (1960), 211–31; Foley, *Controlling London's Growth*, Chapters 1, 2, and 3; and Ruth Glass, 'The Evaluation of Planning: Some Sociological Considerations', *International Social Science Journal*, 11 (1959), 393–409.

[3] See Foley, 'British Planning', pp. 221–2.

variables such as manpower distribution or levels of welfare expenditures. The administration of development control by the LCC was clearly meant as an exercise in physical planning. One planning officer put it quite succinctly. 'Town planning is not economic planning. The legislation is quite clear on this point. We must pay attention only to planning factors.' Economic and social planning, insofar as it was done, was the concern of the central authorities.[1]

The attempt to divorce town planning from social and economic planning can be seen in the limited interest planners and Planning Committee members had in involving the planning machinery in capital budgeting, i.e. in the allocation of resources for the building of capital works.[2] There was in fact a budget supplied with the 1951 *Development Plan* (and the *Review* as well) but most of the work was done by the Comptroller's office rather than by planning officers and the whole operation was not taken very seriously.[3] One planner indicated the prevailing attitude when he commented that 'not only were planners not concerned, but neither was the Committee. They simply didn't think it was their job.' A member of the Planning Committee supplied the basic reason. 'It is not a town planning decision to decide on local authority priorities. Town planning is not to be involved directly and consciously in the setting of social priorities.'[4]

Within this broad concern for the physical environment two approaches to planning can be distinguished. The first is suggested by the remarks of a former member of the Planning Committee who responded to a question about the objectives of town planning with the following.

Planning's role is to regulate land use by setting standards which permit good neighborliness. As a result you have day-lighting codes and fire and safety regulations and you must also protect social amenities. Planning is regulatory.

In general, this approach is designed to promote and protect amenity.[5] Planning is to be concerned, as one Committee member put it, with the

[1] There was a sense, at least amongst some professional planners, that town planning was already concerned with more than physical planning, even if this was not widely recognized. And it was contended that it ought to be even more consciously concerned. One LCC planner commented, 'planners are being drawn more and more into social and political problems and questions of priorities. We are using blinkers less, i.e. solely being concerned with physical planning. The trend now is more toward a positive approach, and allocating the community's resources.'
[2] The attempt to concentrate on physical planning is of course relevant to understanding the analysis in Chapter 5 of the exclusion of certain issues in planning discussions.
[3] One member of the Committee recalled that 'the whole matter of *Development Plan* budgeting was thought farcical. The Committee's attitude was "let the comptroller have a go if he wants to".'
[4] It is very likely that this limited concern with capital budgeting was related not only to ideas about the proper concerns of town planning, but was also connected to a realization that much of local authority financing depended on decisions made at the central level. The incentive to support and promote capital budgeting is low when there are strong constraints on the local authority as to what can be spent where.
[5] Foley, in a discussion of the various strands of British planning thought, defines amenity as a 'quality of pleasantness of the physical environment'. He says that amenity embraces a

'preventing of outrages'. Good design, plenty of open space and a share of the sunlight are the hallmarks. It is this approach to planning that was evidenced in the case studies when the LCC showed itself greatly concerned with the design of the various buildings. This is town planning as an extension of architecture. As one text on the subject states: 'town planning... is architecture applied to town building which includes all the problems of design, scale and arrangement of individual buildings and reciprocal relations.'[1]

The second approach to town planning takes a broad view of the physical environment of the city. The basic perspective is that large cities are not very satisfactory places in which to live. Amongst other things, the residential densities are too high and the result is unhealthy living. As a Committee member put it in reference to the crowded conditions of working-class living at an earlier time, densities must be controlled in order to see that 'the errors of the Victorian period should not be repeated'. This view was the basis of the stand taken by the second Chairman of the Planning Committee in the World's End case. If the amenity approach is called aristocratic in orientation, this approach can be seen as a manifestation of a concern for the living conditions of the working class.[2]

Both of these approaches to town planning share an 'anti-urban' bias.[3] Town planning should aim at the goal of as many people as possible living in semi-urban conditions, i.e. in low density housing with plenty of open space. The best-known expression of this bias can be seen in the ideas of the garden city movement which aimed at decentralization of urban areas by building satellite cities.[4] An early and extensive exposition was in the Barlow Commission Report, as well as in the two advisory plans for the London area prepared by Abercrombie (and Forshaw). These ideas also underlay the *Development Plan* for London.

spectrum from 'restriction against nuisances' to a 'positive notion of visual delight'. 'British Planning', p. 220. Mandelker in *Green Belts*, however, says that 'amenity...comprehends more than aesthetics' (p. 32). It is very likely that this emphasis on the protection of amenity is part of an aristocratic attitude toward land use. Emphasis on design and open space is likely to be associated with an aristocracy with close ties to the land and a concern for the preservation of its beauties. See Altshuler, *City Planning*, p. 439, especially the quote from Charles Haar on 'aristocratic interest in land use' which is taken from his (Haar's) book, *Land Planning in a Free Society: A Study of the British Town and Country Planning Act* (Cambridge, Mass., 1951). V. S. Pritchett says, simply, that 'the landed peers worship space, buildings and grass...' *New Statesman*, 10 May 1968.

[1] James W. R. Adams, *Modern Town and Country Planning* (London, 1952), pp. 2–3.
[2] Historically this was expressed in attempts to promote public health. On the relationship between public health and town planning see Ashworth, *British Town Planning*, Chapter 3.
[3] Glass, 'Evaluation of Planning'. See also Hall, *London 2000*, Chapter 2.
[4] See the discussion of the movement in Foley, *Controlling London's Growth*, pp. 14–16. The garden city ideas and the anti-urban bias have been subjected to challenge in the recent past (Glass, 'Evaluation of Planning'), but at least up until the time covered by this study (1965) these ideas still dominated the thinking of those who operated the planning machinery. See also Westergaard, 'Structure', p. 129.

Some lines of disagreement within the planning authority can be distinguished, two being of particular interest, viz. those between the political parties and those between officers and members. It has already been said that party differences in planning were not great, but there were in fact some disagreements. The major ones were as follows: Conservatives were more willing to allow high densities, partly in order to promote, as one Conservative put it, 'a more economic use of land'. Conservatives were probably inclined to be more lenient on office building being more worried about London's status as a world commercial center. And in house-building, Conservatives were more chary of the reactions of middle-class residents to council house building. These were the differences in planning itself and they were largely a matter of emphasis. In areas related to planning, Conservatives were less interested in treating council housing as a straightforward social service and felt that it should be made more economically viable.

One of the difficulties in detailing party differences in planning is that as the Labour Party held a majority for so long any disagreements the Conservatives might have felt were likely to be muffled by their minority position, which on occasion was perceived as more or less permanent. The consensus then might be interpreted as simply another way of discussing the majority party's views. There is no easy way to settle this problem. However, it is worth repeating that some of the major aspects of thinking about planning derived from a traditional concern with amenity of which at least some Tories were very much the custodians. Furthermore, as a matter of fact, the Conservatives did cooperate with the Labour Party on a whole series of planning matters.

There were also some disagreements between planners and members of the Planning Committee taken as a whole. These too can be briefly listed. Again, density was a major source of dispute with planners being somewhat more lenient than the Committee, particularly its Labour members. The disagreement between planners and members in the World's End case illustrates the point. Some of the disagreement can be traced to the planners' impatience with density standards that tended to be rigidly applied; on occasion planners were willing to make concessions based on particular circumstances, whereas members were more afraid of the dire consequences for living conditions if standards were relaxed. This may in turn have rested on a feeling by members that density standards were ends to be achieved, part of the definition of a good environment, while planners apparently looked on them more as a means to such an environment defined in other terms. In general, however, differences between planners and members were about means, not ends. Both accepted the consensus as defining the general goals of planning for London.[1] Planners were to interpret what one

---

[1] See Altshuler, *City Planning*, Chapter 9 and Catherine Bauer Wurster, 'Introduction' in Melvin M. Webber *et al.* (eds.) *Explorations into Urban Structure* (Philadelphia, 1964), p. 10. See also Foley, *Controlling London's Growth*, Chapters 1–3.

of their members talked about as 'well-defined objectives'. As a long-experienced member put it,

planners were to interpret these planning principles. They were not people who could think up or invent new approaches...One needs an over-all philosophy, a planning philosophy...Planners under the LCC were to imaginatively interpret this social philosophy. This helps account for the cooperation between planners and members and that's why we had planners.

Not only were planners to be involved in this interpretative process but so also were those members, particularly the Chairman, who were willing to devote the necessary resources to obtain the required competence.

An explanation of the origins and persistence of the planning consensus would require a study in itself. However, some relevant factors have already been isolated. In London, the comparative certainty of the political environment and the associated autonomy of members made a consensus on planning ends and means possible. Elected representatives did not find the upholding of the consensus unacceptable in terms of their political fortunes. A similar consensus on land use and related matters in large American cities would be difficult if not impossible; one of the fundamental features of the political process in these cities is the sensitivity of participants to the divergent interests of the citizens. Beyond these kinds of considerations we can also point to the recruitment process of members.

From the analysis presented in the preceding chapter one would expect that the only important recruitment mechanism for candidates for the LCC would be the two major political parties. This is in contrast to even partisan American cities where nominations often reflect the ability of candidates to gain support from ethnic or business organizations, for example, since political parties in such cities are often coalitions of local interests. In London, even though recruitment was done through *constituency* parties, there were few attempts by organized groups to exert influence in the process. Therefore, the rather heterogeneous collection of views characteristic of American urban representatives and aspirants was less likely to be present.

The analysis of recruitment needs to be coupled with some facts about the nature of the member's job. As noted, LCC members were unpaid, although they could get some compensation for expenses. Those who wished to stand for office had to have the kind of job which allowed leave from work on a regular basis and which provided either sufficient income to offset any loss of earnings while attending to Council business or which did not reduce income during Council work. In short, those with middle-class occupations, especially professional men, had a substantial advantage. Other groups who had the necessary characteristics were housewives, retired people and trade union officials. Of these, housewives were likely to be middle class, having the necessary articulateness and confidence to stand for office. This applied to retired people as well. In short, the only major source of working-class representatives were trade union leaders who would be helped by their unions. This situation is reflected in data on the class background of LCC candidates in the 1961 election.

Table 6.*   *Social class – all candidates, 1961 election*

| Party | Percentage in social class | | | | | Unclassified | | Not available % | No. (= 100%) |
	I	II	III	IV	V	Re-tired	House-wife		
Conservative	54.0	23.8	9.5	—	—	2.4	9.5	0.8	126
Labour	27.0	28.6	18.2	0.8	1.6	11.1	12.7	—	126
Liberal	37.6	29.0	10.1	1.5	—	1.5	14.5	5.8	69
Others	11.1	16.7	33.4	5.5	—	—	5.5	27.8	18
ALL %	38.0	26.5	14.2	0.9	0.6	5.3	11.6	2.9	100
No.	130	89	48	3	2	18	39	10	339

Class I: Professional (barristers, architects, business executives, etc.); Class II: Intermediate (teachers, draughtsmen, shopkeepers, etc.); Class III: Skilled (toolmakers, bricklayers, shop assistants, etc.); Class IV: Partly skilled (hall porters, window cleaners, bus conductors, etc.); Class V: Unskilled (night watchmen, dockers, builders' laborers, etc.).

* From Sharpe, *Metropolis Votes*, p. 39. This table is reproduced by permission of the author and the Greater London Group, London School Economics. In addition, there is evidence to suggest that the Labour leadership on the Council made a conscious effort to recruit middle class candidates.

Councilors then tended to be middle class and this likely helped account for the similarity of their views on planning, especially the emphasis on semi-urban environments and the concomitant preference for certain housing styles.[1]

To summarize to this point in the analysis: arguments have been presented to show that members typically shared a deliberator role which placed emphasis on discussion of the merits of alternative courses of action as the appropriate mode of Council decision-making. In the subsequent discussion the role was treated as a set of behavioral dispositions, a set of 'paths' within which councilors viewed the balance of costs and benefits (particularly as they arose from their political environment) of delegating or exercising authority. It was argued that the former was acceptable in terms of

[1] Aldermen were not recruited in the same manner as elected councilors being selected by the parties on the Council. However, the points about the class bias of the pool of those available to serve would apply. As to planners, their adherence to the consensus is to be largely explained by the fact that the consensus constituted the principal substance of the professional values they were committed to serve.

the implications of the role prescriptions as long as members doing the delegating perceived that those to whom effective authority was to be given shared their policy ends and their conception of the public interest.

Several points remain to be discussed. First is the behavior of those to whom effective authority was delegated; until now we have concentrated on analyzing the factors associated with delegation. Second is the relationship between partisan and non-partisan behavior on one hand and delegation and its associated factors on the other.

From the preceding analysis it follows directly that those members to whom effective authority was delegated tended to act as deliberators, i.e. follow the role prescriptions. For them it was not a question of whether to exercise authority or not; that had already been decided in effect by their assigning considerable value to intrinsic and public service benefits. The principal determinants of their behavior then were the role prescriptions.[1] The senior planners who played an active part in planning decisions also tended to treat them as problems to be analyzed rather than as an exercise in overcoming differences in interests which were to be taken as givens of the situation. This followed from their conception of the public interest, their professional training and the political world in which they operated. Unlike bureaucrats in American cities, their need to take positions which would increase or protect their standing with the citizenry was virtually non-existent. Those whose cooperation they sought, particularly the more active representatives, would have been largely insensitive to any demonstration of public support for the views of officers.

Turning to the second point, the relationship between the member in his deliberator role and decisions taken on a non-partisan basis presents no problem; indeed this has been the implicit context of the preceding discussion. However, in the case of decisions taken on a partisan basis, the impact of the role and its related behaviors may not be so clear. Clearly, in partisan decisions, it is the majority party leaders and particularly the Chairman, who are the principal actors. What requires explanation is the relationship between the fact of this party leadership and the deliberator role and attendant factors. We are now in a position to add to the analysis of the political parties offered above and, moreover, confront the difficult task of explaining the majority party's extensive reliance on senior officers for advice. To argue that a disciplined majority party would simply command officers' advice as being useful to reaching decisions does not explain why the advice would be regularly taken by party members without careful and

---

[1] Of course, these members did not invariably act as deliberators. There were 'situational' factors which also shaped their behavior; see Chapter 7. These situational factors are in part another way of discussing members' relationship with their political environment. The incentives arising from the environment have been shown in general not to point to behavior at variance with the role prescriptions. However, there is obviously a good deal more to be said here: satisfactory theory would suggest when departures from role prescriptions would occur and why.

continuing consideration of its likely impact on their political positions, as was in fact the case on the LCC. In both cases, the existence of party leadership and the reliance on advice of senior officers, we are again dealing with delegation to those with perceived competence, time and interest, by members who occupied a deliberator role and whose calculus of costs and benefits pointed to such delegation. And again, as with decisions taken on a non-partisan basis, it would appear that (majority) party leaders and senior officers most often reached decisions through analytic processes, rather than bargained solutions which reflected the interests of diverse constituents and groups associated with the party. The principal contrast to non-partisan decisions was that the focus of discussion was somewhat different; the concern for the city as a whole as given direction by the consensus on planning means and ends was seen through the filter of party advantage. This was the case for example in the World's End decision where the second Chairman was concerned both with adhering to appropriate city-wide planning standards and trying to score some partisan advantage over the Conservatives in the borough and on the Council.

CONCLUSION

Some of the basic features of the process of land use decision within the LCC were shaped by the certainty of the political environment of representatives. In comparison to American cities, the extent to which effective authority was delegated and decisions reached by deliberation was great. An analytic mode of coordination predominated. The explanation for these differences is to be found in the complex interactions between characteristics of the political environment, representatives' assessment of them, and their legislative role. For large American cities the crucial consideration in explaining the manner in which effort is coordinated in reaching decisions is the uncertainty of the political environment. Careful study would no doubt reveal that the decentralization and bargaining characteristic of such cities is related, albeit in complex ways, to the comparatively greater uncertainty of the political environment. For London, the affective dimension of the typical role of councilors, the balance of incentives pointing to delegation and the deliberative behavior of those to whom effective authority was delegated all depended to an important degree on the certainty of the political environment.

7. THE AUTHORITY AND THE APPLICANT: PROBLEMS OF CHOICE

It might be expected that given the legal powers concentrated in the planning authority, the relatively certain political environment of representatives, and the mode of coordination, decisions on applications for permission to develop would have been simply announced by the authority without any extensive contact with applicants. The authority would seem to have been in a position to define its ends and to ask that applicants include these considerations without change in their proposals. This was the case in many applications for small-scale development, i.e. development which would have little impact on the surrounding areas. Here the procedure by and large was to apply in a straightforward manner the standards laid down in the *Development Plan*. However, with applications for large-scale development and, specifically, those submitted by large commercial developers and by borough housing authorities, as one planning officer put it,

no application was straightforward. Developers were always seeking variations in the standards. There was always plenty of negotiation.

On its side, the planning authority was also interested in negotiating. Applications for large-scale development represented opportunities to change land use patterns that were difficult to turn down. The authority often found itself not simply laying down rules for development but trying to convince applicants to modify their proposals.

The negotiations, particularly on the large-scale developments that are of concern here, revolved around the content of the constraints the authority would impose on applicants. These constraints set additional ends for applicants besides those they would serve if there were no planning system. This applied to both borough housing authorities and private developers. As a result, applicants, for example, were forced to consider ends other than commercial viability or additions to the housing stock of the borough. The constraints were for the authority one means by which to achieve its general purposes. In large-scale developments, then, the authority had two closely related tasks. It needed to formulate its own views on the application, i.e. define the content of the constraints, and in the negotiations it needed to convince applicants of the soundness of its views. The latter followed

141

directly from the fact that applicants, whether public or private, were quite independent in their decision to build or not. Permission to alter the land use pattern was not sufficient; they needed incentives to do so.

The case studies suggest that in fact the planning authority's record in negotiations was uneven. In both cases, applicants persuaded the LCC at various junctures to accept aspects of developments about which it had strong doubts. A principal feature of these negotiations was that the authority was not a forceful advocate. In the nature of the case, it had to make some concessions to applicants. However, the cases indicate that the authority made some concessions not out of a need to get applicants to act on the permission but as a consequence of its difficulty in deciding what it wished to see done. This would appear to have been true in the St Giles development with regard to the extent of the office space allowed and in the World's End case with both the level of density and open space required.

The authority's limited skill in advocacy stemmed in large measure from what might be called its 'intellectual' problems. Applicants were able to capitalize on the resultant ambiguity in its position on applications. Moreover, in consequence of its intellectual difficulties, the authority made operational choices in development control which were ill-suited to achieving such goals as it had defined. In general, the authority's difficulties with applicants were part of a broader phenomenon, viz. the problems it had in relating its choice of means in development control to a series of policy goals that would define the ends of planning. The principal concern in the following discussion is to examine the form of these intellectual difficulties, their roots and their consequences.

By focusing on intellectual difficulties, the implication is that 'political' problems both in and outside of the authority were at a minimum. This indeed is a central conclusion to be drawn from Chapter 6: the autonomy of representatives and the prevalence of delegation and deliberation meant that the authority was little constrained either by external forces or internal disagreements in defining its position on applications. The planning agency was in a position to order means and ends in terms of a consideration of the substance of planning and, taking note of the need to negotiate, was in a position to enforce those orderings. An extension of the analysis presented in Chapter 6 (and 5) which supports this conclusion will be our first task with a discussion of the authority's intellectual difficulties succeeding. Arguments about the latter must be seen in the context of powerful economic forces which helped shape land use patterns in the city. These have been outlined in the introductions to the case studies. It is likely that any public authority would have great difficulty in controlling the workings of a highly developed land use market with anything like complete facility.[1]

[1] See Chapter 8 for additional discussion of this point.

EXTERNAL AND INTERNAL CONSTRAINTS

The predominant mode of negotiation between authority and applicant was discussion based on or in search of common substantive principals.[1] While some bargains were struck, the predominant style of settlement was through cooperation rather than contention and thus the relative political influence of the actors was less important than their persuasiveness. The clarity with which ends were defined was consequently of paramount importance. Planning politics revolved around the relative abilities of participants to argue their case.

The World's End case offers evidence to support this description. In general, applicants spent a good deal of time trying to convince the planning authority that their requests were consistent with good planning. In the Chelsea case in particular, there was little attempt to exert influence which relied on inducements extraneous to the matter at hand. Among other things, the Borough Council did not attempt a public campaign aimed at convincing the planning authority that its (the authority's) course of action was politically unwise. Similarly, there is no clear evidence that developers were in the habit of aiding the cause of a political party in return for sympathetic consideration of an application. Developers might induce a member of the Planning Committee to bring their application to the attention of a planner who might be sympathetic in negotiations, or they might attempt to promote a quicker review of their proposals. The overwhelming amount of contact, however, was with planners and other officers where discussion of the various features of the proposed development was the order of the day.

An examination of the situation of the metropolitan boroughs and of private developers provides additional support for the argument. If the Chelsea case is representative, the tactics of the boroughs, apart from reasoned argument, appear to have been limited to the following: working for an inquiry before the Minister in order to take the matter out of the hands of the planning authority; asking members of the LCC who were elected from the borough to keep track of their case within the LCC and to present the borough's arguments; trying to speak with the Minister directly, or perhaps with one of his representatives. The position of the boroughs was succinctly put by one of the senior officers of the Chelsea Council who, when asked why the borough did not attempt to strike a bargain with the LCC, replied 'what have we got to bargain with?'

Commercial developers also had limited means with which to bargain. The St Giles case unfortunately clouds the issue with 'extraneous' legal problems, but even here, aside from using the LCC's legal complications

[1] The term 'substantive' is important. It is possible, as Banfield points out ('Note on a Conceptual Scheme', p. 306) that cooperation can take place on the basis of an agreed-upon procedural principle or the 'rules of the game'.

as a lever, the developer did not resort to other means of influence. His ability to do so was limited. In general, whether developers were business corporations seeking a new home or commercial development companies, they did not have the great involvement in local politics characteristic of their American counterparts which might be used to further their interests. For example, their episodic involvement via applications for development made it difficult to offer 'side-payments' to the authority in return for concessions; their ability to make concessions in other areas of local politics or even on a future development was limited.

Commercial developers, however, did have some resources at their disposal with which to bargain. Aside from bribery, which is difficult to ascertain but which seems to have been minor in incidence,[1] the developer could use the following devices. He could serve the planning authority with a purchase notice which, upon ministerial confirmation, would require the authority to purchase his property.[2] He could do so if refusal of permission or the conditions attached to a permission prevented him from obtaining a 'reasonably beneficial use' of his land.[3] Since the property might be very expensive, and the planning authority's funds were limited, the threat of a purchase notice could be used to extract concessions. Along similar lines, a developer who wished a particular type of permission on a large site might threaten to make use of an existing permission for a section of the site which was never used.[4] Here, the authority might grant concessions on the basis of its desire to see the area treated as a whole. Finally, as in the St Giles case, a developer might offer to assemble land which the authority would like to see redeveloped as a whole, but for which purchase it lacked powers (or resources). All of these worked as inducements because the authority lacked some measure of legal powers or because of shortage of funds. To this degree, concessions made by the authority did not stem from intellectual difficulties. However, since in the nature of the case the

[1] This is based on responses by planners and members to questions about the extent of bribery. They came up with one case in which a Chairman of the Planning Committee was thought to be acting improperly and was later exonerated. No other cases were referred to. However, there have been cases in other cities (Manchester, Cardiff, Teeside and Glasgow) where members of planning committees have been prosecuted for taking bribes. Of course, using incidents which have become public knowledge through prosecution is hardly a satisfactory way of estimating the extent of bribery, nor is asking the targets.

[2] This is assuming he is applying for permission on property which he in fact owns. As noted earlier, a developer may apply for planning permission for a site he does not own. This is often done to see whether it would be worthwhile to purchase. Previous to 1959, a developer could apply for permission without notifying the owner of the site.

[3] Cullingworth, *Town and Country Planning*, p. 86.

[4] A planning permission does not attach to the person who applies for it. Rather, it applies to the land so that anyone, if he purchases the land, can develop in accordance with the permission. The 1968 Planning Act appears to make this practice rather difficult since it requires that detailed proposals must be submitted to the authority within three years of outline permission being granted. If this does not happen, the permission apparently lapses. See Sharp, *Ministry*, p. 150 and *The Times*, 17 December 1969.

possibility of using such levers was limited, an understanding of the authority's lack of success in negotiations must focus on additional and more pervasive factors.

The nature of the relationship between authority and applicant followed from the characteristics of London politics described in preceding chapters. The authority was largely able to disregard any attempts by applicants to inject what it interpreted as non-planning considerations. While applicants may not have cooperated by choice, they lacked by and large other alternatives. The applicants could convince the authority of the desirability of their own ends, provide courses of action when the authority was in doubt, or convince the authority that its own ends should be ordered in a different fashion. The striking thing about the London situation was that, unlike American cities, those promoting development did not think automatically in terms of trades which would bring in considerations outside the matter at hand. The characteristic style was to discuss the merits of the particular project and to negotiate within its boundaries, not to offer inducements or promote costs to the authority which were extraneous to the case under consideration.

Internal decision-making

The case studies reveal instances of disagreements among those to whom effective authority had been delegated. For example, in the St Giles case the planners and engineers involved held different views about the appropriate width for the roundabout. In the World's End case, the Chairman of the Planning Committee and the planners disagreed as to how large a concession should be made to the Chelsea Council. On the basis of such instances, it might be thought that a principal reason for the authority's difficulties in negotiations and more generally in relating means to ends was to be found in the structure of decision-making within the Council. In particular, the need to gain the agreement of a variety of organizational members might result in decisions on applications which would provide little specific guidance for planners in negotiations or contradictory guidance. It is clear that the need to coordinate the several participants did on occasion produce the kind of results noted. However, this would be a significant barrier to defining sufficiently specific and consistent decisions only if the usual mode of dealing with internal disagreements was bargaining. But, as argued in Chapter 6, those members to whom effective authority was delegated tended to follow the prescriptions of the deliberator role. The principal exception to resolution of differences through discussion was on some of the occasions when officers other than planners played a major part in a decision. As the St Giles case suggests, both engineers and comptrollers had sufficiently different approaches to land use problems so that on occasion

145

deliberative approaches proved inadequate and bargaining was resorted to. Again, the St Giles case is illustrative, with the changes in the width of the roundabout being the particular example.

ORIENTATIONS TO POLICY CHOICE

The planning authority's ability to set its own ends and define appropriate means for achieving them was not limited by a need to make concessions to influential actors outside the Council nor to applicants, nor did internal decision-making processes prevent analysis of what was at issue. Rather, the manner in which planners and members conceived of the problems of choice posed by applications for permission to develop made it impossible for the authority to adequately cope with the complexities involved in relating development control decisions to its broad purposes. The appropriate place to start an analysis of these intellectual difficulties is with a description of the considerations the authority took into account in reaching a decision, particularly the purposes development control was designed to serve. This will amplify the earlier discussion of the consensus on planning principles.

Substantive considerations

The principal statement of the consensus on London planning as it applied to development control was to be found in the *Development Plan*. It was this document that was to guide the authority in setting the constraints for applicants. The *Plan* specified several standards to be used in the control of development. These control standards for daylighting and plot ratio were not meant to be ends in themselves, but rather means to some higher order ends.[1] The standards were to be varied as other factors in a development impinged. There was, however, no indication given as to the principles which the variations were to follow. Certainly the objectives that development control was to serve, as set down in the *Plan*, were of little help in this regard.

The job of development control as stated by the *Plan* was

to ensure...through cooperation with and between developers that, as far as possible, all new development in the Administrative County conforms to the general principles set out above and makes its contribution to a better London.[2]

These general principles were, in the first instance, a statement of the basic principles of planning for London as formulated by the Barlow Com-

---

[1] *Analysis*, pp. 237 and 239. Density zones were also control standards. They do seem to have been thought of as ends in themselves. On density zones see below. The use zones also appear to have been thought of as ends in themselves.

[2] *Analysis*, p. 5.

mission and adopted by the Government, i.e. the restraint of London and the dispersal of its population and industry. More specifically, under the heading 'main objectives' statements like the following are found.

(i) Character and Function
To preserve the best of existing London, to respect and develop its structure and major uses and to remedy its manifest defects, so enhancing its individual character and improving its efficiency as the Commonwealth center, the capital city, a commercial and industrial center, a port and a home for millions.
(ii) Communities
To recognize the existing community structure of London and, as circumstances allow, to intensify its character by developing a system of communities, each comprising several neighborhoods and being as self-contained as possible without endangering the sense of healthy interdependence between them.
(v) To provide sites for houses and flats for those in urgent need and in association with these to provide sites for ancillary purposes such as shops, markets, churches and licensed premises.[1]

It would be rather difficult to use these 'objectives' as statements of the ends which development control was to serve since, in practice, it would not be easy to tell just what any of the statements called for. However, the goals for population density and for open space were in fact more adequately defined than those mentioned, i.e. progress towards them could be measured. But, in the *Plan* there was no explicit consideration of how these goals were to be related to the others noted above. For example, was control of density to be relaxed to provide 'sites for houses and flats for those in urgent need'? We shall return to the general point below. For the moment, the important consideration is that the *Plan* set out a large number of considerations in the form of both ends and means which the authority needed to consider in reaching a decision on a development control application. In addition, there were also a series of specific proposals for such uses as schools and roads, the St Giles traffic scheme being one example. Insofar as applications affected these proposals for capital development, some evaluation might be required about the importance of the latter *vis-à-vis* what might be gained or indeed lost from the former. This was one of the issues presented by the St Giles application. Therefore, especially in larger developments, the authority often had to consider not only the general guidance provided by the *Plan*, but the proposals of the Council itself for capital improvements.

Important additional sources of considerations for the authority were to be found in the values instilled during the professional training of planners and other officers and in the policies that were announced subsequent to the *Plan*. Both of these served either to interpret some of the very general

[1] See *Administrative County of London Development Plan* (London, 1951), *Statement*, pp. 1–3.

aims of the *Plan* or to supplement particular aspects of it.[1] As an example
of the latter, the civic design criteria noted in both of the case studies are
to be found in a policy adopted by the authority subsequent to the approval
of the *Development Plan*. These criteria were an attempt to give substance
in one area to the idea of promoting amenity. The policy of holding down
office development in the central area – discussed in the St Giles case – was
also a policy adopted by the LCC after the *Plan* was approved; it added
additional ends for the authority to serve by going substantially beyond
what was only vaguely implied by the consensus in terms of a central area
policy.

As for professional values, in the World's End case the question of how
open space was to be handled turned on professional judgement.[2] Presumably
professional criteria, however determined, required that all of the space be
provided in the first phase of the development, i.e. on the Cremorne site
and the adjoining area, rather than allowing some to be provided in subsequent development of the Lots Road area. Similarly, the attempt by planners
to see that the central island of the roundabout at St Giles Circus was left
without a building – insofar as it was aimed at preserving or enhancing
the existing view – must be counted as an attempt to apply professional
criteria, in this case of an architectural kind.

Another source of considerations that the authority took into account
in arriving at control decisions was the Ministry's policies in various planning
matters and, on occasion, its decision on aspects of particular applications.
Several points are worth noting about the Ministry's role. First, the Ministry
played a very limited part in the reaching of decisions on individual applications for development. Except for occasions when a grant or permission
was required under the Planning Acts, the planning authority was autonomous. Second, on the level of planning policy the Ministry played a
larger part. Having approved and indeed revised the *Development Plan* to
its own specifications, the Ministry was committed to the broad principles
set down there.[3] However, as the *Plan* could not cover non-local aspects
of planning for London, that is those that arose from national considerations
such as the relationship between the south eastern region (of which London

---

[1] The Town and Country Planning Act says: 'Where an application is made to the local planning
authority for planning permission, that authority in dealing with the application, shall have regard
to the provisions of the Development Plan, so far as material to the application, and to any other
material considerations' (Town and Country Planning Act, 1962, Part II, paragraph 17.)

[2] Of course, the *Development Plan* itself was based very much on what can loosely be called
professional criteria. The basic features of the *Plan* were a product of the training and preferences
of a select group of planners, and especially of Abercrombie. See Chapter 2. As well, professional
values were to be found in the planning policies the LCC adopted.

[3] It should be noted that in arriving at decisions in public inquiries on a planning appeal, the
Ministry does not feel bound to uphold a development plan. Appeals are at least partly conceived
of as enforcing considerations of equity, i.e. as having a judicial emphasis as well as a policy
emphasis. See Mandelker, *Green Belts*.

is a part) and the rest of the country, the Ministry regularly made its views known on such matters to the authority. Similarly, the Ministry also set out its views on such questions as more intensive use of land and the development of town centers; these views might derive from national policy consideration, from the successful experiences of local planning authorities or from its own research. In general, Ministry pronouncements and policies supplemented the goals of the *Plan* or interpreted them in light of national considerations. As a result, in some cases they were at variance with policies of the LCC as happened, for example, in the World's End case on the matter of higher densities.

Insofar as Ministry policy and local policy did not agree, some of the difficulty the planning authority had in ordering its ends and selecting means to serve them would be attributable to the former authority's independent influence. While the necessary evidence is absent to establish with any accuracy the extent to which the Ministry advocated competing policies for London planning, two factors, aside from the existence of the consensus, suggest that the Ministry's behavior was not an important source of the authority's difficulties. First, the authority had substantial problems deciding what to do even when competing policies were not evident. Second, the Chelsea case demonstrates that the authority felt quite capable of taking an independent line in disputes with the Ministry.[1] While this concern for independence clearly did not eliminate possible contradictions in policy – the Ministry did have substantial resources – it does suggest that the LCC attempted to interpret Ministry policy according to its own lights.

Economizing

The principal task of the planning authority was to translate the various considerations which were to guide land use control into decisions on particular applications, i.e. into definitions of the constraints applicants must be convinced to observe. The process of translation principally involved relating control decisions to some set of ends. The burden of designing decisions fell largely on planners, and such other officers whose competence was required, in consultation with those few representatives who took an active part. The evidence of the case studies reveals, however, that those involved did not cope successfully with the problems presented. In practice this meant either that the authority entered negotiations with applicants unclear about what constraints it wished to set or that it selected constraints that were ill-suited to serving its principal policy aims. Examples of the former have already been given. The latter can be seen in the use of liberal

---

[1] This observation was confirmed by a former junior Minister in the Ministry of Housing and Local Government. See also Young's comment on this in terms of the independence of the London Labour Party. Young, 'Political Party Organization'.

planning permissions for office space to promote the road-building program, as illustrated at St Giles, while at the same time pursuing a policy of reducing traffic congestion. While such permissions might stretch resources for road-building, any substantial number of them (and it was done for several important intersections) would clearly be self-defeating as more traffic would be generated at precisely those points where the aim was to reduce congestion.[1] No serious attempt was made to ascertain at what point major costs in congestion would be incurred nor even whether the wider thoroughfares could accommodate increases in traffic to provide even the same level of movement as existed previously. The course of the negotiations detailed in the case studies suggests that the authority reworked its position more in response to the arguments of applicants and less in response to its own continuing calculations about how decisions on the applications might be used in the service of some broad ends.

Demonstration that the planning authority had the difficulties noted can be undertaken in another manner. Consider the question: what would be required for the planning authority to be able to choose with any accuracy and consistency means to serve its ends and concomitantly to have a clearer idea of the constraints it wished to see applicants meet? To the degree that the authority did not possess the requirements, which shall collectively be called 'economizing', it must have been unable to cope with the problems presented. Looking at the problem in this manner enables us to supplement the examples provided by the case studies and to show that, in general, the authority consistently fell short in the manner already indicated.

The form of the argument needs to be made explicit. Economizing is construed as referring to attributes possessed by members of an organization, which may be held to a greater or lesser degree, and which, where appropriate, may be exercised with greater or lesser skill. Extent of skill and possession taken together indicate the degree to which an organization economizes. The more an organization economizes, the greater its efficiency, which in this context means that the organization can define appropriate means within the development control process to serve its ends and by extension be relatively clear about what constraints it wishes applicants to serve. Insofar as this last is the case, then the authority would be a stronger and consequently more successful advocate in control negotiations.[2] All but the last statement is considered to be a matter of definition, i.e. they are taken to be analytical truths. The initial question posed – 'what would be required...' – is here treated then not as a question to be answered by

---

[1] As a matter of fact it depends on whether all that is being built is a larger building or one that will accommodate more people. The LCC operated on the principle that more space meant more people.

[2] The authority could be a forceful advocate by simply selecting in an arbitrary fashion some set of means and pursuing them without great interest in the consequences. That however would be quite at variance with the basic tasks it had defined for itself.

empirical observation but by an assertion of the order of: to get A you need B because A *is* B. Although somewhat simplified, this is the type of reasoning employed. The last statement is treated as a simple empirical relationship as it concerns the determinants of the outcome of negotiations between two parties. What is required then is to ascertain the extent to which the LCC, or more accurately its principal members, engaged in economizing. In the whole discussion matters of definition need to be carefully distinguished from empirical problems. This is particularly important in the discussion of problems of rational choice where analytical and empirical truths are often confused.[1]

As just noted, given that planning is purposive behavior, i.e. activity directed toward the achievement of an end or ends, and this much at least seems to be agreed upon,[2] it can then be treated as synonymous with attempts to be efficient and to economize. Somewhat differently stated, if we agree that planning is meant to replace (or supplement) a market system, the identification becomes clearer. A market is an economizing mechanism[3] and therefore that which replaces it performs the same function, whether well or ill, consciously or otherwise. Planning *is* economizing. As long as both economizing and efficiency are understood as being concerned with problems of choice where multiple goals are present and not simply with a narrow notion of saving resources then no major problems should arise. Efficiency and economizing are concepts which can be applied to *any* kind of choice problem and are not confined to economic problems as these are generally understood.[4]

The informing assumptions of economizing are that 'public policy problems can best be solved by trying to understand them'[5] and that policy choices are problems of *allocation* of scarce resources. The central concept is efficiency which may be defined in its most general sense as the 'ratio

---

[1] For example, Lindblom's conclusions concerning the problems of synoptic decision-making may be simply restatements of assertions about the intellectual capacity of human beings. It is not at all clear that analytical truths about *individuals* is the appropriate way to attack problems of *collective* decision-making. However, the important point is that Lindblom is not clear whether this is the form of his argument, or whether his analysis is built upon *observations* of collective decision-making. Or both. But then the problem is to disentangle the arguments. See *The Intelligence of Democracy* and (with David Braybrooke) *A Strategy of Decision*.

[2] See Yehezkel Dror, *Policy-Making Re-Examined* (San Francisco, 1968), Part II.

[3] Cf. Dahl and Lindblom, *Politics, Economics and Welfare* (New York, 1953); Paul Deising, *Reason in Society* (Urbana, Ill., 1962), Chapters 1 and 2; and Chapter 8 below.

[4] See particularly, Ludwig von Mises, *Epistemological Problems of Economics* (Princeton, 1960); Alan Schick 'The Road to PPB: The Stages of Budget Reform', in Robert T. Golembiewski (ed.), *Public Budgeting and Finance* (Itasca, Ill., 1968); Dahl and Lindblom, *Politics*, Chapter 1. In general see Diesing, *Reason*.

[5] Albert O. Hirschman and Charles E. Lindblom, 'Economic Development, Research and Development, Policy Making: Some Converging Views', in Etzioni (ed.), *A Sociological Reader on Complex Organizations*, 2nd ed. (New York, 1969), p. 92. It should be noted that Hirschman and Lindblom are not characterizing their own views but those held by others.

between valued input and valued output'.[1] This concept provides the logical core of economizing, and discussion below of additional attributes is meant to draw out some of the implications. In organizational terms, planning is an attempt to institutionalize efficiency by directing the efforts of members of the organization to the definition of organizational goals (valued outputs) and the least costly means of achieving them (valued inputs).[2]

Professional planners in the economizing conceptions are the members of an organization that carry the principal burden of analysis. They have what might be termed an economizing mentality, i.e. an outlook on policy choice which sensitizes them to the central problems in linking means to ends in an efficient manner. This outlook is the basic constituent of economizing. It is in the service of this conception that the particular skills and data noted below are put to use. Some of the hallmarks of such a mentality are an awareness of the need to: (1) define ends empirically so that progress toward them can be measured; (2) evaluate the correspondence between means and ends, i.e. examine the complex chain between a policy choice and its consequences in light of the ends being aimed at; (3) take into account a 'wide' range of values involved in the decision under consideration and not to treat whole classes of direct consequences as being costless; (4) be aware that ends are often logically competing and that as a consequence choices must be made between serving one or another, or at least giving up some of one end to achieve some of another; (5) be aware that all ends compete because of scarcity of resources and that therefore all choices are costly in terms of opportunities foregone;[3] (6) concomitantly, see that ends need to be weighted, and that therefore policy choices are between combinations of ranked ends.[4] Overall, economizers see that the central problem of public policy involves *choices* in how we use our resources in the pursuit of a variety of goals. They are aware that the choice is never between pursuing any possible end to complete achievement, but of choosing combinations of ends from the myriad things we would like to do with our limited resources.

The perspective on cities logically associated with planning as economizing is to see them as dynamic organisms in which interdependency is the key factor. Cities are seen to be networks of interdependent uses of space in which alterations in the physical (or socio-economic) environment in one area will produce effects in other areas. The emphasis on interdependency of land use parallels several of the basic concerns of the economizing ap-

---

[1] Dahl and Lindblom, *Politics*, p. 29. For present purposes allocation encompasses decisions about *any* type of policy ends including explicitly distributive ones. Efficiency in this view is 'grand' efficiency. See Peter Steiner, 'The Public Sector and the Public Interest' in Robert Haveman and Julius Margolis, *Public Expenditures and Policy Analysis* (Chicago, 1970).

[2] Or alternatively, getting the most of valued output per unit input.

[3] In economic theory these are known as opportunity costs.

[4] For additional discussion, see Harry Johnson, 'The Economic Approach to Social Questions', *The Public Interest*, 12 (1968), 68–79 and Diesing, *Reason*, pp. 43–56.

proach. The fact that alterations in land use in one part of the city have repercussions in other parts indicates the likelihood that many choices in the service of some particular end or ends will have negative consequences for the achievement of other ends. This in turn means that some value must be assigned to the various ends so that, given their competitive quality, choices can be selected which will tend to maximize gains. Also, the fact that individual choices have consequences beyond the policy ends under consideration suggests the need to trace out the various major level effects and thus to gather the appropriate data to do so. There are other links between economizing and the dynamic view of cities but it is sufficient to emphasize that both focus on complex interdependencies, in one case of land use, in the other of ends and means. When economizing is applied to land use the very stuff of the interlacing of ends and means *is* interdependence in the use of land.

An interest in certain kinds of expertise is also logically associated with the presence of the mentality. In order for an authority to evaluate its present decisions in terms of its policy ends, data would be required on the impact of similar decisions in the past. Some type of monitoring system would be necessary the running of which would require some knowledge of the handling of social science data. As well, in order for an authority to evaluate with any degree of precision alternative courses of action, including the proposals of applicants for development permission, it would need to be able to predict the likely consequences of various alternatives. Again social science competence would be important for rendering existing data in policy-oriented forms, e.g. in models of housing markets or traffic flows, as well as for analysis of the alternatives in light of what theoretical knowledge exists. Finally, planners and a planning agency would also have an interest in techniques for refining the consideration of alternative decisions, broadly the tools growing out of economic analysis. These might include the more sophisticated techniques of cost–benefit analysis and program budgeting.[1]

The conception of planning in London

Both the perspective on cities that underlay the consensus on planning ideas for London and the concomitant view of policy choice differed from the economizing conception outlined above. An essentially static view of cities prevailed which did not point to complex interdependencies; hence the competitive quality of policy decisions was obscured. It is, however, easier to state than to demonstrate that the planning ideas did not emphasize interdependency. In the first instance, it must be clear that at the very

[1] For additional discussion of economizing, particularly on the possibility of choices being made in this manner, see Chapter 8.

broadest level the idea of an interrelation between jobs, housing and open space was in fact present in the original advisory plans prepared by Abercrombie, as well as in the *Development Plan* for the County of London. However, this was the level of either the whole metropolitan area or of the County and consisted mostly of the reasonably elementary perception (but not perhaps elementary at the time) that employment and housing are closely related. However, there was little discussion about interdependencies *within* the urban area itself, i.e. how changes in one part of the city would affect activity in another part, or other activities within the same area. The focus was the metropolitan area or the city as a whole, rather than the relationship between one part of the city and another.[1] Indeed, this latter would have required considerably more information than Abercrombie and his associates had available at the time, as well as certain skills they lacked.

If we interpret the Abercrombie plans and the *Development Plan* as essentially regulatory, a similar conclusion may be reached on the conception of policy choice. The plans were, at least in part, designed to enforce a standard of environment. There was relatively little concern about the effects the enforcement of these standards would have, for example, on movement in London. The use of land would follow criteria which were based not on a consideration of the relationship between land uses, but which were essentially environmental standards that would be applicable to land 'anywhere'.[2] It was as if a building was being designed and the standards were set down with minimum consideration of the kinds of traffic (people and goods) which would be moving through the building: aesthetic criteria would dominate. A sense that the enforcement of these environmental standards might be costly in terms of other ends and that choices might have to be made between the standards and the other ends was largely absent. In general the Abercrombie plans and the *Development Plan* concentrated on active ends, i.e. the goals noted in the discussion of the consensus, and had little to say about the relationship between these ends and a host of contextual ends that might come up in any actual land use decision or to which the authority might have attached value even at the time when the *Plan* was constructed.

A similar analysis can be applied to the development control procedures. They were not designed for consideration of alternative proposals for the use of a particular site. For example, the planning authority when faced with an application which conformed to commercial zoning standards was not to say that shops might be preferable to offices but must accept it, assuming other criteria were satisfied. As the cases show, the authority did

---

[1] See Foley, *Controlling London's Growth*, p. 172.

[2] Abercrombie thought in terms of one density level for all London. See *County of London Plan*.

indeed on occasion attempt to alter the content of applications by trying to alter the balance of land uses. However, the orthodoxy was clear.

Planning legislation is not designed to foster consideration of alternatives. If the LCC wants to use the land for something else other than what the application is for, about the only way we can do anything is to get some local authority [the LCC itself or a borough council] to purchase the land and amend the *Development Plan*. We just can't say that the land ought to be used another way. This wouldn't stand up at inquiry.

The traditional view of the planner is that he is to take a look at an application and if it fits the [development] control standards then it is to be passed.

The aim, as these comments by a councilor and a planner indicate, was, again, to enforce certain environmental standards. Planning in general and development control in particular was 'simply' to serve a particular set of ends.

An additional aspect of the thinking about London planning is important to consider. There appears to have been a real reluctance to attempt to empirically define policy ends. This was reflected in the injunction of the Ministry to phrase the objectives of development plans in general terms.[1] Moreover, development plans were, as already noted, supposed to serve as general guides to decision in development control not as precise statements of ends. The actual decisions were to take account of a variety of (unspecified) considerations which were somehow to be brought together with the relevant regulations and objectives of the plan.

The best way to summarize the preceding discussion is to say that practitioners of London planning and those actively concerned with its operation did not focus on the allocative functions of land use control. For some of these, planning was largely a regulatory process in the service of a social vision. For others, the regulatory process was to be the place where the social vision was constantly to be interpreted. In either case the allocation decisions that were continually being made did not receive significant attention. The first conception was associated with a more rigid view of the use of the development control machinery: it was to be used to enforce the *Development Plan* which was the concrete expression of the vision. The second conception gave full play to the concern for flexibility and tended to be more creative. In either case the skills called for on the part of officers involved in development control, and particularly planners, were not those designed to cope with allocation problems. In the narrow view, the planner was to be an administrator applying rules already laid out. The usefulness of technical expertise of any description would be at a minimum. In the second, he was to be the principal interpreter and exponent of a set of agreed upon values. This conception of the planners' professional role was

[1] Mandelker, *Green Belts*, p. 52.

set out in some detail by a member with long experience on the Planning Committee.[1]

Planners are professional philosophers, not technical experts. It's probably because of the history of the setting up of the planning department. There were practically no professional planners when we started so we had to use the existing Council officers. So, we sent them to post-graduate courses...Planners are imaginative philosophers. This may have been built up because of the kind of men who were put into the roles by necessity. This has persisted even when we had trained planners.

Planning under the Labour Party dominated LCC was about changing London as a matter of principle...The Town Planning Act came about because of the Labour Party seeing changes were needed in the face of London in the public interest. Planners were to interpret these principles.

While it is not clear precisely what talents planners were to have in order to interpret the planning principles, the emphasis would appear to have been more on some quality of judgement which would come from experience rather than on technical skills. Associated with the limited concern with problems of allocation, and the concomitant role of planners, was the lack of emphasis by the planning authority on the collection of data about the city and on the development of the associated skills. Support for this observation may be found in the history of the St Giles development. As noted, a striking point about the case was that the authority lacked data on the impact of the office building on congestion in the area. In general, the authority lacked this kind of data and planners were not trained to provide it.[2]

The applicants

While the planning authority had difficulty in formulating the content of the development control constraints and thus was often a weak advocate, applicants for planning permission had less difficulty in defining their ends. They had fewer goals to serve and these goals were better defined than those of the authority. In general, applicants reaped the advantages of repetitive calculations; their goals tended to be stable and the situations in which they attempted to achieve them were generally similar. As their calculation problems were comparatively simple, they could argue their position persuasively and with clarity. In short, they were relatively successful economizers.

A distinction needs to be made between commercial developers and borough housing authorities. The ends of the former are relatively easy

---

[1] See also the discussion in Chapter 6.

[2] Mandelker notes that at the time of his study, English planning authorities generally lacked these data. See *Green Belts*, p. 139. See also Lloyd Rodwin, *The British New Towns Policy* (Cambridge, Mass., 1956), Appendix A.; Ruth Glass, 'British Planning', p. 401; Donnison, *Housing*, p. 325. See also Chapter 4 above.

to describe. The St Giles case suggests that the goals of commercial developers were by and large defined as achieving the maximum amount of profitable floor space and the most profitable mixture of uses. The tendency of the commercial developer was to try to maximize his profits within the constraints perhaps of his aesthetic tastes; his attachment to other goals, especially if they took up profitable space, tended to be slight. The ends of the metropolitan boroughs were also relatively well-defined compared to those of the planning authority, but somewhat more complex than those of commercial developers. The boroughs' behavior was shaped by the fact that they were housing authorities whose job was to provide adequate housing for the population within their boundaries. Given the great shortage of vacant land, the expense of land in the County and the other factors noted in the World's End case, the boroughs tended to favor higher density developments than the LCC in order to meet housing demand in their areas.[1] This aim was given added impetus by the existence of a housing shortage in virtually all boroughs. However, as the Chelsea case suggests, the boroughs were to some degree also inclined to support planning principles such as increasing open space; this followed in part from the fact that they were involved in the construction of the *Development Plan* and had some minor responsibilities in the administration of planning.

The boroughs had a clearer ranking of their policy ends than the LCC when it came to housing; they would, under pressure of events, sacrifice planning principles to the need to rehouse. The following comment helps establish the point. It was made to the LCC by a spokesman for the organization that represented the metropolitan boroughs in dealings with the central government and the County Council. The spokesman for the body, the Metropolitan Borough Standing Joint Committee, said that his organization

feared that the County Council's density standards might in some cases be too rigidly applied. Broadly speaking, restricted densities encouraged good planning, but resulted in more people being displaced by development schemes than could eventually be rehoused. This led to overspill problems that could not be coped with by the boroughs.

There is some possibility that this simplification of the end-system of the boroughs is too drastic. Being a public body and concerned with its own maintenance, it clearly had more ends than have been stated. Perhaps the best way to make the point is to say that in its housing activities the boroughs had few active ends and a host of contextual ones.

Not only did applicants have fewer ends than the planning authority to consider, but they had a calculus by which to judge the acceptability of the authority's proposals; the ends the applicants wished to serve had

---

[1] As the LCC was a housing authority, high density developments were also attractive possibilities for it to consider. But such proposals had to be weighed against its planning aims.

clear empirical content. This was especially true of commercial developers who could judge the proposals in terms of their profitability.[1] For the boroughs the comparable measure was housing units. Within limits, a proposal could be graded by the number of housing units allowed.

All of the above is summarized in a remark by a planner with long experience in development control.

Developers have enormous influence because planners don't have the answers. When a developer knows what he wants it is difficult to stop him. Often the planner doesn't know his own mind.

The comparative certainty on one side and the comparative uncertainty on the other meant the applicants helped to determine the content and the extent of the constraints which the planning authority imposed on them.

CONCEPTIONS OF PLANNING: PERSISTENCE AND CHANGE

Now that the planning authority's limited effectiveness as an advocate has been established, we may investigate some of the roots of the intellectual difficulties which defined its problems in negotiations. It is not very useful to say that the principal reason the authority did not manage too well was because it did not engage to any great extent in economizing. Relevant here are the earlier remarks about analytical truths. Moreover, if we ask the question, 'why didn't they do so', the answer surely is the banal one that they did not realize there was an alternative. All that we have done is to impose a framework on the behavior of the authority which is not rooted in the perceptions and understanding of its members. As a cause of why the authority's effectiveness was limited, such an approach tells us little about the behavior of the members of the organization. It is a cause in form only. To understand the roots of the authority's limited effectiveness we need to understand the factors that were associated with the way organizational members approached planning. In principle, what is required is a review of the development of the planning movement and the adoption of land use control by government as well as an analysis of the factors which promoted the persistence of the views which informed the movement and which were associated with planners occupying an interpreter's role. The first task is beyond the scope of this study. However, some relevant remarks have been made elsewhere in the study.[2] Moreover, there is in fact a comprehensive study of the matter.[3]

The second task has the following aspects. We must account for the persistence of the facets of LCC planning which have been isolated above

---

[1] For some reservation on the argument that business corporations have well-defined ends, see William Dill, 'Business Organizations' in March, *Handbook*, pp. 1073-7.

[2] See Chapters 2 and 6.

[3] See Ashworth, *British Town Planning*.

and, in particular, the forces making for persistence, and change, in the content of the planners' professional role. Persistence as much as change requires explanation. It does not seem useful to assume that the social world is generally in an equilibrium state and thus only change requires analysis; if anything, the reverse seems a more useful assumption. Focusing on the planners' role is useful for several reasons. Stability in the content of the planners' role would be an important and likely consequence of stability in other areas, such as the political environment of representatives, and by examining persistence in role content our attention is drawn to salient characteristics in these areas. A similar point can be made about change in the planners' role. Also, any change in the content of the planners' role itself would clearly be an important source of change in ideas about planning in general and planning for London in particular.

Beyond the (theoretical) reasons noted for focusing on change in the content of professional roles, it was the case that towards the end of the LCC's tenure a variety of relatively slight[1] changes in the approach to planning began to appear. Among them may be noted: cracks in the consensus; greater concern for data gathering and analysis; reservations about the static conception of the city; and most generally, and to some degree encompassing these, a change in planners' conception of their role toward greater involvement with allocation problems. This last was shared and even promoted by some of those concerned with planning matters, particularly academics in the relevant disciplines.

Economics, technology and the political environment

The land use problems that the planning authority faced, and which it thought it faced, provide a useful starting point for the discussion of stability and change. The housing situation in London in the post-war period up to the mid-sixties has already been described.[2] The shortage of accommodation and the presence of a substantial amount of sub-standard property meant that planning under the LCC was very much tied to improving the housing situation. The consensus on London planning provided at least some guidelines for what was essentially a job of rebuilding the environment. The static conception of the city and the lack of data presented relatively few difficulties to a planning authority whose central concern was to find vacant sites and build houses or to replace slums with satisfactory accommodation. However, the changing nature of land use problems in the city revealed some of the difficulties with the consensus. This happened when the authority began to concern itself with the functioning of the central

[1] That is compared both to what took place under the GLC and to what has transpired in American planning.
[2] See Chapter 3.

area, and particularly with the problem of the movement in the central core, a concern prompted by increasing use of automobiles in the downtown and what was thought to be increased congestion generally. It might be said that the orientation of the authority began to shift in the sixties from rebuilding, improving or conserving the environment to 'controlling' it. The problem was no longer simply to build houses or increase open space and keep a loose watch on commercial development, but, for example, to understand how traffic was generated and how the flows could be controlled. However, the impact that a change in the problems confronted was likely to have on thinking about planning was in fact dulled by the weakness of the data gathering machinery. The consensus persisted longer than it might otherwise have because the data required to understand what was happening were in short supply. Nor was the theoretical framework necessary to give the data meaning available.

The relative certainty of the political environment of LCC representatives also had consequences for the persistence of the planners' role and for. planning ideas generally. As long as councilors faced such an environment they had little incentive to demand from planners a different set of skills nor dismantle the consensus the planners were supposed to interpret.

The impact of a high level of certainty in the political environment can best be seen by a consideration of the effects of a *reduction* in this level. This could come about through a decline in the economic vitality of the central core which might impinge on citizens in such a way as to direct their attention to government.[1] Or, it might come through direct alterations in the political environment, perhaps induced by government in the form of a proposed large-scale change in land use, for example, a new motorway system. Again, increased citizen sensitivity to racial matters prompted by the influx of large numbers of colored immigrants might also result in a direct change in the political environment. In any case, a necessary corollary for our purposes is that these changes in the pattern of citizen concerns be accompanied by an increase in citizen activity otherwise there would be no change in the level of certainty. This in turn would require changes of the kind discussed in Chapter 5, such as alteration in pertinent citizen norms or increasing availability of information about the conduct of local affairs.

There are at least two possible linkages leading from a reduction in certainty to an alteration in the content of the planners' role. The first, and simplest, would involve planners developing skills in justifying allocative decisions in order to serve the interests of representatives under increasingly varied pressures from citizens for reduction of congestion, for more housing, etc. Planners' roles would alter in response to such skills becoming a valued

[1] See the discussion in Chapter 5.

political resource for councilors. Alternatively, and both may occur simultaneously, planners might perceive such calls for assistance on the part of representatives as 'political' pressures, i.e. competition and contention between members trying to get planners to serve their (individual member's) particular political interests. Planners might then invest resources in developing a more clearly defined expertise with which to counter the claims of members in order to retain their position of influence in land use decision-making. Planners would presumably try to work for a planning process which gave scope to the skills they would be developing, i.e. a planning process where their expertise in the analysis of complicated choice problems would dominate.[1] This would be at variance with what members preferred, a bargaining situation likely being more to their tastes, but whatever the outcome it would be a process more attuned to allocative considerations than was the case under the LCC.

It is possible to construct an analysis similar to the preceding this time at the elite level. Again, a reduction in the level of certainty in the political environment is pertinent but the principal generating force in this view would be existing elites rather than new citizen groups and their leaders.

The early justifications for town planning in England had less to do with arguments about the need to apply expertise to achieve the proper use of land and more to do with the government controlling land use in the public interest. The arguments were not primarily in support of the expertise that government could bring to bear but concerned the value of government control itself; performance was a less important criterion than who was responsible for execution.[2] Furthermore, the content of this public interest, at least for London, rested on a convergence in aims of major social strata. Upper-class, upper-middle-class and working-class spokesmen could advocate and applaud a policy which tried to make the capital city less 'urban' by providing homes for the working class at high standards of amenity, either within or outside the city. These broad goals were not finally compatible[3] but the convergence could be maintained as long as progress was clearly being made in the provision of local authority housing. Both the original justifications and the convergence of aims meant that a planning profession making claims about its expertise in problems of land use allocation or, in general, trying to move away from the consensus would have

---

[1] This is relevant for an understanding of the situation of the planning profession in the United States. American planners tend to be more advanced in their repertoire of skills than their English counterparts. This in part probably reflects their desire to establish independence from the claims of elected representatives. See also the discussion below on client-controlled professions.

[2] In general, see Beer, *British Politics*, Chapter 9. On the particular point see Glass, 'The Evaluation of Planning', pp. 397–8; Ashworth, *British Town Planning*, pp. 323–7; Rodwin, *British New Towns Policy*; and Foley, *Controlling London*.

[3] See Chapter 8.

great difficulties.[1] Planners, or indeed any critics of the existing policies and approaches, would have had great problems building a constituency either at the local or national level, given the broad and embracing agreement among the spokesmen for major strata. However, should this agreement have lessened significantly (as in fact happened under the GLC) uncertainty in the political environment would increase markedly and shifting coalitions made up of less encompassing social groups would be the order of the day.

The planning profession

Within the context of the LCC itself there was little incentive for either planners or councilors to alter the situation. Planners, especially senior ones, already had a significant amount of influence without having demonstrated great expertise in handling the problems of land use allocation while members did not face any significant challenges from the electorate. However, if we turn to the organization of the planning profession the picture was different. Changes in the profession, particularly in the 1960s, clearly presaged important alterations in the role of planners and ideas about planning. The latter two became apparent in the middle and late sixties.[2]

The largest single component in the post-war planning profession in London, and in the rest of the country, was planners employed by local authorities. Moreover, a considerable number of planners were not trained by full-time attendance at planning schools but did part-time courses while engaged in a variety of occupations.[3] In general, the profession in the post-war period and until the early sixties followed closely the model of what might be called a client-controlled profession.[4] In such a profession, advancement and prestige depend primarily on the favor of the client. In terms of

[1] It is worth noting in this context that until recently expertise probably counted for less in terms of influence in policy-making in England than in the United States. The idea of skills arising out of job experience instead of academic training is a common theme in discussions of the civil service, as is the idea of the generalist administrator. See the *Report* of the Fulton Committee. (*The Civil Service*, vol. I, 1966–8, Cmnd. 3638, 1968). Along the same lines, the limited interest the authority took in collecting data about the city stemmed not only from financial constraints and from the nature of the planning consensus, but also likely had roots in the low status accorded to research in the service of policy-making and administration. See Shils, *Torment*, especially pages 40–1.

[2] See Cockburn, 'Opinion and Planning Education' (Centre for Environmental Studies, IP 21, London, 1970), Chapters 2–6.

[3] See Cockburn, 'Opinion and Planning Education', p. 25. In 1960, 49 per cent of planners in Great Britain were employed by local authorities. The rest either worked for non-local public agencies, taught, or were in private practise. Of these remaining 51 per cent, over 18 per cent were overseas and thus presumably had little impact on the profession. From data supplied by the Royal Institute of Town Planning.

[4] Discussions with Terry Johnson of Leicester University greatly facilitated the following analysis. The client-controlled and colleague-controlled models (see below) are meant to be ideal typical cases. Actual professions are mixtures of the two; what is at issue here is to ascertain the degree of mixing.

Table 7. *The change in the number of planning courses**

	Prior to 1965-6	1970-1
Number of planning and planning-related courses offered in Great Britain	28	107
Offered by universities	10	70
Offered by other than universities (e.g. polytechnics)	18	37

* Data from the Royal Institute of Town Planning and from Cynthia Cockburn, 'The Provision of Planning Education' (Centre for Environmental Studies, IP 15, London, 1970).

the English planning profession, a number of consequences can be delineated. Development of new techniques and approaches, which would likely be great in a profession in which prestige and position depended importantly on colleague approval, was limited. Moreover, what ideas that were generated, principally from those working as independent planners or from people in collateral disciplines, were slow in transmission to practitioners because of the existence of few full-time institutions for the teaching of planning and the corollary, few professional journals.

In the early sixties the profession began to change. The growth in the number of full-time planning faculties, particularly in the universities and polytechnics as shown in Table 7, and the growing interest by social scientists in urban problems, meant an increase in the number of planners (and others) who had career-related incentives to develop new techniques and approaches. Recruitment patterns to the profession also were beginning to alter. The older generation of planners tended to have engineering or architectural backgrounds which were compatible with the physical design emphasis of planning. By the middle 1960s practitioners and, even more so, students with social science backgrounds were more in evidence. Concern for the theoretical underpinnings of planning was more likely to flourish in this new soil, as was a recognition of its non-design aspects. Table 8 provides supporting evidence on changes in recruitment.

Injection of new approaches and techniques did not only depend on the activities of the independents but also on the response of some local authority planners to the changes within the profession. To generate new ideas was now professionally rewarding as was learning the new techniques and concepts; there was now a 'market' for such endeavors. In short, elements of what may be called a colleague-controlled profession began to appear. As a consequence, by the middle to late sixties the consensus on planning for

Table 8. *Origin of entrants to the town planning profession**

	1951	1962	1966	1969
Architects, engineers, surveyors	77.0	77.5	36.0	29.4
Geographers, sociologists, economists	7.9	22.5	29.4	41.6
Direct entry planners	15.1		34.6	28.8

* Data from Cockburn, 'Opinion and Planning Education', pp. 22–4, and from the Royal Institute of Town Planning. 'Direct entry planners' refers to persons who did their undergraduate degree or its equivalent in planning.

London was thought by many observers and practitioners to be inadequate to the task of managing land use in the city. More sophisticated data-based analyses cast in an allocation framework began to appear not only in London, but within other local authorities. As a result of the changeover to the Greater London Council, the old planning machinery was dismantled, and the new arrangements were designed to take account of the intellectual changes that had taken place.

8. PLANNING, VALUES AND RATIONALITY

The principal task of the social sciences is not simply to build theory, but to build theory that is meaningful to men living in political communities. One way to answer the question of whether the theoretical enterprise is moving in the right direction is to ask whether it speaks to the significant concerns of such men. What is deemed to be significant will inevitably be a mixture of what groups of citizens define to be so, and this will vary, and what the social scientist himself takes to be of central importance. Relevant here then are the historically grounded problems of political philosophy such as participation, distributive justice, representation and the like, as well as the central ethical concerns of economic (and other social) theory, viz. rationality and efficiency in the use of a community's resources. In this chapter the various values just noted will be considered in the context of the organization and functioning of the LCC. A social science which has little to contribute to the discussion of such matters is trivial in the most profound meaning of that term: it has little to say about some of the deepest concerns of mature men and about concerns of men who are perhaps less reflective but who most often know whether their political lot is an acceptable one.

VALUES AND POLITICS

A useful way of beginning the evaluation of land use planning in London is to summarize some of the major features of politics in this city and in the large American cities that have been of interest in this study. This will point to the aspects of the planning process which are important in explaining land use patterns and their consequences as well as emphasizing those features which are of intrinsic interest. The features, the patterns, and the consequences of the latter, will provide the principal focus for the evaluation.

The major characteristics of land use politics in large American cities can be briefly listed:[1] (1) there is intense conflict; (2) ethnic and racial divisions are often important; (3) there is generally a high degree of public participation in comparison with urban politics in other countries;[2] (4) authority to make land use decisions is dispersed; (5) self-interest, broadly

---

[1] In general, see Banfield and Wilson, *City Politics*, and Williams, *Metropolitan Political Analysis*.
[2] Cf. Almond and Verba, *Civic Culture*, p. 188.

or narrowly defined, is, and is thought to be, the dominant motive for participation. In general, land use politics in American cities involves a number of actors with influence whose cooperation must be assured before anything important can be done, although the poor and unorganized have tended to play a limited part here. Concomitant to the multiplicity of actors is the widespread use of local government as a kind of holding company or arbitrator, not as an initiator of policy. Clearly, some mayors do more initiating than others and become heavily involved in pushing for a particular policy, but this is by and large only after some measure of agreement among important and interested parties is reached. Whether a mayor pushes openly or not, with or without vigor, the process by which policy is made remains more or less the same. It follows that the mayors are not often involved with the definition of the problem and the initiation of solutions. Finding problems and defining and making proposals is by and large the job of others. The mayor's primary job is usually to assemble the requisite influence in order to carry out the agreed upon approach.

Land use politics and politics in general is a full-time occupation for its practitioners in urban America. Amateurs who can only afford limited investments of time and effort do not often go far. There is a constant need to mend political fences, build alliances and cement constituencies. The strategies employed are various and the required adroitness, which professional politicians exhibit on a regular basis, is not easy to attain. The atmosphere might be characterized as one in which actors are regularly climbing, or trying to climb, over the dying political bodies of their opponents. In short, land use politics and politics generally is a very intense experience. It is a more or less visible process with activity and passions running high.

We can note some of the more obvious results of this pattern of land use politics as they affect various groups within American cities. Without going into any of the subleties – which are often important – it is not unreasonable to say that even though (and maybe because) there is a fair degree of access to government, the better-off generally benefit most from the operation of land use politics. While this has been changing, in the past it was certainly the middle class and the downtown merchants who fared the best from urban renewal projects, and from other forms of land use control. Those who generally have fared the worst in land use decisions have been the poor, and particularly poor Negroes. Not only have they often been displaced without adequate rehousing provisions being made, but little accommodation has been built to serve them directly.[1] However, stronger emphasis on citizen participation has given the poorer sections of cities increasing advantages, and the general openness of the system also makes it possible for those who feel deeply distressed at least to bring particular projects to

---

[1] See, e.g., Wilson, *Urban Renewal*, Chapters 19–22.

a halt if not to do anything positive. So far, for the worse off, however, land use politics has been more prominent in its promise of influence than in its substance and in the benefits that would follow.

As we have seen, land use politics in London was different. There was a well-defined political leadership which was mainly governmental in composition. Occasional actors outside government did gain access and have some influence on policy-making, but for the most part the groups that did exist spent their time on the outside looking in. Land use politics was a much less intense experience than in American cities. There were fewer cross-cutting issues, fewer issues, fewer actors, and less publicity. Amateurs could still earn a political living.

Most importantly, the result of the various features of London politics discussed in previous chapters was that the local authority took the lead in the definition of problems and in the initiation of policies to deal with them. A large measure of activity at the local level consisted of attempts to reach agreement on what was the best thing to do for the area under administration. While there were differences of opinion within the authority, it was a politics in which there was a regular attempt to assert some definition of the public good which was not derived from the competing views within the public itself. More so than in American cities, the stakes of action and the incentives used to coordinate activity were non-material. In contrast to American urban politics, the emphasis was on 'solving' problems rather than managing conflict in the local society. Concomitantly, the administration of services was a more prominent function of local government than that of conflict management. In general, there was a closer correspondence between the content of the discussion about policy and its final shape.

The basic features of politics in London and large American cities are or were associated with differences in the level of certainty in the political environment of elected representatives. The central proposition based on this environmental characteristic, which is at the core of explanations about the pattern of politics in the various cities, is the link between low certainty and bargaining as the predominant mode of organizational coordination on the one hand and high certainty and an analytical mode on the other. This relationship is built up from a series of lower level propositions concerning the incentives for representatives, and from propositions about the role and values of representatives, the last two also having roots independent of environmental characteristics.[1] What is central about London in comparison to American cities is the propensity of representatives to deliberate and delegate.

The characteristics of the development control process were to an important degree products of these more general features of London politics

[1] At least as they have been treated here.

and to that extent the shape of land use policy and its impact can be traced back to these wider patterns. But development control was only one aspect of the planning system, albeit the central one at the local level, and only one element in the set of public and private forces which was at work. The explanatory power of development control characteristics for explaining land use patterns and their impact is, then, limited. In this sense the succeeding examination of the consequences of planning policy and related problems is much broader than would be presented if the only consequences considered were ones which could be traced back to the impact of development control. The discussion then must be largely descriptive and evaluative rather than explanatory. The same conclusion is prompted by having, effectively, only two cases with which to work. Moreover, the description and evaluation must proceed from a point of view outside the organization. Particularly, we cannot consider the extent to which the authority served ends it set for itself since discussion in preceding chapters has turned on the authority's inability to be very clear about such matters.[1]

These remarks indicate the limits of what the extent of the LCC's economizing can explain in the context of this study; its principal relevance is in the analysis of the development control negotiations and this is a piece of a larger puzzle. However, since the concept is used in Chapter 7 to show that the authority could not handle the choice problems inherent in development control, problems which are common to reaching a decision on any complex question, clearly issues of general import are being raised. Even if we need to treat them in a fashion which rests only indirectly on the operation of the LCC, not to address them, particularly by considering whether any organization could have done better, would reduce the importance of the analysis in Chapter 7. If no organization could do any better, it is of less consequence that the LCC didn't. This issue will be taken up below, after a description and evaluation of the results of the LCC's attempts to control land use.

Efficiency and distribution

Some vocabulary is required if the analysis of land use policy is to achieve any precision. Policy outputs may be thought of as the end products of

---

[1] This by itself does not eliminate the possibility of discussing organizational effectiveness from the organization's point of view. Since many organizations to a greater or lesser degree share this inability, or indeed prefer not to be very clear, it does not seem very useful to simply give up talking about effectiveness defined in this manner. But suggestions to cope with the dilemma, which run from looking at role systems (Herbert Simon, 'On the Concept of Organizational Goals', *Administrative Science Quarterly*, 9 (1964), 1–22) to investigating patterns of agreement among the actors concerned with the activity (Philip Kronenberg, 'Interorganizational Behavior', Department of Political Science, University of Indiana, 1970 and Thompson, *Organizations*), do not give much help in terms of performance measurement, although they are of greater use in other respects. We seem to be driven back to criteria that gain their significance from sources other than whether the organization consciously pursues them.

governmental activity. Government produces these outputs but the explanation of such characteristics of the outputs as the mix of types of activity or the level of commitment may depend on non-governmental factors.[1] There are two types of outputs that are of interest here, viz. those produced by the public authority being discussed and those produced by the total number of authorities who have some responsibility for performing the governmental function for the area in question.

Policy outcomes can be thought of as the consequences of policy outputs: a reduction in racial tension may be a consequence of an increase in housing expenditure for low-income dwellings.[2] The line between outputs and outcomes is not always clear and the distinction will often depend on the purposes for which it is required. The distinction is particularly important if we are trying to evaluate the performance of an organization, especially a public authority, since it makes sense to evaluate in terms of what the organization can to some degree control. Outcomes are more significant, but in the short run at least, outputs are more appropriate subjects in evaluating governmental performance.

Cutting across the distinction between output and outcome is that between goals the organization defines for itself and those defined for it by the wider society however construed. As noted, the last concerns us here. These supra-organizational goals may refer to both substantive policies as well as to prescriptions for the way in which the organization should carry on its business.[3] Under the heading of substantive policies the principal evaluative criteria are distributive and efficiency judgements. Roughly speaking, the latter refers to *what* is done, i.e. to allocation, while the former refers to *who* gets it, i.e. distribution.[4] For the conduct of the organization's business, the criteria of concern here are degree of participation and representativeness of decisions. Each of these criteria present complex problems of definition and measurement, and caution therefore needs to be exercised in interpreting the following discussion.[5]

[1] Dennis J. Palumbo and Oliver P. Williams, 'Predictors of Public Policy: The Case of Local Public Health', *Urban Affairs Quarterly*, 2 (1967), 75–92.

[2] A crucial problem is the relationship between various outputs and outcomes. Political scientists studying public policy often seem to act as if the relationships were not problematic and thus they concentrate on the former seemingly indicating it is the more interesting of the two.

[3] These distinctions owe much to discussions with Robert Backoff and Bernard Mennis of the University of Pennsylvania.

[4] It is worth emphasizing that the term efficiency is being used here in a more restricted sense than in the discussion of economizing in Chapter 7 and below. In the latter cases the term encompasses the relationship between means and ends without specification of the types of ends. As noted in Chapter 7, these may include distributive goals. In the present discussion, efficiency is restricted to the realm of the allocative function. See Richard Musgrave, *The Theory of Public Finance* (New York, 1959).

[5] The literature on efficiency and distributive judgements is quite large. Good discussions with appropriate citations can be found in Steiner, 'The Public Sector and the Public Interest' and Brian Barry, *Political Argument* (London, 1965). Citations for participation and representative decisions are noted below.

Output and outcomes: efficiency. The lack of adequate data makes discussion of the output of the planning authority very difficult.[1] The problems presented by the quality of the data are matched by the difficulty of establishing a relationship between permissions granted and what was built[2] and of defining the benchmarks necessary to ascertain the value of what was done. The difficulty of establishing a relationship in the area of public housing can be circumvented by simply concentrating on the numbers of local authority dwellings erected.[3] This would come within the boundaries of an output, albeit of a kind for which the planning authority was only partly, and in a small way, responsible. However, the difficulty of establishing benchmarks is not so easily overcome. Should we wish to inquire into the degree of efficiency, we would need data from other producers of the product, and on a cross-national basis the problems become quite dramatic. Outside of public housing we cannot even usefully talk about outputs (except for permissions granted) since what was built depended very much on market forces, and this comes under the heading of outcomes.

The relationship between planning and the market was a kind of loosely organized competitive coexistence. Some of the outcomes of this shifting mixture of government control and market allocation can be briefly described. At the most general level, there were considerable commercial and residential changes, with the planning authority probably having less impact on the first than the second. The latter conclusion and the analysis which supports it, to repeat an earlier point, should not be construed as *explanations* of the outcomes, but largely as descriptions of the authority's efforts to affect land use patterns. Among other things, explanations would require a complex analysis of the relative impact of market and political characteristics in the context of multiple cases. The same points apply to the discussion below of the distribution of outputs and outcomes.

The authority's limited efforts in the commercial area are indicated in the remarks of a planner with long experience in central area development.

By and large, the rebuilding of central London with some exceptions has been done on the background of existing conditions. We haven't tried to turn the place upside down.

In central London there wasn't great war damage so the opportunity for great chunks of renewal was not present as it was in other parts of London. As far as I can tell there is no great demand for striking changes anyhow. At least newspapers and discussions in Parliament don't suggest that there is. The general weight of opinion seems to be to keep central London more or less as it is. It is only inside the planning profession that there has been a call for central area planning. This tends to be a set of professional responses rather than an evaluation of what is

[1] Cf. Chapter 7.
[2] See GLC, *London Statistics, 1955–64*, p. 157 for summary data on planning permissions.
[3] See GLC, *London Statistics, 1955–64*, pp. 98–102.

desired by the population, what is financially possible and what would be the social costs of massive renewal. This is fine because the chances of doing anything basic are about zero. There is no political priority for central area development and no economic viability so nothing has been done. And furthermore land use in the central area is extremely haphazard due to constant renewal over a thousand year period. It would be very hard to do a comprehensive approach.[1]

Some figures on the growth of office space in the central area suggest the extent of the changes in commercial development. Between mid-1948 and the end of 1954 permission to build offices was granted to the extent of well over 20 million square feet. Permission to convert existing buildings to office use added another six million square feet. The total was almost three times as great as the office space lost because of the war.[2] From 1955 to the end of 1963[3] approximately another 36 million square feet was added through rebuilding, extensions and new buildings plus almost 4 million from changes in use. The total permitted from mid-1948 to 1963 was about 70 million square feet[4] which allowed an increase of substantially more than 50 per cent over office space in the central area just before the war.[5] Given that the LCC and the government responded rather late to the heavy investment in commercial space, at best the planning authority might have influenced to some small degree the dimensions of the boom.[6] Of course, the extent of building is not the only thing the authority concerned itself with, and insofar as it was able to affect the placing of the buildings by its use of zoning, it might have had some impact. But here the relevant question would be whether the behavior of developers really was altered since by and large the zones followed existing uses. The same is true of the aesthetics of the new building; it is unclear to what extent developers would have behaved very differently. At any rate it would be difficult to argue that the results, however explained, were in any way superior to those, for example, in New York.

There are several reasons which help account for the relatively greater efforts by the authority in residential development. First, and most importantly, the interest in shaping commercial and downtown development was more recent and less well formed as compared with the strong traditional emphasis on residential living in the thinking of town planners and other

[1] Some of these factors apparently no longer hold as the GLC has recently discussed a renewal scheme for Piccadilly Circus in the heart of the central area. There are also plans for the renewal of Covent Garden.

[2] Marriott, *Property Boom*, p. 169.

[3] In 1964, the central government instituted a ban on permissions for office development in the London area.

[4] GLC, *London Statistics, 1955–64*, p. 158.

[5] Cf. Stevens, 'The Central Area', p. 183. By way of comparison, in a similar period, about 50 million square feet of office space was added to the stock in New York. See Edgar M. Hoover and Raymond Vernon, *Anatomy of a Metropolis* (Garden City, N.Y., 1962), p. 107.

[6] Marriott, *Property Boom*, p. 169.

students of urban life: there were fewer well-defined ideas about what the downtown area should look like. The feeling displayed in the World's End case that some proposals (in this case high densities) were simply unacceptable, almost regardless of context, had no parallel in the area of downtown development. Second, the limited private effort in house-building made attempts to influence patterns of residential development quite plausible. As to what was actually accomplished in residential development, the general trends for the last decade of the LCC's existence are quite clear. A great deal more housing was constructed by public authorities than by private developers and of the public share the LCC built well over half giving it more than half of *all* housing built for Londoners in the period. The totals are as follows: there were 226,076 dwellings built in London and on out-County estates from 1955–64; of these just under 30,000 were built by private parties including housing associations; of the rest the LCC built 116,576[1] which was some 35,000 more than it built during the inter-war period. The total housing effort for the period was about 25 per cent of the units in existence in the years immediately preceding (although, of course, due to replacement, these did not constitute a net addition).

Output and outcomes: distribution. If we shift attention from allocation of public goods to their distribution, the discussion is complicated not only by the factors already alluded to but by the serious problem of the extent to which we can aggregate benefits (and costs) across individuals so as to arrive at a judgement about how various groups are faring. Here we shall simply assume, principally because it is such an important topic, that it is possible to talk meaningfully about such matters.[2]

It is possible, in principle, to simply make some general, i.e. *community-wide*, distributive judgement either against some standard or by longitudinal comparison. In this case we would be simply aggregating the distributive outcomes across all individuals in the community, rather than within subgroups. Doing the latter doesn't dispense with the problem of defining a community standard for a just distribution, since even if we say that we

---

[1] The rest were built by the metropolitan boroughs. See GLC, *London Statistics 1955–64*. By comparison, in New York, which has the largest public housing program in the country, of the total number of dwellings, 8 per cent were built by public authorities. David Dreyfuss and Joan Hendrikson, *A Guide to Government Activities in New York's Housing Markets* (Santa Monica, California, 1968), p. 3. These measures of outcomes are clearly not very satisfactory. Total units built gives us no information about demand or need, and either, or both, of these should be included if we wish to make meaningful comparisons. Unfortunately, while data on units built is readily available, the additional, and crucial, data is not.

[2] Interested readers will certainly want to pursue the complexities involved. Useful discussions are: Jerome Rothenberg, *An Economic Evaluation of Urban Renewal* (Washington, D.C., 1967), particularly Chapter 2; E. J. Mishan, *Cost–Benefit Analysis* (London, 1971); and Henry Aaron and Martin McGuire, 'Public Goods and Income Distribution,' *Econometrica*, 38 (1970), 908–20. For a discussion of distributive judgements in general, see Barry, *Political Argument*, Chapters 6–9.

are only interested in how one or two specified groups are faring, this assumes at least an implicit standard for the rest of the community, viz., that we are not concerned with their positions. They will be rewarded to the extent of their efforts might be the implied standard, while the groups at issue deserve special consideration. However, focusing on sub-groups does ease the problem of aggregating benefits and costs across individuals since the fact of group membership suggests some similarity in preferences, or at least greater similarity than across the population. Aggregation within groups is likely to be less arbitrary. Focusing on sub-groups within the community also has obvious policy advantages, since public policy is often directed at particular categories within the general population.

The problem of *which* groups in the community to focus on is as complicated as the ones just noted, especially for London and cities like it. In a political system where the various sections of the community are not very articulate concerning their own interests, and in some cases not articulate at all, what criteria shall be used for deciding upon which groups to consider? Moreover, aside from the problem of weighing benefits and costs within each group, how shall we decide what *are* benefits and costs in the absence of even the crude guidance of the articulated interests of various groups.

Even with all the unanswered questions, it still seems worth pursuing the distributive question. The strategy adopted here is simply to assert the importance of several groups or divisions in the community, drawing on American experience as a guide and to infer, again using American experience, what outcomes they might consider to be important, both as to benefits and costs. In addition, it would be well to keep in mind the distinction between outcomes and outputs and the extent the LCC may be said to be responsible for the latter.

1. (The working class.) The record of the impact of development control on the housing supply is mixed. Given the general shortage in London,[1] moves to increase the supply of standard housing were clearly in the interests of the poorer sections of the community as they were and are the group that suffers most from a shortage of such housing. On the positive side, there was widespread agreement on the need to build council housing and insofar as development control helped to effect the substance of this agreement, many of the poorer members of the community gained. Furthermore, the planning system was not used to give approval to the procedure of turning land used for low cost housing either into commercial buildings or housing for the better-off;[2] there is no evidence of the kind of behavior

[1] See Chapter 3.

[2] In fact, the Minister in 1955 said the following. 'Throughout the County, permission (temporary or permanent) will not, except in very special circumstances, be given for a change from residential use of any residential building which can still be used, with or without adaptation, for residential purposes of any kind.' Quoted in the *Review*, p. 154. See also Stevens, 'Central Area', p. 197.

often found in American cities, of using urban renewal projects to subsidize the better-off at the expense of the worse-off. Along similar lines, the worse-off did well in the rehousing process (this comes outside the authority of the planning agency); public projects were generally not started unless there was housing available for those displaced. On the other hand, planning policies worked to restrict the supply of housing available to the working class in London. This was partly by intention and partly as a result of an overall policy of dispersal which was not very successful.[1] The results were, among other things, crowded living conditions, continued significant use of substandard housing and high rents.[2] Of course, all of this cannot be laid at the feet of development control, but it contributed to the situation. Two of the major values that development control sought to serve were: (1) a limitation of residential densities and (2) an increase in open space. The result was to restrict the number of housing units built and the amount of land on which housing could be provided. Of course, other values were served by doing this, such as promotion of any intrinsic values of open space (see below) or the presumed value of living in low rise buildings and single-family dwellings.

Raising the densities allowed in the provision of residences would clearly have had a direct effect on council housing, and given that this housing served the worse-off, these increases would be a clear gain for this group. In the area of private development the gain would have been less direct. It might come about, for example, through a filtering-down process where some of the better-off move into high density 'luxury' apartments and the abandoned standard housing go to the worse-off. This could also be done for single-family dwellings; density levels could be increased here as well. It must be said however, that there is some possibility that a looser housing market might attract more people to London and offset any gain made by increased residential building. Also relevant here is the question of how many people could be added to a site if the density increased. If the density level were raised from 150 p.p.a. to 200 p.p.a., and this were done without any dual use of land, the gain in numbers might not be worth the loss of amenity.[3]

Also important here is that the housing program in London in the 1950s, having more or less exhausted bombed sites and open spaces (ones that

[1] See Hall, *London 2000*, Chapter 4, and Westergaard, 'Structure', pp. 127–8.

[2] Donnison comments (*Government of Housing*, pp. 335–6): 'Those most likely to lose the battle for housing space were the families with the lowest incomes and the largest numbers of dependents to support, particularly if they were compelled by shift work or social ties to live in central parts of the town.'

[3] The argument that higher density living is unacceptable because it is unhealthy will not serve here. Of course, this is not the only point to be made in defense of low limits on densities, but on the issue of health alone, the supposed adverse effects of high densities seem to have been overdrawn. See Glazer, 'Housing Problems', p. 26, and Donnison, *Government of Housing*, p. 287.

were not designated for recreational purposes), switched its emphasis to slum clearance. As a result, the council house program, whose output was reduced in size by land shortage, was used more and more to rehouse people who were being displaced due to Council projects, and less and less to house people off the waiting list. It is not clear that it was the worse-off who were, and are, the consistent beneficiaries of this switch. At least some of the people who had to be rehoused lived in satisfactory housing on the edges of the slums and may also have had reasonable incomes. Furthermore, even some of those in the 'slum' houses have had more than minimum incomes. Rehousing according to who had to be rehoused rather than according to income probably deprived those among the worse-off who were not being moved of some subsidized housing space. Again, however, the planning authority played only a small part here; even town planners cannot manufacture cleared spaces.

Overall it is probably best to distinguish between the 'respectable' working class and the poor. The former gained considerably more from land use and housing policies than the latter. They tended to get the better council houses[1] and more importantly the very poor tended to be more transient and thus to loose out in a process which gave attention to established inhabitants of development sites.[2]

2. (The middle class.) It has already been said that the better-off subsidized the housing of the worse-off to some degree, and that this was not seen as a major grievance that needed to be articulated in the political arena. The better-off did, however, get some benefits from the workings of development control, for example in the area of open space and the promotion of amenity and civic design. It may be that the policy of keeping and promoting open space helped support high rents for those properties in the vicinity and this would clearly benefit those of the better-off who owned such property. Moreover, it may well be that the better-off were, and are, more frequent users of the open spaces preserved and promoted by planning. They may also derive more pleasure from amenities and beautiful buildings (although they may be more willing than the worse-off to pay for the pleasure they get). And finally, emphasis on open space, amenity and design may

---

[1] See Burney, *Housing on Trial*.

[2] See Donnison, *Government of Housing*, p. 335. To some extent town planning also failed to serve adequately the housing need of three other groups, viz. single people, the young and the old. In terms of the type of housing to be promoted, the principal aim of town planning was to encourage the building of houses with garden space for families. The groups just noted, however, can probably be well served by high density, high-rise flats (with elevators for the old). Insofar as planning discouraged the building of such housing, it reduced the possible supply of housing for these groups; less accommodation could be provided less rapidly by constructing houses. Since these high density projects would also have released more land for family-type dwellings, the approach did not do as much as it might have to improve the lots of families either. See Donnison, pp. 274ff. For a critical view of proposals for high density development (200 p.p.a. for example) see Hall, *London 2000*, pp. 97ff.

well help to preserve and promote the property values of the better-off. The justification often presented for the benefits received by the better-off is that the worse-off are, or ought to be, equal beneficiaries, at least in terms of aesthetic pleasure and use. It is difficult to evaluate this argument. It would be useful to determine whether those living in crowded, substandard housing who pay more than the bare minimum for rent prefer, for example, the preservation and expansion of open space to more immediate rehousing in satisfactory quarters. As for downtown development and maintenance, considered as an amenity it may be that the middle class gets greater benefit from the continuation of an active, exciting central area where there are also varied shopping facilities.

3. (Neighborhood groups and downtown merchants.) A distinction must be drawn between those living on the actual site and the surrounding residents. Both were alike in the sense that neither had very much access to the policy-making machinery, but the former fared better insofar as they were assured of rehousing in council buildings if they were displaced by council projects. Neighboring residents, however, did less well than their American counterparts. If they found a development in their area unacceptable, they had considerably less ability than American neighborhood groups to force a reconsideration. In other words, external costs of development were given little consideration. However, it is not clear whether *all* such external effects felt by those living around a development site, or indeed by anybody, should count as costs. For example, should we give any weight to those who object to living next door to poorer neighbors? As Mishan says, it is a question of choosing between grounding our calculations in utility or ethics.[1] As for downtown merchants, the relevant points have already been set out.[2] We need only repeat that the policy ends of development control, viz. limiting the growth of London and dispersing its population and jobs, were ultimately antithetical to their economic interests. However, the merchants did not feel the impact of the policies and in consequence were little concerned by development control.[3]

A more explicit discussion of the distribution of the costs of planning than that given above is even more difficult to formulate than on the benefit side. This is not least because appropriate data are almost completely lacking. The only data available, which among other deficiencies are hardly specific

---

[1] Or more precisely, in one ethical criteria or another. Mishan, *Cost–Benefit*, Chapter 45. We may decide to give some weight to those who raise objections because of their neighbors' social characteristics, if we include a value criteria which takes account of political stability or viability. Cf. Wildavsky, 'The Political Economy of Efficiency', in Austin Ranney (ed.), *Political Science and Public Policy* (Chicago, 1968).

[2] See Chapter 5.

[3] More accurately, since the target population of the *Plan* was not very different from the then present population of the County, it might seem that merchants ought to have been interested in increasing the population of the County.

Table 9.   *Rates income in London 1963–4**

	Household income group (per year in pounds)						
	Under 312	312– 519	520– 779	780– 1,039	1,040– 1,559	1,560 and over	all
Percentages of households in each group	11.4	11.4	8.2	15.8	29.8	23.4	100.0
	Averages: per year						
Household income	240.5	405.6	663.8	906.4	1,276.3	2,115.1	1,146.6
Income tax, surtax and national insurance contributions	7.0	11.2	71.2	97.5	146.9	296.1	136.8
Disposable income	233.5	394.4	592.6	808.9	1,129.4	1,819.0	1,009.8
1963–4 rates	21.1	26.0	31.7	28.9	31.2	44.7	32.2
	Percentages						
Rates as a percentage of household income	8.8	6.4	4.8	3.2	2.4	2.1	2.8
Rates as a percentage of disposable income	9.1	6.6	5.4	3.6	2.8	2.5	3.2

* From: Committee of Inquiry into the Impact of Rates on Households, *Report*, Cmnd. 2582 February 1965, p. 80. Note that the rates are generally paid by those who occupy the property, not those who own it. Local authorities can tax owners, but the latter can then recover the rates from the occupiers.

to planning nor very wide-ranging in its definition of cost, is the distribution of local authority taxes (rates). These data, presented in Table 9, are, however, suggestive in that they reveal the distinctly regressive nature of local authority rating, which is the principal means of local revenue-raising. This, however, needs to be seen in the context of the progressive nature of national taxation and the provision of 'free' social services by the central government.[1]

Representativeness

On the basis of the preceding discussion no general assessment of the distribution of benefits and costs of the outputs and outcomes of planning is possible.[2] However, an assessment which is related to a distributive judgement can be hazarded by reinterpreting the problem as a question of the representative quality of the decisions made. In this case we ask how well the decisions made by the local authority accord with the policy preferences of the citizenry. Both kinds of judgements speak to the question of the

[1] See Richard Kirwan, 'London's Political Economy and the Problems of Inner London', Centre for Environmental Studies, London, WN 261, 1971.
[2] Indeed, as already suggested, it is an open question whether one can in principle be arrived at using this kind of analysis. Among others see I. M. D. Little, *A Critique of Welfare Economics*, 2nd ed. (London, 1957) and E. J. Mishan, *Welfare Economics: An Assessment*, 2nd ed. (New York, 1969) as well as the works cited in footnote 2, p. 172.

correspondence between governmental action and citizen preference. And both present many of the same difficulties of definition and measurement.

A discussion of the representative quality of decisions must deal with at least two qualities of the views of the public under consideration, viz. 'sharedness' and 'intensity'. The first simply asks how many people hold a particular view. The second asks, given differing views, what is the intensity with which individuals adhere to their views? A representative decision needs to take into account both these dimensions.[1] Now it is possible that in a particular case, these two qualities will be in conflict. For example, one value is widely held in the population but only weakly so, while other values are intensely felt but by smaller groups of people. This often seems to be the case in American cities when it comes to land use decisions for public housing. There is very likely widespread agreement that all people should be decently housed, and very deep concern among residents as to who shall be housed where. And the residents often disagree rather strongly on the latter. What then is a representative decision?

In London the situation seems to have been rather different. A good case could be made that the problem of making representative decisions in London was eased by the fact that there was little intense conflict over land use. The quality of sharedness is much more difficult to document. Hard evidence is not available which would allow a statement that the authority was promoting widely shared values. Regardless, those who were involved in making land use decisions in London could more easily claim that their decisions were representative because by and large they did not need to concern themselves with working out intensely held, and often contradictory, views about what should be done. If land use politics involved deep-seated conflict, this claim would be less plausible, assuming the governmental machinery still worked in the manner described here. A relatively closed system was more acceptable in London than it would be, for example, in Chicago or New York because it did not deny a complex political reality, as it would in the two American cities.

PLANNING AND RATIONALITY

A great deal of the discussion in this study, particularly in this and the preceding chapter, can be brought together in the following manner. The analysis has been informed by placing planning within the context of economic rationality, or economizing as it has been called here. This conception

---

[1] See the excellent discussion by Wilmore Kendall and George W. Carey, 'The "Intensity" Problem and Democratic Theory', *American Political Science Review*, 62 (1968), 5–24 and the references cited therein, especially Robert Dahl, *A Preface to Democratic Theory* (Chicago, 1956). See also Rae and Taylor, *Political Cleavages*, Chapter 3 and James Buchanan and Gordon Tullock, *The Calculus of Consent* (Ann Arbor, 1962), particularly Chapters 5–8. In general, see Hannah Fenichel Pitkin, *The Concept of Representation* (Berkeley, 1967).

of rationality with its focus on ends and means has suggested the shape of the analysis pursued, from the questions asked to the categories utilized in the answers offered. It might be argued, particularly by practitioners and observers of English planning, that the whole discussion has been misplaced since planning, at least in London, was not about economic rationality at all, or about it in a very small way. Rather it was oriented around something that might be called political or even legal rationality. The examination of this claim, and related matters, will provide a useful conclusion to this study, as many of the issues raised will be relevant to the fundamental problem of rationality for societies.

The attack on the application of the concept of economic rationality to public affairs often takes the form of asserting that policy ends cannot be adequately defined and the necessary quantification can't take place and therefore – so it is implied – we, practitioners and observers alike, must be looking at the problem in the wrong manner and some alternative must be found. The initial points are often well-taken, but the conclusion derived from them is misplaced. The objections raised merely point to the proposition that varying degrees of exactness are possible for different problems; they do not indicate, nor can they without additional analysis, that alternative approaches to understanding and evaluating policy-making are appropriate. Because we do something inexactly, even poorly, is not by itself an argument for the desirability of some other approach. We may be able to perform much better within the context of some other view, but unfortunately our performance (and understanding) may be irrelevant to our purposes. In short, an alternative approach must be put forth which attacks the fundamental conceptions of economic rationality as applied to public policy, particularly its concern to relate means to ends in an efficient manner. This is a much harder task than observing that it is difficult to quantify in a meaningful way, for example, the costs and benefits of alternative transportation schemes. In fact, it is sufficiently difficult so that well-argued alternative stances from which to understand and judge policy-making in public authorities are not easy to come by.[1]

What then is meant by political rationality? Since it is difficult to isolate fully argued and coherent conceptions from people concerned with London planning, a liberty must be taken by imputing a conception of political rationality (and legal rationality; see below). Let us say that this form of rationality focuses on the structural characteristics of public organizations and particularly on their flexibility in moving between different types of decision processes when confronted with varying types of problems.[2] One

---

[1] Lindblom's work, cited above, is a prominent exception.

[2] This conception draws on Diesing, *Reason*, particularly Chapter 5. The discussion here owes much to his work. Aside from economic, political and legal rationality, Diesing also specifies a social variety.

appropriate question to ask in evaluating a public authority is then, does it have the capacity to move, for example, between persuasion and bargaining when circumstances require? Political rationality may also be said to encompass the other forms as it refers to the capacity of an organization to move between the various types of decision processes appropriate to the types of rationality.

The strongest objection to viewing the planning authority principally through the perspective of political rationality is that it obscures what seems to be generally accepted as a fundamental attribute of planning, viz. the attempt to improve the performance of public organizations. Planning is irreducibly about the *product* of organizational activity, even if that product is defined at the most general level of citizen welfare. This applies whether planning is (loosely) characterized as having broad social and/or distributive goals, as was the case under the LCC, or more specific operationally defined objectives. The nature of the objectives is of no consequence in this context, only the logic of choice. In short, planning is only secondarily about the flexibility of organizational structures.

A similar objection holds for viewing the planning authority through the perspective of legal rationality, which involves the application of general rules to specific cases. This suggests its seeming connection with planning, and particularly development control, where planning standards are applied to individual cases and a review process is incorporated which may inquire into the 'fairness' of the decisions made. However, again the centrality of means/ends thinking is obscured, in this instance because legal rationality is only marginally concerned with the *effects* of decisions: the question is whether some rule applies and if it does then the decision follows. To interpose the consideration that some unacceptable consequences might follow would be, generally, to impair justice. Of course this simplifies, but it is crucial to legal rationality that it is essentially present-oriented and that considerations of effects must be built into the rules, otherwise they become extraneous considerations. Care is taken that the latter do not supplant the rules themselves.

Although economic rationality is central to understanding and evaluating planning, both political and legal rationality do provide appropriate perspectives. This is the case particularly with political rationality, especially in situations where the public authority needs to devote considerable resources to managing conflict as well as efficiently providing goods and services. In this case politics can carry the principal burden of integrating the society in response to a relatively low level of integration at the social level. In such a community the political system is much more salient and carries a greater burden than in communities where the appropriate integratory sentiments and habits of cooperation already exist to a high degree. In such situations, the level of political rationality of public authorities in general and planning authorities in particular will be of considerable importance; the authority will need to be flexible enough to move between making decisions which further integration and those which increase efficiency. In this sense, the political rationality of planning authorities in American cities is central to understanding and evaluating them.

If economic rationality provides the appropriate lens through which we must view planning, this still leaves open the question of the extent to which it is possible to *be* rational in a means/ends sense. Quite apart from difficulties which grow out of considerable dispersal of authority and influence,[1] as a matter of analytical capability, how successfully can organizations economize? The inquiry cannot end here, however, since, regardless of the extent to which a public authority can economize, there is still the further problem of implementing its efforts given the presence of independent actors, particularly in the private sector. This issue has already been raised in connection with the negotiations between the planning authority and applicants and in the discussion above of outcomes, but the analysis can usefully be extended to encompass some general considerations. Consideration of problems of implementation involves in part an examination of the manner in which private market forces put limits on planning. This in turn leads to an analysis of the merits of markets versus governmental choice, of which planning is a particular type. These questions are also important to the arguments just presented about the centrality of economic rationality. If economizing is difficult, impossible or very costly, political and legal rationality become more attractive modes of analysis. There are then two contexts within which the evaluation of economizing must proceed: the various conceptions of rationality and the alternative logics of social choice processes.

When the possibility of organizational economizing is raised, it is sometimes argued that a kind of super-rationality, an ability to calculate beyond the capabilities of men, is being advocated. At bottom in this kind of argument is often the observation that defining 'all' relevant ends and considering 'all' possible means is costly and rational men and organizations trying to be rational do not bother to do so.[2] First, the observation itself clearly does not tell us whether individuals or organizations *can* analyze extensive combinations of ends and means. Second, and more importantly, all the observation appears to mean is that organizations and men attempting to be rational realize that there is some trade-off between more costly analysis of the choices before them and the benefits that may accrue from additional increments of doing so. Arguments concerning the costs of extensive analysis, then, are by no means determinate for the question of whether it is possible to economize since they merely indicate that resources which go into analysis

---

[1] See particularly Meyerson and Banfield, *Politics*.
[2] See, for example, Braybrooke and Lindblom, *A Strategy of Decision*, Chapters 1–3.

constitute costs just as much as resources that are used to serve what ends are chosen. Both kinds of costs need to be taken into account.

The arguments just presented concerning the costs and benefits of extensive analysis apply to the whole apparatus of Braybrooke and Lindblom's strategy of 'disjointed incrementalism' from which many critiques of economizing draw their inspiration.[1] In one sense, the various aspects of the strategy all involve judgements about the costs of continuing analysis compared with the benefits, i.e. belong within the context of economizing. Each is a way of reducing the costs of decision-making, but each increases the probability that we will miss some choice which is superior to the alternative chosen. Clearly, the problem here is how the existence of superior alternatives is to be known, i.e. how are the costs of not proceeding to be calculated? If we *knew* what the benefits to be gained were (assuming a superior alternative is in the offing), surely we would continue our analysis, but it is precisely because we do not that we wish to halt it. This is a conundrum of formidable dimensions, but unless we attempt some judgement about what may be foregone if we do not proceed with our analysis, we are left with accepting as satisfactory whatever comes out of our incremental procedures. There is no 'outside' vantage point for evaluation. To argue, as Lindblom appears to do,[2] that as long as the incremental strategy is utilized in the context of multiple bargainers and advocates we may accept the consequences, is either to accept the existing distribution of political influence as being approximately justified, or to face the question of on what grounds we might argue that it be changed. To establish the grounds is surely as formidable a task as dealing with any of the complexities involved in economizing.

If the possibility of economizing is now seen to involve not only calculations about ends and means, but calculations about calculation, this may be counted as an advance in understanding, but it by no means resolves the possibility issue itself.[3] Some general considerations may be offered in this regard. While it may be conceded that no organization can be the compleat economizer, organizations undoubtedly differ in the extent to which they are successful in this respect, or so it is clearly being argued here.[4] If we grant this, then those who argue that discussion of economizing is pointless have a more difficult argument to make than is usually offered, for they

[1] Braybrooke and Lindblom, *Strategy of Decision*.

[2] See *The Intelligence of Democracy*.

[3] The discussion immediately preceding is relevant to comments sometimes made by planners, and by observers of the profession, that planning can't be equated with economizing (or something like it) since this places too great a burden on planners. The argument amounts to not much more than that planners would rather not bother thinking about the costs of search and information gathering. If not all relevant ends or means are considered, then this should be because it is too costly to do so given the likely benefits. If such judgements are not made explicitly they are perforce made implicitly. The problem is still an economizing one, even if it is not faced.

[4] See, e.g. Alan Schick, *Budget Innovation in the States* (Washington, D.C., 1971).

must demonstrate that even if organizations vary in the manner noted, all the results are so far from being efficient as to be valueless in some sense. That is, even though organizations vary in orientations to the problems of choice and in skills, the problems are so complex and the capacities of the human mind so limited that all efforts are equally futile. On the basis simply of casual observation, it appears that this conclusion does not hold for some areas of public policy, for example water resource development.[1] Therefore, at the least some distinctions are required for when the line of argument is useful. Moreover, for this kind of argument to be successfully executed requires the demonstration that no level of efficiency is possible which would also in some sense be worth it. The last, of course, necessitates some separate and complex judgement about worthiness, but that aside for the moment, the usefulness of the argument from human capability would seem to depend on a chain of careful deductions based on well-established empirical premises about the problem-solving capacities of men in social contexts. As indicated earlier, conclusions about individual capabilities outside of an organizational context are not appropriate: the problem is not atomistic individuals but men interacting within organizations. Neither the complex deductions nor the necessary data are present in anything like a sufficient manner in existing discussions.[2] At this juncture an appropriate method of coming to grips with the whole question is by observation, viz. an examination of a variety of attempts by complex organizations to achieve some measure of efficiency. This is no mean task, but the difficulties of carrying the job to a satisfactory completion are not sufficient objections in this context. As long as we do not have adequate theories on the basis of which we can settle the matter, analyses of planning organizations in action have some interest. In short, extensive empirical work is called for.

The last point needs to be extended. Given that the whole matter can be construed as an empirical question, it is not useful to discuss only the possibility of economizing. We need to ask: what are the benefits and costs of economizing as compared to other ways in which societal choices may be made? While economizing may be difficult and costly, if other alternatives are inferior, then it clearly is to be preferred.[3] This is in effect a restatement of the question concerning the extent to which it is 'worth' trying to be efficient given complex societal choice problems. It is not possible to give a coherent answer except by considering the alternatives. Some of the issues

[1] See Arthur Maass *et al.*, *The Design of Water Resource Systems* (Cambridge, Mass., 1962). A similar argument can be made for the size of the unit under administration, e.g. cities versus large nations. In general, see Alice Rivlin, *Systematic Thinking for Social Action* (Washington, D.C., 1971), particularly Chapter 3; and Schultze, *The Politics and Economics of Public Spending*.

[2] Herbert Simon and his colleagues are attacking part of the problem. See, for example, *Models of Man* (New York, 1957).

[3] The discussion here assumes that the agency attempting to economize has legal authority to make choices for the community and, internally, is sufficiently hierarchical to employ the logic.

involved in this enormously complex area will be highlighted if we consider the following. What is meant when it is contended that planning authorities are limited in their efforts by the workings of the private market? This is what we have called above the problem of implementation.[1]

The most straightforward interpretation of the limits set by private market forces is as follows. There are consumers, and producers who respond to them, who attempt to serve their preferences in the market place and these preferences are at variance with the planning authority's ends. The authority cannot get what it wants because the distribution of preferences among economic actors and the pattern of incentives are such that behavior which runs counter to its goals results. The most crucial point here is the part played by consumers. Even if there were no market system, and assuming some form of democracy, these consumers would still voice their preferences in a political market place through interest groups, political parties, voting and the like. The question of the limits imposed by the market, then, means in effect an examination of alternative ways in which the preferences of citizens may be ascertained and implemented.

From the planning authority's point of view, the existence of a market system produces at least two *advantages*. First, the price of goods and services (with adjustments made for market imperfections which may be quite severe) can sometimes be used as indicators of citizen preferences in policy areas where the authority must make decisions. House prices established in the private market would be an obvious example. In this sense, if the market did not exist, the authority would have to invent one or devise alternative means of establishing preferences.[2]

Second, the market provides a means through which the authority can implement its preferences. This can be done by manipulating prices directly, or by setting various constraints (as in development control) which will in turn affect them. Again, if the market didn't exist, the authority would have to construct a replacement, in this case some means by which citizens could be induced to perform a variety of actions. This would generally involve some form of governmental regulation and, while little enough is known about the comparative advantages of each mode, there is some reason to think that economic incentives work more smoothly than government prescription or proscription in many cases.[3]

[1] Another aspect of the general question of implementation, not considered here, is getting subordinates in government agencies to carry out directives. See, for example, James Q. Wilson, 'The Bureaucracy Problem', *The Public Interest*, 6 (1967) 3–9.

[2] For a useful discussion of the advantages and disadvantages of using such price information (shadow prices) for public decision-making, see Julius Margolis, 'Shadow Prices for Incorrect or Nonexistent Market Values', in Haveman and Margolis, *Public Expenditures*.

[3] See, for example, Thomas Schelling, 'The Ecology of Micromotives', *The Public Interest*, 25 (1971), 59–98; William Niskanen, *Bureaucracy and Representative Government* (Chicago, 1971) and Charles Schultze *et al.*, *Setting National Priorities: The 1973 Budget* (Washington D.C., 1972), Chapter 15.

The counterpart of these two tasks, ascertaining preferences and inducing behavior, in the case of a planning system where the market is absent would presumably be performed through leaders of interest groups and other political formations. The extent to which citizen preferences are reflected through group political processes is likely to be more limited than through a well-functioning market. This is principally because groups must generally make *collective* expressions of preferences in which some citizens will obviously be disadvantaged, unless there is a unanimity rule, in which case more than likely nothing at all will be done. Moreover, the citizens who are disadvantaged will not be a random sample, but will no doubt reflect the initial distribution of material resources in the community.[1] The counterpart difficulty of the latter in the market place also rests on the distribution of resources, but the deprivations of limited income in this case seem less severe than those of having limited political influence when influence is the *only* currency that will count in the expression of one's views. As for the authority trying to promote preferred behavior by regulation, some comments have already been offered.

The above considerations are not, of course, the only ones necessary to raise in this context. Issues ranging from the nature of consumer preferences, conceptions of citizen welfare and the public interest, to the causes of market failure are relevant since in the final analysis the problem being addressed is who and what is to count as being valuable in choices that are to be made within and for the community.[2] The advantages that accrue to the planning authority from the existence of a market system, or its absence, can hardly be counted as very important unless it can be argued that both what it gains and its own ends are to be deemed valuable; and this requires a judgement rooted in some general criteria dealing with the community's good and the legitimacy of its choice processes. Consideration of the limits imposed by markets and the possible alternatives that grow out of such an analysis requires no less than an examination of alternative arrangements for societal choice and the value premises underlying such proceedings.

The same conclusion is arrived at if we dispose of the implicit assumption in the discussion until this point, viz. that *government* choice is required. Planning is one method by which communities may make decisions, but the advantages of such a collective decision process must be weighed against those of non-collective choice processes, particularly markets but also private

---

[1] See, for example, Grant McConnell, *Private Power and American Democracy* (New York, 1966), and, in general, Mancur Olson, *The Logic of Collective Action* (Cambridge, Mass., 1965).

[2] A sampling of the relevant literature would include the following: Bertrand de Jouvenal, 'Efficiency and Amenity' in Kenneth J. Arrow and Tibor Scitovsky (eds.), *Readings in Welfare Economics* (London, 1969); Sidney S. Alexander, 'Comment' in Julius Margolis (ed.), *The Analysis of Public Output* (New York, 1970); John Kenneth Galbraith, *The Affluent Society* (Boston, 1958); Francis M. Bator, *The Question of Government Spending* (New York, 1960); and Virginia Held, *The Public Interest and Individual Interests* (New York, 1970).

cooperative arrangements.[1] As well, there are other types of governmental processes, particularly those characterized by less concentration of influence and authority and more bargaining than is true of planning.[2] It is no more useful to assume that collective or governmental choice of any particular type is appropriate without considering the alternatives than it is to simply ask whether planning or economizing is possible or worth it. Each (and they involve the same issues) must be considered in the context of alternatives which also have strengths and weaknesses.

To turn full circle in the analysis and to return to London, each of the considerations raised above is to be viewed in the broad context of economic or means–ends rationality. But as noted, to adopt this viewpoint itself requires a choice between other kinds of rationalities through which political structures may be understood and evaluated.

In the London of the 1950s and early 1960s, considerations of political rationality were, in fact, less important, both for participants and observers. For reasons that hopefully are now apparent, the planning authority was free to work within the framework of economic rationality. Indeed, should the flexibility of the authority to move between different decision processes have become important, it might not have fared very well. An increase in the level of uncertainty in the political environment would have required, for example, a greater investment in conflict management, i.e. using decisions to maintain and enhance community stability. (By the end of the 1960s, in fact, the political dimensions of planning were becoming more important as land use decisions were increasingly seen to involve questions of social advantage to particular groups which needed to be resolved as well as achievement of 'planning' goals.) For conflict management to have achieved any success it is likely that public officials would have needed to become more responsive to spokesmen for organized groups and have greater information about community sentiments. It is possible that the operation of the LCC would have altered in response to increased uncertainty and conflict, but it is more plausible to argue that the norms which directed attention to consideration of the community as a whole would have persisted for some time in the face of the changing political realities.[3] While such inflexibility might not distinguish the London planning authority from a host of other organizations, if we add its limited success within the framework of

---

[1] See the following: Michael Polanyi, *The Logic of Liberty* (Chicago, 1951); Buchanan and Tullock, *Calculus*; Buchanan and Robert D. Tollison (eds.), *Theory of Public Choice: Political Application of Economics* (Ann Arbor, 1972); C. D. Foster, 'Planning and the Market', in Peter Cowen (ed.), *The Future of Planning* (London, 1973) and Otto A. Davis and Morton Kamien 'Externalities, Information and Alternative Collective Action', in Haveman and Margolis, *Public Expenditures*.

[2] See, for example, Lindblom, *The Intelligence of Democracy*.

[3] The evidence from the GLC suggests that this indeed has been the case.

economic rationality (the very great complexities of both judgements being noted) then an overall evaluation must look to be unfavorable.

However, a more useful judgement might well be that the authority's implicit claim that serving the public interest in land use control could best be achieved by *public officials* defining its content and the best means of reaching it, which is essentially a claim in the context of land use policy about economic rationality, was at least plausible given the lack of obvious competitors for the task. And if public officials did not live up to their claim, they were saved many of the political consequences. Their shortcomings went largely unnoticed and unpunished, their claims largely untested. A different, more populistic and participative kind of political system would have tested them, large American cities being an appropriate example, and very likely have vitiated the planning system as a result.[1] But then the virtues of a politics in which statements of *public* purpose, even if ideologically debased, are the principal currency of politics would be lost. The gain would be a citizenry more vigilant of its interests as *it* defines them and more active in their pursuit.

[1] On the intrinsic value of participation see e.g. Peter Bachrach, *The Theory of Democratic Elitism: A Critique* (Boston, 1967).

INDEX

Note: references to America are entered as such; other references concern London or Britain.

Abercrombie, Professor Patrick, 21, 53, 135, 148n
advisory plans for London, 21–3, 135
aldermen of LCC, 16, 138n
allocation of public goods
    decision-making as problem of, 151, 152, 154
    efficiency judgements relate to, 169, 170–2
Almond, G., and S. Verba: *The Civic Culture* by, 98, 99
amenity, 134n–135n
    planning tradition concerned with, 22, 133, 134–5, 148
American cities, 5–6, 7
    bargaining in, 123, 124, 140, 167
    bureaucrats in, need to consider their standing with citizens, 139
    cleavages between citizens in, 78n, 80, 84–9 *passim*, 176
    councilors in, constrained by constituents' views, 74, 76, 130, 137
    land use politics in, 165–7
    litigation in local government affairs in, 59n
    local government arbitrates rather than initiates in, 166
    participation by citizens of, 94–5, 98, 99, 100–1, 165–6
    patronage in, 120
    pluralistic concept of public interest in, 124, 132
    political parties in, 110
    uncertainty of political environment in, 4, 5, 114–15, 140, 167
    zoning in, 13
analytical mode, in organizational coordination, 3–4, 167
anti-urban attitude, traditional in planning, 133, 134–5, 161
applicants for planning permission, 25n, 156–8
    appeals by, 25
    constraints to be observed by, 141, 143–5, 149, 150
    guaranteed legal standing at inquiries, 104
    negotiations between planning authority and, 141–5

architects
    as negotiators for developers, 63
    planners with experience as, 163–4
architectural/aesthetic dimension of planning, 18, 22–3, 135
Ashworth, William: *The Genesis of Modern British Town Planning* by, 18
auditors (District Auditors) of local authority accounts, 112
autonomy
    of elected representatives, 75–8, 113, 115, 127, 137; acceptance of, in political culture, 96–7, 126; consonant with role of deliberator, and holistic concept of public interest, 128
    limited, of local authorities, 111, 112
    of planning authority, 148

bargaining mode, in organizational coordination, 3–4, 118
    link between uncertainty of political environment and, 167
    resources of developers for, 144
    unacceptable in London, 122, 123; lack of 'items' to bargain over, 127
    usual in America, 123, 124, 140
Barlow Commission, 146–7
    anti-urban bias of, 135
    and central area of London, 53
    and distribution of industry, 20–1, 22
Beer, S.: *British Politics* by, 97
Beveridge Committee, on social insurance, etc., 21
bribery, in planning cases, 144
building licences, ending of (1954), 54
business *v.* social improvement interests in municipal politics
    in America, 84–5, 86n
    in London, 50, 85–7, 176

car ownership, increase in, 87
    and scheme for World's End site, 43
case studies, 6, 10–11

189

central area of city
business interests and, 84–7, 176
growth of office space in, 170–1
planning in, 53–6
traffic problem in, 55, 87, 150
central government
attitude of, to London, 13, 15
large share of, in decisions, limits organization of local interest groups, 109–10
and local authorities, 109–13, 114; and local authority finance, 86, 134n
planning permission not needed by Ministries of, 25
social services provided by, 177
Centre Point tower block, 73; *see also* St Giles Circus
certainty of political environment
high level of, in London, 4–5, 77, 91–2, 114, 140; linked to autonomy of councilors, 129, 137, and to delegation of authority and deliberative behavior, 5, 118, 167; possible effects of reduction in, 160–1
low level of, in America, 4, 5, 114–15, 140; linked to bargaining, 167
Chambers of Commerce, 50, 101, 102
Chelsea, 27–8
Conservative majority on Council of, 28, 32
Cremorne Estate in, 33, 35, 36, 39, 148
housing in, 31–2
Lots Road area in: open space in, 148; zoned as industrial, but could be rezoned as residential, 41, 45–6, and combined with World's End area, 42, 43, 44–5, 47
merged with Kensington (1965), 46n, 51–2
World's End housing scheme in, *see* World's End
Chelsea Society, not represented at World's End inquiry, 49–50
Chicago, number of employees of city of, 18
cities, as dynamic organizations with interdependency as key factor, 152
citizens
cleavages between, 78, 94; *see also* ethnic groups, neighbourhood, political parties, social class
hierarchical and collectivist attitudes of, 96–7
interest groups among, *see* interest groups
market system as means of ascertaining preferences of, 184–5
participation of, in politics, *see* participation
sharedness and intensity of opinions of, 178
City of London, 13, 15–16
advisory plan for, 21n
Cole, Margaret: *Servant of the County* by, 13, 76n
comprehensive development areas (CDAs), under 1947 Act, 24, 26

possibility of declaring St Giles Circus as, 58n, 60, 61, 114
Comptroller's Department of LCC (finance), and St Giles Circus schemes, 60, 61, 69, 145
compulsory purchase orders
alternative to (St Giles Circus), 58
required by CDA designation, 59
used as threat: by developers to owners of land, 72; by LCC to developer, 71n
consensus
in analytical mode of organizational coordination, 3
in London planning, 137, 146, 153; advisory plans pave way for, 22; difficulties with, 159–60, 163–4
in London politics, 7
Conservative Party
attitudes of councilors of, to planning, 136
control Chelsea Borough Council, 28, 32
on LCC (Municipal Reform Party), 16n
voting for, 88
cost–benefit calculations
on delegation by councilors, 129–31, 138
on distribution of public goods, 173, 176–7
on value of extensive analysis of ends and means in economic rationality, 181–2
councilors (elected members) of LCC, 16
attendance record of, 129
autonomy of, *see under* autonomy
behavior thought appropriate for, 122, 123
of both parties, involved in decisions, 117
cost–benefit calculations on delegation by, 129–31, 138
deliberative role of, *see* deliberation
election of: (1961), 87–8; election little dependent on personal reputation, 107; elected as party men, 119–20, not in neighbourhood interests, 80–1
holistic concept of public interest held by, 124–5; consonant with autonomy and deliberative role, 128
motives for candidatures of, 129
no publicity for, 130
partnership of officers and, 117
recruitment of, 76, 137
seek support inside Council rather than from constituents, 107
social class of, 138
unpaid, 17, 130, 137
County of London, 13, 21; map, 14
advisory plan for, 21–3
credit squeeze, 31

data, lack of machinery for gathering and analysing, 22–3, 159, 160, 164

decision-making (choosing)
  in American cities, 5–6; process public, and
    citizens participate, 100–1
  collective, 8, 10, 151n, and non-collective,
    185–6
  competitive quality of, 153
  deliberation, bargaining, and inducements in,
    118
  economic rationality compared with other
    methods of, 183
  efficiency and economizing concerned with
    problems of, 151
  extensive analysis of ways and means in, 182
  internal disagreements in, 145–6
  not a party matter as a rule, 121, 122, 126
  as problem of allocation of scarce resources,
    151, 152, 154
  process of, not open to newspapers, 105, 106
  small numbers involved in, 116
delegation of authority, to planning officers, or
  subset of councilors and officers, 3–4, 118
  association of, with reaching decisions by
    deliberation, 5, 118, 167, and with will-
    ingness of party members to acquiesce
    in decisions of party leaders, 119
  cost–benefit calculations on, 129–31, 138
  effective as long as concept of public interest
    is shared, 139
deliberation as method of reaching decisions, 4
  association of, with delegation of authority, 5,
    118, 167, and with certainty of political
    environment, 5, 167
  consonant with autonomy, 128
  implies dominance of those with expertise,
    132, and existence of standards, 123
  requires freedom from constraints of pro-
    moting constituents' interests, 123
  see also role
density of population
  in advisory plans, 22
  in Chelsea, 27; in Chelsea housing scheme,
    35–49 *passim*
  differences of opinion on, 136
  in *Development Plan*, 23–4, 135, 146n, 147
  effect of limitation of, on council housing, 174
    175n
  pressure for increase in standards of, 32–3,
    157
  zoning for, *see* zoning
depressed areas, 20, 53
developers, commercial
  bargaining resources of, 144
  and density, 32
  goal of (profit), 156–7, 158
  not involved in local politics, 144
  at St Giles Circus, *see under* St Giles Circus
  seek to vary standards, 141

development charge (1947 Act), 23
  abolished (1953), 54
development control, 9, 25
  to enforce *Development Plan*, 155
  impact of, on working-class housing, 173–5
  procedures of: explain land use patterns to
    limited extent only, 168; not designed
    for consideration of alternative pro-
    posals, 154–5
Development Corporations, for new towns, 26
Development Plan for London, 23–6, 32, 141
  anti-urban bias underlying, 135
  attitude of LCC to views of different groups
    on, 101–2
  based on professional criteria, 148n
  budget with, 134
  and central area, 53–4
  in Chelsea inquiry, 47, 48
  development control to enforce, 155
  little discussion of interdependency in, 154
  Metropolitan Boroughs involved in making,
    157
  overspill in, 86
  St Giles Circus scheme and, 59, 61
  standards established in, 146
  zoning in, 131
distribution of public goods, 169, 172–7

economic growth
  concern of business men with, in America,
    84, 85
  planning officers and (London), 85
economizing (economic rationality), ability to
  choose means to obtain ends, 149–53
  applicants relatively successful at, 156
  planning and, 178–9
education
  central finance and local practice in, 111
  participation of parents in, Britain and
    America, 100
  for participation in politics, Britain and
    America, 98, 99
Education Committee of LCC, 17
efficiency, definitions of, 150, 151–2
efficiency judgements, relating to allocation,
  169, 170–2
Electricity Board, London (1950), 76
engineers, planners with experience as, 163–4
Engineer's Department, LCC, and road layout
  at St Giles Circus, 58, 64–9 *passim*, 145
ethnic groups in municipal politics
  in America, 78n
  in London, 78–80
ethos, Anglo-Saxon Protestant middle-class:
  emphasizes 'good government', not poli-
    tics, 125
Euston Centre, no public discussion on, 2

expanded towns, under 1947 Act, 26
expertise
  arising out of job experience, 162n
  delegation to those with perceived, 132, 140
  and economizing mentality, 153
  LCC respect for groups with, 101, 103

Forshaw, J. H., chief architect, LCC, 21n, 135

garden city movement, 20, 135
Gas Board, London (1950), 16
Greater London, advisory plan for, 21, 22
Greater London Council (GLC), succeeds
  LCC, ix–x
  institutes scheme for purchase of council
    houses by tenants, 90n
  planning under, 91, 164
  as traffic authority for London, 55n
green belt, in advisory plan, 22
ground rent
  from developer to local authority, 64n
  for St Giles Circus site, 71

highways, in advisory plan, 26
hospitals, administration of, 113
households: size of, and housing demand, 29
housewives, on LCC, 137–8
housing
  council: in America (public housing), 87,
    89–90; beneficiaries of, 84, 173–5; den-
    sity controls could be relaxed for, 147;
    general acceptance of government obli-
    gation to provide, 90; as percentage of
    total built, London and New York, 172;
    rents of, 50n, 90, 108–9; sites of, 88–9;
    state subsidies for, 19, 31; tenants'
    associations in, 94–5
  emphasis on, in planners' thinking, 171–2
  improvement of, by owner occupiers, Chel-
    sea, 27, 31, 33, 48–9
  some of central area rezoned for (1955), 54
  supply of, and demand for: Chelsea, 31–2,
    47–8; London (1951–61), 28–31
  Housing Committee of LCC, 104

immigrants, colored: in London, 79–80, 91n
implementation, problem of, 184
industry: dispersal of, from central London, 53
information on planning activities
  lack of, hinders public participation, 105–8,
    129
  see also newspapers
interest aggregation, in political parties, 83–4
interest groups in municipal politics
  American councilors elected to represent, 137
  cleavages between, London and America,
    78–91

functional and pressure, 101–3
high predictability in demands of, 91–2, 114
influence of, limited by large share of central
  government in decisions, 109–10
limited in activity, 3, extent of organization,
  92–3, and number, 94
interviewing, x–xi, 6, 7, 11
Irish in London, 79
Islington Borough Council, proposed housing
  development by, 2–3

Joseph, Sir Keith, Minister of Housing and
  Local Government, 32, 40

Kensington, Chelsea combined with, in Metropolitan area reorganization, 46n, 51–2

Labour Party
  control LCC (1934–65), 16n
  housing allocation by LCC under, 84, 175
  voting for, 88
land for housing, scarcity of, 29
Leader of LCC, 17, 119
  in St Giles Circus case, 116
legal structure of planning machinery, not
  favourable to public participation, 103–5
litigation
  on acquisition of land at St Giles Circus, 59,
    62, 63, 64, 70
  less common in local government affairs in
    Britain than in America, 59n
local authorities (county boroughs, county
  councils)
  auditing of accounts of, 112
  central government and, 109–13; and finances
    of, 86, 134n
  percentage of population attempting to
    influence, Britain and America, 98
  planning departments of, 23
  politics of, emphasize solution of problems
    rather than management of conflicts, 167
Local Employment Act (1960), assists manu-
  facturers to move to depressed areas, but
  not offices, 53
Local Government Acts: (1888), 13, 16; (1894,
    1899), 15
London, 13
  concept of planning in, 153–6
  idea of limiting growth of, 19–20, 20–1, 22, 26
  movement of population out of, 87
  see also central area, City of London, County
    of London, *Development Plan*, Metro-
    politan Boroughs, *etc.*
London County Council (LCC), 13
  as advocate in negotiations, 9
  appeals from decisions of, 25–6

central government and, 15, 112n
and Chelsea Borough Council, 28, 31; and
World's End site, 35–48 *passim*
committees of, 16–17; chairmen of, 119
and density standards, 32
as housing authority, 84, 157, 172, 175
leadership of, 17, 119
and Ministry of Housing, 24–5, 148–9
planning under, largely tied to housing situation, 159
and problems of choice in development, 168
and St Giles Circus development, 56–73
passim
succeeded by GLC, ix–x
see also councilors of LCC, officers of LCC
London County Council Staff Association, 18
London Government Act (1965), 46n
London roads, Nugent Committee on, 69n
London Trades Council, 102n
London Transport Board (1933), 16, 113
and Lots Road power station, 44, 47
and St Giles Circus development, 70

majority opinion, in political culture, 96, 97
market in land use, 142
advantages of, to planning authority, 184–5
planning meant to replace or supplement,
151
relation between planning and, 9, 170, 181
Marriott, Oliver: *The Property Boom* by, 2, 63n,
71n, 73n
Metropolitan Board of Works, 13
Metropolitan Boroughs, 15
applications for planning permission by, 25,
141, 143
and density standards, 32, 157
and housing, 157, 158, 172
involved in making *Development Plan*, 157
local politics in newspapers of, 108n
Metropolitan Boroughs Standing Joint Committee, 32, 157
Metropolitan Water Board (1902), 16
middle class
in Chelsea, 27
impact of development control on, 91, 175–6
on LCC, 125n, 138
voting by, 88
Ministry of Housing
and *Development Plan*, 24, 148n
and local authorities, 111, 114
and LCC, 24–5, 148–9
rezones some of central area as residential 54
and St Giles Circus, 61, 62
and World's End scheme, 40, 41–2, 44–5, 149
Ministry of Transport, traffic authority for
London area, 55n, 56
and finance of St Giles Circus roads, 58

one-way scheme of, and St Giles Circus
roundabout, 72
Municipal Reform Party (Conservatives), on
LCC, 16n

neighbourhood interests in municipal politics,
America and London, x, 80–1, 83, 176
new towns, 22, 26
newspapers
decision-making process not open to, 105,
106
lack information on London municipal politics, 105
national focus of, 108
officers and councilors not to give information
to, 106–8
Nordlinger, E.: *The Working-Class Tories* by,
96–7
Nugent Committee, on London roads, 69n

office buildings
best commercial investment, 65
boom in building of, 54, 171
employment in, not necessarily increased as
much as space, 55–6, 150n
LCC policy to restrain amount of, in central
area, 55, 56, 148
post-war planning and, 53–4; 1947 Act
allows 10% increase in, 60
at St Giles Circus, 60–1, 65, 66, 150
officers of LCC (local government civil servants), 16, 17–18
see also planners
open space, 24n
application of professional criteria on, 148
in Chelsea, 27, 28; in Chelsea housing
schemes, 36, 37, 44, 45, 47, 142
in *Development Plan*, 147
effect of increase of, on council housing, 174
organizations, analytical and bargaining modes
of coordination in, 3–4, 118
Oxford Street Association, 85n–86n

Parliament, and London, 13, 15
participation by citizens in politics
in America, 6; self-interest dominant motive
for, 165–9
none in World's End case until inquiry, 74
not encouraged by legal structure of planning,
103–5, planning administration, 102,
108–9, political structure, 103, or shortage of information on planning activities,
105–8
political culture and, Britain and America,
94–5, 100
probable effects of increase in, x, 11–12, 187
socialization of children and, Britain and
America, 98–9

patronage, 118
  in London involves only unpaid posts on
    committees and boards, 120
planners, planning officers, 8, 18
  autonomy of, 3
  chairmen of LCC committees in contact with,
    119
  delegation of authority to, 74–5, 187
  developers and, 143
  LCC Planning Committee and, 136, 145
  as major participants in decisions, 116–18
  not to speak to press, 106
  partnership between councilors and, 117;
    councilors do not publicly criticize, 105;
    councilors willing to defer to, 121;
    councilors share concept of public
    interest with, 132–3
  role of, 155–6, 158–61
  training and attitudes of, 139, 147, 152, 156
  trust in, 133
planning, 1–2, 7–8
  as attempt to improve performance of public
    organizations, 180
  authority and concentration of influence
    required for, 11–12
  concept of, in London, 153–6
  confined to physical, as opposed to social and
    economic aspects, 109, 133–4
  early history of, 18–21; tradition in (anti-
    urban and concerned with civic amen-
    ity), 133, 134–5
  meant to replace or supplement a market
    system, 151
  as a profession, 162–4
  as purposive behavior, 151
planning authority, LCC, 23
  advantages of private market forces to, 184–5
  autonomous (except where Ministry of
    Housing involved), 2, 148
  in negotiations: with applicants for planning
    permission, 141–5; with developers, 75;
    made concessions because of indecision
    on its own aims, 142, 149
Planning Committee, LCC, 3, 17, 104, 105
  acts by reviewing and modifying recommen-
    dations of planners, 74, 75
  Chairman of, 119; in World's End case, 36,
    37, 41, 135, 140, 145
  disagreements between planners and, 136,
    145
  'particular' interests on, 125
  and St Giles Circus scheme, 68
planning permission, 9
  attaches to land, not to applicant, 144n
  compensation for revocation of, 54
  decisions on applications for, 141
  public inquiry on refusal of, 25–6, 40n, 104

plans for London, *see* advisory plans, *Develop-
    ment Plan*
plot ratio (relation of floor space to land area),
    55, 64
  in St Giles Circus scheme, 65, 57, 70
police, administration of, 113
policy, public
  efficiency in, 170–2
  distribution in, 172–7
  outputs and outcomes of, 168–9
  as product of conscious choice of ends and
    means, or as aggregation of interests, 1
  representativeness of, 177–8
political culture
  attitudes of, on participation by citizens,
    Britain and America, 94–5, 100
  differences between, Britain and America,
    101n
  evidence of changes in, x
  importance of 'political deference' (trust in
    authority) in, 96–7
political parties
  American: decentralized and non-program-
    matic nature of, 110
  class voting for, 88
  differences between, and cooperation be-
    tween, on planning, 136
  disciplined and hierarchical, 119–20; loyalty
    and strong organization important in,
    97, 107
  expect autonomy in elected representatives,
    76; representatives described as belong-
    ing to, 77, 113
  interest aggregation in, 83–4
  on LCC, 119–22, 139–40
  long and effective service to, as means of
    advancement (in unpaid positions), 120
  as main cleavage between citizens, 78
  not usually involved in planning decisions,
    121, 122, 126
  see also Conservative Party, Labour Party
politics
  full-time occupation in America, 166
  public purposes as principal currency of, 187
  relation of planning and, 1–2
population of London area
  changes in, 26, 27n, 28–9
  density of, *see* density of population
  idea of limiting the size of, 21, 22
  target for, in *Development Plan*, 24, 176n
Port of London Authority (1908), 16
power station (Lots Road, Chelsea), in housing
    schemes, 37, 38, 39, 57
  proposed modernization of, 41, 44, 46
private enterprise
  government attitude towards, 29n–30n
  in housebuilding, 29; in Chelsea, 31

professions, client-controlled and colleague-controlled, 162–3
public inquiries
on Chelsea housing scheme, 46–9
on *Development Plan*, 25
on refusal of planning permission, 25–6, 40n, 104
public interest
delegation of authority dependent on shared view of, 139
holistic concept of, 124–5, 128; shared by planners and councilors, 132–3, and by American planners, 132, and reformers, 124
pluralistic concept of, held by American councilors, 124, 132
public utilities
administration of, 113
and planning authority, 25
purchase notice
by owner of land unable to obtain 'reasonably beneficial use' owing to refusal or conditions of planning permission, 60n
threat of, used to extract concessions, 144

rates, 15
as percentage of household income for different income groups, 177
redistribution of, between London boroughs, 81–3
rationality, ix
economic (economizing), 149–53, 178–9, 181; cost–benefit calculations on extensive analysis of ends and means in, 181–2; costs and benefits of, as compared with other ways of making societal choices, 183; variable success of different organizations in, 182–3
legal, 180
planning and, 10, 11
political, 179–80, 180–1, 186
rents for council housing, 50n, 90, 108–9
representativeness, of local authority decisions, 177–8
representatives, elected, *see* councilors
role
of deliberator, 123, 126, 138, 145; autonomy and holistic concept of public interest consonant with, 128; implies deference to expertise, and hence delegation, 132; political realities consonant with, 124, 128
of planners, 155–6, 158–61
Royal Fine Arts Commission, and St Giles Circus development, 70n

St Giles Circus
in *Development Plan*, 56, 59, 61, 62, 65; map, 57; in *London Traffic Congestion*, 56, 58

Engineer's Department of LCC and road lay-out at, 58, 64–9 *passim*, 145
LCC sets about acquiring land for roundabout under old legislation, 58–9, 63; resulting litigation, 61, 62, 63; developer and litigants, 64, 70
no organized group arguing against decision to develop, 74
office space at, 60–1, 65, 66, 142; permission to increase, contrary to policy of reducing traffic congestion, 150
planners want to leave island unbuilt on, 60, 138, 148, 149
plot ratio at, 64, 65, 66–7, 70
possibility of CDA at, 58n, 59, 60, 61, 114
private developer considered by LCC, 60, 61, 62; negotiations with developer, 63–4; developer to provide land for roads in exchange for liberal planning permission, 64–5, and 150-year building lease (with no arrangements for revising ground rent), 71; development scheme submitted (24-storey block), 65; scheme revised with wider roads on two sides and 30-story block, 66–7, 68; further revision for 50-ft roads all round and 34-storey block, 69; final stages of negotiations, 70–2; roundabout made useless by one-way traffic system, 72; building completed, tower° block unlet, 73; developer's profit, 73; planning authority not successful bargainer with developer, 75
satellite towns, 20
school, in World's End site, 38
Scott Committee, on land utilization in rural areas, 21
Sharpe, L. J.: *A Metropolis Votes* by, 87, 88
slum clearance, 30, 175
social class
of candidates for LCC, 138
limited impact of, on housing policy, 87–9, 91
as main cleavage in electorate (expressed in political parties), 78, 113
and voting, 88
social dimension of planning, 18–19, 22
social science, increasing number of planners with background of, 163–4
social status: demonstration of superior, more difficult in America than in Britain, 89
socialization of children: involves less questioning of authority, and less concern for participation, in Britain than in America, 98, 99
Special Areas Act (1934), 20
standards: existence of, implied in process of deliberation, 123

suburban shopping centres, increased investment in, 87
suburbanization, inter-war, 19

taxation, by local authority, *see* rates
Tottenham Court Road, one-way traffic in, 72–3
Tottenham Court Road underground station, developer of St Giles Circus and, 70
tower blocks
  Centre Point, 73
  proposed for Chelsea World's End site, 37, 38n; power station and, 43, 45
Town and Country Planning Acts
  (1932), 19
  (1947), 23–6; allows 10% increase in office space, 60
  (1954), and compensation for revocation of planning permission, 54
  (1959), applicant for planning permission has to show that owners know of application, 64n, 144n
  (1968), detailed proposals to be submitted within 3 years of outline permission, 144n
Town and Country Planning Association, 53n
Town Planning Act (1909), 18; revision (1919), 19
Town Planning section of Architect's Department, LCC, 18
trade union leaders, on LCC, 138
trading estates, 20
traffic
  congestion of, in central London, 55, 87
  policy of reducing, contradicted by permission for increased office space, St Giles Circus, 150
Traffic Advisory Committee for London and Home Counties (1924), 16

Uthwatt Committee, on compensation and betterment, 21

Valuer's Department, LCC, 64, 69
voting behavior: social basis of, similar in London and national elections, 87–8

war damage, areas of, 21, 26
working class
  in Chelsea, 27
  impact of development control on housing for, 173–5
  planning as means of improving conditions of, 18, 22
  representatives of, on LCC, 138
  voting by, 88
World's End section of Chelsea, project for housing in, 33–5; map, 34
  application for development of, discussed with LCC, 35–8; rejected, 38–40
  attitudes towards, 40
  environmental standards involved in decisions on, 123
  LCC members for Chelsea and, 126–7
  new scheme for, 41–4; Ministry of Housing calls in application, 44–5; revised scheme, 45–6; inquiry on, 46–50; Minister refuses permission, 51; best features of two schemes combined, and result accepted, 51–2
  public not involved in, until inquiry, 74
  question of density in, 35–40, 42–3, 142, 149, 172
  question of open space in, 36, 37, 44, 45, 47, 142
  question of rents in, 50, 108–9

zoning, for residential or industrial use, and for residential density
  in America, 131
  in central area, 54
  in *Development Plan*, 24, 131, 146n; followed existing uses, 23, 171
  of Lots Road area, Chelsea, 41, 45–6